The
Politics
of
Negotiation

America's

Dealings

with Allies,

Adversaries,

and Friends

The

Politics

of

Negotiation

Linda P. Brady

The University of North Carolina Press

Chapel Hill & London

Library of Congress
Cataloging-in-Publication Data
Brady, Linda P.
The politics of negotiation : America's
dealings with allies, adversaries, and
friends / Linda P. Brady.
    p.   cm.
Includes bibliographical references and
index.
ISBN 0-8078-1971-9 (cloth : alk. paper).—
ISBN 0-8078-4320-2 (pbk. : alk. paper)
1. Diplomacy.   2. Diplomatic negotiations
in international disputes.   3. Negotiation.
4. United States—Foreign relations—
1981–1989.   5. International relations.
6. World politics—1975–1985.   I. Title.
JX1662.B73   1991   91-13
327.2—dc20   CIP

For my parents,

Charles and Helen Brady

Contents

Preface

During the fall of 1980 I served as defense adviser with the U.S. delegation to the Negotiations on Mutual and Balanced Force Reductions (MBFR) in Vienna, Austria. From 1973 until early in 1989, when the unsuccessful talks were brought to a close, members of NATO and the Warsaw Pact met weekly in the Redoutensaal of the Hofburg Palace to discuss the reduction of conventional forces in Central Europe.

The format of the talks required East and West, on alternating Thursdays, to deliver a plenary statement to the delegations of the participating countries. Members of the delegations often gathered in the Hofburg early on Thursday to take part in informal discussions with their colleagues. On one Thursday, as I recall, the discussion turned to politics.

A military representative from one of the Eastern delegations suggested that if the military representatives met together in a separate location for two weeks they could hammer out a reasonable agreement limiting conventional forces in Central Europe. His counterpart on a Western delegation agreed, noting that military officers—regardless of their nationality—shared an understanding of the nature of the military balance in Europe and the minimum requirements for deterrence and defense.

A third military representative, again from the East, remarked that the complicating factor in MBFR was politics. An essentially military issue had been transformed into a political debate, and herein lay the explanation for lack of progress. The nodding agreement of others present suggested the consensus of the group: if only "politics" were eliminated from these negotiations, MBFR might succeed. One way to eliminate politics would be to take responsibility for MBFR away from the politicians and the diplomats and place it in the hands of the military.

The problem, of course, is that it is impossible to eliminate politics from international negotiation. Political considerations influence many aspects of negotiation, from decisions to enter into discussions, to the specification of interests and objectives, to bargaining strategies and concession-making. Put differently, international negotiation does not occur in a political vacuum. Efforts to explain the process and outcome of international negotiation that ignore politics will be at best incomplete and at worst irrelevant.

This book is about international negotiation and the role that politics has played in explaining the success or failure of negotiations between the United States and selected allies, adversaries, and friends during the 1970s and the 1980s. My argument assumes that international negotiation is a political process in which nations pursue their security interests and objectives while attempting to reconcile those interests with their negotiating partners. This reconciliation or balancing of interests requires consensus-building at home and abroad. The process takes one form in negotiations between alliance partners that share, by definition, a common perception of the threat and an agreed security commitment. The process takes another form in negotiations between adversaries that share, also by definition, conflicting interests and perceptions of the requirements for international security.

By far the most difficult negotiations, in my view, occur between "friends"—countries that share neither membership in a formal alliance nor an adversarial relationship. In these cases, the absence of shared perceptions of security interests and the nature of threats to international security impedes the consensus-building necessary for successful negotiations. In all of these cases—whether dealing with allies, adversaries, or friends—history, culture, and politics are foremost in explaining the process and outcome of negotiation.

This book is organized into five parts. Part I consists of two chapters. Chapter 1 briefly reviews American efforts to enhance security through negotiation during the Cold War and identifies two themes in scholarly approaches to understanding negotiation: negotiation as art and negotiation as science. Chapter 2 presents a framework for understanding international negotiation around which subsequent case studies are organized. Elements of the framework include: background factors (history, culture, and the personal characteristics of negotiators and political leaders), context (defined as the nature of the prior relationship between the United States and its negotiating partners), substantive concerns (interests and objectives), process (bargaining and concession-making), and politics. The framework is simply that—a way of organizing the multiple influences on negotiating behavior. It does not purport to be a theory or model of negotiation but highlights those factors that should be taken into account in the development of theories or models of negotiation.

Parts II, III, and IV represent the heart of the book. These chapters offer six case studies that illustrate the role of politics and other factors in explaining the process and outcome of negotiations between the United States and selected allies, adversaries, and friends during the 1970s and the 1980s. In Part II, to examine the process by which the United States negotiates with allies, I have selected negotiations that grew out of the Long Term Defense Program (LTDP) signed by the United States and its NATO allies in May 1978. These negotiations concerned logistical support for a U.S. deployment to the European theater in time of crisis or war (the U.S.-German Wartime Host Nation Support Agreement) (chapter 3) and the debate within NATO leading to the December 1979 decision to deploy new U.S. theater nuclear forces in Europe (chapter 4).

Part III considers two cases that illustrate the problems encountered in negotiating with adversaries. These cases are the Vienna negotiations during the 1970s and the 1980s between members of NATO and the Warsaw Pact concerning conventional forces in Europe (the MBFR negotiations, noted earlier) (chapter 5) and the Geneva negotiations between the United States and the Soviet Union concerning theater nuclear forces in Europe (the Negotiations on Intermediate-Range Nuclear Forces, or INF) (chapter 6). The INF negotiations resulted in a treaty signed by the United States and the Soviet Union in December 1987.

Perhaps the most difficult negotiations in which the United States has been involved are with friends or those that concern "mixed" relationships. These issues are the focus of Part IV. To illustrate the problems of negotiating with friends, I have selected a series of discussions between the United States and several of the Arab states and Israel concerning basing rights and logistical support for a U.S. deployment to the Persian Gulf in time of crisis or war (chapter 7). U.S.

efforts to negotiate with its NATO allies about the defense of Western interests in the Persian Gulf (the so-called out-of-area issue) illustrate the problem of mixed relationships (chapter 8). These relationships are mixed because, while dealing with its European allies (whether bilaterally or within the formal NATO arena), the United States raises issues that fall outside the scope of traditional NATO responsibilities.

My selection of cases is based on several considerations. First, these cases focus on negotiations which have as their objective the signing of a treaty or formal agreement on arms control, defense, or security matters. I have not considered the routine diplomatic exchanges that comprise day-to-day international relations. Second, these cases include recent negotiations in which the United States has been a direct participant. I have not examined negotiations in which the United States has served as a mediator, intermediary, or facilitator. Third, I have deliberately selected certain cases that have not received detailed treatment elsewhere. This is particularly true for the U.S.-German wartime host nation support talks, the conventional arms control negotiations, and discussions with the Arab states, Israel, and the NATO allies concerning logistical support for a U.S. deployment to the Persian Gulf. Finally, in each of these cases I played a supporting role as a civilian employee of the U.S. Department of Defense. The origins of this book lie in my personal observations about the role of politics in these negotiations.

Part V shifts the focus to lessons learned from America's experience in these negotiations and their relevance for negotiating a new security framework after the Cold War. Chapter 9 raises the issue of how the United States should adapt its approach to international negotiation as traditional distinctions between allies, adversaries, and friends break down. As we enter the last decade of the twentieth century, the negotiating process is becoming more difficult, while negotiation is becoming a more essential instrument of foreign policy. The challenge facing the United States in international negotiation is learning how to make politics work for us, not against us.

This book is a product of my experience in Washington, D.C., from 1978 to 1985 and could not have been completed—indeed, it would not have been started—without the support of the Council on Foreign

Relations. I was awarded an International Affairs Fellowship by the council in 1978 and spent the 1978–79 academic year in the Department of State's Bureau of Politico-Military Affairs. My introduction to the real world of policy-making and diplomacy began there. I am grateful to Alton Frye, former director of the International Affairs Fellowship program at the council, and Kempton Dunn, current director of the program, for their support and encouragement.

My "one year" in Washington, D.C., turned into seven. During the six years following my fellowship experience, I held several positions in the Office of the Secretary of Defense, where I had the privilege of working with a number of individuals who exemplify the ideal of public service. In particular, I would like to thank James R. Blaker, Richard Darilek, Norman Eliasson, and Lawrence J. Korb, who taught me valuable lessons about diplomacy and the policy-making process.

I began work on this book while serving as Fellow in International Security and Arms Control at the Carter Center of Emory University during 1986–87. I am grateful to Kenneth Stein, former executive director of the Carter Center, for providing an opportunity to reflect on my experiences in Washington. Ken also introduced me to Paul Betz, of the University of North Carolina Press, who believed that I had something to say and encouraged me to pursue this project to completion. His patience and support, and the editorial assistance of Ron Maner and Mary Reid, helped make this book a reality.

The bulk of the writing was completed at Georgia Tech. My colleagues in the Consortium on Multi-Party Conflict Resolution—an interuniversity research project involving faculty from Georgia Tech, Georgia State, and the University of Georgia—offered useful comments on the conceptual framework. I would especially like to thank Gregory Bourne, Michael Elliott, Dorinda Dallmeyer, and Louis Sohn for their suggestions. Charles W. Kegley, Jr., of the University of South Carolina and Donald Snow of the University of Alabama also made important comments on an earlier draft of the manuscript. The index was prepared by Sharon Smith.

Part I　**Introduction**

There has been a dramatic change in the international environment since the end of the Second World War. In 1945 the "hot war" ended and was soon replaced by a Cold War and its associated security arrangements. Those arrangements provided stability and predictability for forty years. In 1989 the end of the Cold War was signaled by revolutionary change in the Soviet Union and Eastern Europe and the fall of the Berlin Wall.

As it attempts to deal with these changes and the construction of a new security order, the United States will rely increasingly on international negotiation. Although negotiation has been an instrument of American foreign policy since the nation's beginning, it has become even more important as we approach the end of the twentieth century. Resolving conflicts through diplomatic means and ensuring security through negotiation will be major themes in American national security policy in the post–Cold War world.

While the United States has increasingly turned to negotiation to address its security interests, international negotiation has become more difficult because the Cold War framework within which negotiations have been conducted since the end of the Second World War is unraveling. For most of this period, the United States has characterized its negotiating partners as allies or adversaries and has adopted negotiating strategies and tactics designed to achieve its objectives within that framework.

The rise of Mikhail Gorbachev on the political scene in the Soviet Union, growing concerns within the United States about the federal deficit and trade imbalances, and the movement in both Eastern and Western Europe toward greater economic and political independence from the superpowers signal major transformations in the international system that will affect how the United States negotiates and how successfully it can achieve its security objectives through diplomatic means.

The first part of this book examines how the United States has relied on negotiation during the Cold War to achieve national security objectives and why we will rely even more heavily on international negotiation in the future. The introduction also reviews two approaches to understanding the process and outcome of negotiation—negotiation as art and negotiation as science—and describes the advantages and disadvantages of each.

Finally, Part I offers a framework for understanding international negotiation based on the premise that negotiation is a political activity which takes one form between alliance partners who share a common definition of the threat and another form between adversaries who view each other as the primary threat. Perhaps the most difficult negotiations occur between friends who share neither a formal alliance nor an adversarial relationship. In each case, whether dealing with allies, adversaries, or friends, political considerations are critical influences on the process and outcome of international negotiation.

1. Negotiating America's Security after the Cold War

Early in the 19th century, Clausewitz claimed that war was the continuation of policy by other means, and he accurately predicted an increased reliance in the use of war in the politics between nations. Today, things are different: Negotiation . . . could now be said to be the continuation of policy by other means, and it is likely that nations will rely more on this method in the future.
— Gilbert R. Winham [1]

The opening of the last decade of the twentieth century brought with it signs of a revolution in the international political and economic order that had been in place since the end of World War II. Revolutionary changes in Eastern Europe and the Soviet Union signaled the end of the Cold War and the fragmentation of security arrangements that had kept the peace for more than forty years.[2] The Cold War provided American policymakers with a framework for dealing with other nations. The division of the world into two camps—Communist and democratic—and the construction of alliances and other institutional arrangements to support that division simplified the task of identifying friends and enemies. Relationships were clearly defined, and allies and adversaries generally behaved in predictable ways.

The period ahead will be dangerous, as the relative stability and predictability of the Cold War years are replaced by the uncertainty and challenge associated with the dissolution of security arrangements grounded in the Cold War and the creation of a new international order. The pursuit of national security after the Cold War will sorely test the diplomatic, economic, and political skills of the United States. Among the most important of these skills is international negotiation—a willingness to resolve conflicts peacefully through dialogue.

Building a new security architecture in Europe is tied to transformation of the North Atlantic Treaty Organization (NATO) and the

Warsaw Pact and to the creation of new political and economic arrangements for all of Europe. Negotiation will be central to the success of these efforts—whether they take place in the context of NATO and the Warsaw Pact, the European Community, the Conference on Security and Cooperation in Europe (CSCE), or other forums. And the United States will continue to play a primary role in Europe, for both the long and short run.

During the Cold War years the United States had a mixed track record in negotiations with its allies, adversaries, and friends. On the one hand, the United States and its NATO allies successfully negotiated a number of security arrangements during the late 1970s and early 1980s. These agreements were designed to enhance NATO's conventional force posture and, in particular, to better support U.S. reinforcements in the event of crisis or war in Europe. On the other hand, the United States generally was unsuccessful during the same period in its efforts to negotiate greater NATO support for the defense of Western interests in the Persian Gulf.

The SALT I (Strategic Arms Limitation Talks) agreements, signed by the United States and the Soviet Union in 1972, and the treaty on intermediate-range nuclear forces, signed in 1987, are considered by most observers to be examples of the successful use of negotiation in support of American national security policy. However, during the 1970s and the 1980s NATO and the Warsaw Pact were unable to achieve similar success in negotiations about the reduction of conventional forces in Europe.

America's experience in dealing with friends—that is, countries with which the United States had neither a formal alliance nor a history of adversarial relationships—was most frustrating. Efforts to negotiate security arrangements with countries in the Middle East and the Persian Gulf were especially difficult. The limited success that the United States experienced in gaining access to military facilities in Oman, Egypt, Kenya, and Somalia was offset by its inability to negotiate the kind of explicit cooperative defense arrangements in the Middle East and the Persian Gulf that America had with its European allies.

The American experience in negotiating with allies, adversaries, and friends since the end of the Second World War offers lessons for international security negotiations after the Cold War. Certain negotiating skills, such as patience, self-assurance, and the ability to see the problem from the perspective of one's negotiating partner, are timeless and can be taught. Negotiators who practice these skills may enhance their chance of success. But the successful negotiation of international agreements—both during the Cold War and in the emerging security environment—ultimately depends upon far more than negotiators with an impressive repertoire of interpersonal skills.

Successful American negotiators, more often than not, are steeped in the history, culture, context, and politics of negotiation. They know that techniques that work in one situation may fail in another. A negotiating style that is effective with American allies may be ineffective in dealing with adversaries or friends. And negotiating styles that made sense for America's dealings with its allies and adversaries during the Cold War may be inappropriate and ineffective as we move into the new political and economic environment of the twenty-first century. In this new environment, old relationships between allies and adversaries will be transformed, and relationships between friends will comprise more of the agenda of international politics.

This book assumes that the context, or the nature of the prior relationship between the United States and its negotiating partners, influences how common interests and objectives are defined as well as decisions about whether and when to negotiate, when to compromise, and how to structure international agreements dealing with national security concerns. Political factors operate differently and may be more or less critical in explaining the success or failure of international negotiation, depending upon whether the United States is negotiating with allies, adversaries, or friends. Moreover, negotiations between allies about issues that are considered to be outside the scope of the formal alliance relationship reveal their own unique political dynamics.

Perhaps the most important influence on the course and outcome of international negotiation is politics. Negotiations are influenced by (1) international politics, especially the structure of the international system and the perceived global balance of power; (2) regional politics, including the balance of power and perceptions of regional threats; (3) domestic politics, particularly the electoral process and the nature of a negotiating partner's political system; and (4) bureaucratic politics. All of these factors must be taken into account in the design of negotiating strategies and the consensus-building process that leads to the successful conclusion of international agreements.

The prevailing academic view of international negotiation conflicts with what international negotiation actually entails—namely, politics. Many analysts argue that misperceptions of national interests are the fundamental causes of international conflict and that negotiation is a rational process. Recent literature suggests a trend toward thinking that such concepts as the balance of power are irrelevant, when in fact the structure of the international system and the relative capabilities of its members do influence decisions about whether and when to compromise or to rely on instruments other than negotiation to achieve national security objectives. These considerations are just as important in explaining America's dealings with its allies and friends as with its adversaries.

While political considerations often are incorporated in the development of negotiating strategies, some scholars are reluctant to admit that political factors may drive the negotiating process, or at least strongly influence the outcome. This reluctance may stem from a belief that it is easier to manipulate perceptions than to understand or modify political and strategic relationships. In any event, the result has been to "depoliticize" explanations of American success and failure in international negotiation.

The conflict resolution approach to negotiation, which was extremely popular in the 1970s and the 1980s, attempts to define a successful formula for agreement and a set of negotiating tools that can be applied to any negotiation. According to some scholars writing in this genre, negotiating an arms control agreement with the Soviet Union is no different than buying a used car. In my view, this approach—one that neglects critical historical, cultural, and political differences between parties to a negotiation—creates unrealistic expectations about the ability to resolve every conflict and may make already difficult negotiations impossible.

A framework for explaining the effects of history, culture, context, and politics on the process and outcome of international negotiations is the subject of chapter 2. The remainder of this chapter focuses on two issues. First, how has the United States used international negotiation since the Second World War in support of national security policy? And, second, how have scholars conceptualized negotiation, and what relevance do the major themes in the literature on negotiation have for an understanding of the politics of negotiation?

Negotiating Security during the Cold War

Negotiation has been a key instrument of American foreign policy since the close of World War II. Many of the international negotiations in which the United States has been involved have been in support of national security interests and objectives. The primary legacy of the Second World War was an increased American role in international affairs. The growth of United States economic and military power and interests demanded greater participation in the international system. The greatest influence on America's use of international negotiation in support of national security objectives was the outbreak of the Cold War and the policy of containment of the Soviet Union.

The negotiation of the North Atlantic Treaty, signed by the United States and eleven other Western nations in 1949, signaled extensive American military support for the defense of Europe and demonstrated the U.S. commitment to a coalition strategy. Despite greater reliance on international negotiation to achieve security arrangements designed to counter the threat of Soviet expansionism, the United States continued to run the show. American economic and military power in the immediate postwar period enabled the United States to have its way—albeit in the context of negotiated agreements—with its European allies. The Europeans had no other choice.

These relationships remained relatively constant throughout the 1950s and into the 1960s, although by the mid-1960s economic, military, and political changes had occurred that seriously affected how the United States negotiated and with what degree of success. The deepening involvement of the United States in Vietnam, the Soviet achievement of strategic parity by the late 1960s and early 1970s, and the economic recovery and growing independence of the European states and Japan changed the way in which the United States pursued international negotiations in support of its security interests. A perceived shift in the global balance of power resulted in a reassessment of U.S. commitments and strategy—reflected in the Nixon Doctrine—and increased support for negotiated settlements in Vietnam, with the People's Republic of China, and with the Soviet Union.

These shifts in the balance of power led to greater reliance on negotiation with American allies. No longer could the United States take for granted the automatic support of its allies for U.S. policies abroad. The economic successes in Europe and Japan and the greater political independence that followed led the United States to rely increasingly on negotiation to achieve its security objectives, even when dealing with countries that shared a formal alliance relationship. Disagreements between the United States and its European allies were especially serious on issues that extended beyond the NATO area, narrowly defined. Efforts by the United States and its European allies to coordinate policies to combat international terrorism or to support Western interests in the Persian Gulf illustrate the problem.

By the late 1960s and early 1970s the United States began to take the Soviet Union more seriously as well and to turn to negotiation to settle differences. This shift became most obvious in 1969 when the Nixon administration began to pursue its policy of détente. Among the most important achievements of that period are the SALT I agreements on strategic nuclear forces.

The situation also led in the 1970s and the 1980s to greater reliance on negotiation with friends—that is, countries (many of them in the Third World) that were perceived as neither allies nor adversaries. The decline in U.S. economic and military power was paralleled by a more active role in international affairs for many Third World countries who sought to maintain their independence from both the United States and the Soviet Union. Whereas once the United States could have imposed its wishes on these states (the original Panama Canal treaty stands out as a prime example), during the 1980s America came hat in hand to discuss basing arrangements, logistical support, and other security agreements.

The revolutionary changes that struck Eastern Europe and the Soviet Union in the late 1980s and early 1990s have further complicated the negotiating environment for the United States. The talk of new political parties and market-oriented economies among Eastern

Europeans, the opening of the Berlin Wall, and the unification of Germany represent long hoped for events that should be welcomed by the United States. But they also signal the end of the Cold War and the beginning of a critical period of transition to a new international order.

This transition will ultimately change the nature of America's relationships with its allies, adversaries, and friends. Former adversaries may become friends, if not allies. Former friends may become allies. And, over the long term, former allies may become adversaries. For example, in mid-1990 major changes in East-West relations were reflected in NATO's proposal to the Warsaw Pact that members of the two alliances declare that "we are no longer adversaries."[3] While conflict between East and West was far from over, there were clear signs that the relationship was changing, and for the better.

These shifts in the international system will make international negotiation a more attractive and sought-after option for the United States. At the same time, however, the successful pursuit of American national security interests through international negotiation will become more difficult. Approaches to negotiation that worked in the 1940s and 1950s will not work in the 1990s, in large part because the political environment in which international negotiation occurs has changed in ways that weaken America's ability to successfully influence negotiating outcomes.

This does not mean that the United States is doomed to failure in international negotiations in the post–Cold War world. It does mean, however, that we must pay more attention to understanding the historical, cultural, social, and political dynamics of international negotiation. Negotiation is an exercise in understanding the past, as well as the situation at hand. Unfortunately, little systematic attention has been devoted to how the United States has used negotiation to deal with allies, adversaries, and friends, to what explains America's success or failure in international negotiation during the Cold War, and to how understanding the politics of negotiation can better position American policymakers in the emerging security environment.

The Art and Science of Negotiation

The problem of understanding negotiation has occupied diplomats and scholars for centuries. Diplomats have devoted thousands of memoir pages to the phenomenon of negotiation, the existence of national negotiating styles, and characteristics of good and bad negotiators. Historians, philosophers, economists, sociologists, psychologists, and political scientists have been intrigued by the ways in which individuals, groups, firms, and nations attempt to resolve their differences by peaceful means.

Despite the attention devoted to the subject, there is little consensus among those who study negotiation about the dynamics of the process. Many historians highlight the unique nature of every negotiating situation and argue for a case by case approach that emphasizes the historical context within which negotiations take place and the cultural, social, and political differences between negotiating partners. Some scholars, including many economists and sociologists, conceptualize negotiation as a rational process consistent with the assumptions of classical game theory, in which the intellectual challenges are understanding the impact of concessions on the negotiating process and determining what is a rational decision in the realm of strategic choice. Others, most notably psychologists, urge that scholars pay greater attention to the personalities of individual negotiators and characteristics of the social-psychological environment in which they find themselves. Finally, some political scientists suggest that international negotiation is a political phenomenon in which domestic factors such as public opinion, interest groups, and electoral politics strongly influence the process and outcome of discussions.[4] Two major themes emerge from this literature: negotiation as art and negotiation as science.

Negotiation as Art. Diplomatic history is rich with analyses of international negotiation. Many of these efforts are the products of historians; others are represented by the memoirs of diplomats and negotiators. Some emerge from the literature on international organizations (particularly the United Nations) and international law and on the role of conciliation and mediation in international politics.[5] Some schol-

ars have focused on conceptualizing negotiation as a political phenomenon.[6] Others have singled out the problems of negotiating with
particular countries (such as Japan or the Soviet Union) or types of
countries (for example, Communist or democratic).[7] Collectively, these
studies represent the traditional approach to understanding negotiation. This approach treats negotiation as an art.

Scholars who adopt a traditional approach to understanding international negotiation share several important assumptions about the
nature of negotiation, factors influencing the process and outcome of
negotiations, and the objective of their studies. First, most of their
efforts are descriptive in character and based on close observation and
reconstruction of events or firsthand experience. The unique qualities of each negotiating situation tend to be emphasized. Moreover,
scholars who adopt a traditional approach generally discuss specific
negotiations in terms of their historical context. Such factors as cultural differences, national styles of behavior, and the personalities of
individual negotiators often are singled out as having major effects on
the process and outcome of negotiations.[8]

A second distinguishing feature of the traditional approach is the
tendency to view the actors or parties to a negotiation as multidimensional, rather than unitary. One must look beyond the ambassador as
representative of a single national entity and consider the multiplicity
of actors, interests, and constituencies that underlie every negotiation.
The composition of delegations, bureaucratic or organizational interests at home, domestic public opinion and interest groups, and the
interests of allies (or adversaries, given the nature of the issue under
consideration) all shape negotiating objectives, strategies, and tactics.
The existence of multidimensional actors with multiple interests contributes to the complexity of international negotiations because parties
must negotiate on at least two levels: internally, in order to form a
domestic consensus about the objectives of the negotiation and the acceptability of various outcomes, and externally, with the other party,
in order to settle on jointly acceptable outcomes.[9]

Third, and related to the second point, the environment within
which negotiations occur is central to the traditional approach to
understanding international negotiation. Parties to a negotiation cannot be isolated from the broader political and social contexts within

which that negotiation takes place. This means, for example, that the relationship between a delegation and the home government is critical to the development of successful strategies and tactics for dealing with counterparts on the other side. It means, further, that negotiations generally take place in the context of a longstanding relationship between two countries. The nature of that relationship—whether friendly or unfriendly—will influence decisions about when to negotiate, whether to adopt a hard line or a soft line during the talks, and the value of linking the issue under discussion to future problems that may be addressed by the two sides. It also means that the important political role played by negotiations in a democratic society, particularly during an election year, will influence decisions about negotiating strategies and tactics.[10]

Fourth, scholars who adopt a traditional approach tend to describe the process of negotiation as incremental or trial-and-error, rather than rational and systematic. Parties to a negotiation may explore numerous avenues while searching for an agreement, often in informal and unpredictable ways. Moreover, the outcome of a negotiation does not always represent a rational convergence of positions but may be the result of political compromise. This approach is consistent with the assumption that negotiations represent unique events that reflect the cultural, social, and political differences between the parties. Stated differently, there is no single formula to describe the process of successful negotiation. There also is no precise body of knowledge about negotiation or skills that can be taught in the abstract. This implies that successful negotiators are born, not made, with important implications for the education and training of professional diplomats.

Finally, traditional approaches to understanding negotiation adopt an admittedly practical orientation to the subject. The aim of these scholars is not to develop a general theory of negotiation but to derive lessons for policymakers who will confront negotiations about specific issues with particular countries in a unique historical and political context. This does not mean that scholars who adopt this perspective avoid generalizing entirely. However, the generalizations that emerge from their research are situationally based, rather than universal. Thus, propositions may be offered about how best to deal with the Japanese, the Soviets, the Chinese, or America's European allies, or the appropriate strategies for trade, arms control, or military bases negotiations.

The strengths of this approach to understanding negotiation are many. In the first place, traditional studies capture the richness of international negotiation in great substantive detail. Because such studies are often written by individuals who have firsthand experience, they may offer a perspective not found elsewhere. Detailed analyses of the negotiating behavior of individual countries or studies of specific negotiating situations can provide the basis for drawing more general conclusions. And these studies often are particularly useful to policymakers because of their practical, rather than theoretical, orientation and their real world referents.

But viewed from another perspective, the strengths of the traditional approach to understanding negotiation represent weaknesses. The detail present in these studies and the emphasis on the uniqueness of negotiations make it difficult to generalize across countries or negotiating situations. While memoirs of negotiators provide valuable insights, they may be slanted in support of personal, bureaucratic, or national interests. A focus on multidimensional actors and multiple interests enables a comprehensive description of the negotiating process of use to policymakers but makes it difficult to develop more general theories of negotiation. At the same time, viewing negotiators as born, not made, means the results of these studies actually are less policy relevant than at first thought.

Negotiation as Science. The behavioral revolution during the 1950s and the 1960s ushered in a new era in research on international politics and foreign policy. The field of negotiation was not immune from these trends. Economists, game theorists, sociologists, and experimental psychologists sought to develop general models or theories of bargaining and negotiation. A common assumption underlying many of these efforts is that negotiation is closely associated with the kinds of problems addressed by the classical theory of games. Some scholars have focused on the effects of hard versus soft bargaining strategies on the concession-making process, while others have addressed the problem of strategic choice—that is, determining what behavior is rational in the context of the negotiating game. Taken together, these studies represent the scientific approach to understanding negotiation, an approach whose primary objective is the development of theory.

During the 1970s and the 1980s many advocates of a more scientific approach to understanding negotiation were attracted to the concept of conflict resolution. These scholars stress the importance of scientific analysis as the first step in the resolution of ongoing international conflicts. They believe that understanding the dynamics of conflicts of interests, the role of perceptions, and the ways in which conflicts end will provide a basis for dealing with real world conflicts in a constructive way. Many of these studies are highly abstract, in the tradition of classical game theory.[11] Others have attempted to incorporate social and political variables in the analysis.[12] Yet others draw from the "self-help" literature on negotiation for individuals that began to appear during the 1970s.[13]

Although there is great diversity in the writings of scholars who view negotiation as conflict resolution, most studies written from this perspective share the following characteristics. First, these studies focus on the development of formal models or theories of international negotiation. The use of scientific method, experimental techniques, and laboratory simulation characterize much of the conflict resolution literature. Scholars who adopt this approach emphasize similarities across a large number of negotiating situations, rather than the unique qualities of each case. The objective is not the explanation of single cases but the development of generalizations about what kinds of behaviors lead to success in negotiation (that is, to the resolution of conflict). William Zartman attributes progress in research on negotiation to use of the scientific method: "The problem of explaining the outcome of negotiation has intrigued students for centuries, but little progress toward a solution has been achieved until recently. Probably the reason is that for a long time analysts asked their questions and sought their answers in terms of specific cases and so were thrown back to situational and historical descriptions of essentially unique events."[14] Application of the scientific method permits a focus on theory and the analysis of negotiation as a general phenomenon, rather than the study of specific cases.[15]

A second distinguishing feature of the scientific approach is the tendency to view actors or parties to a negotiation as unitary, rather than multidimensional. The assumption is that nations or governments involved in negotiations are analogous to individuals. Thus, there is no need to focus on the roles of internal, bureaucratic actors or public opinion to help explain negotiating behavior. The structure of the game, including the values each player attaches to alternative outcomes (or payoffs), explains strategic choices. This assumption simplifies the analysis because unitary actors are less difficult to simulate than multidimensional actors and thus are easier to deal with in a laboratory or experimental situation.[16]

Third, the conflict resolution approach generally pays less attention to the environment or situational context within which negotiations occur than does the traditional approach. Scholars often "black box" the environment in order to reduce the number of variables that must be considered. The primary focus is on the interaction of two or more parties to a negotiation. The influence of strategy and tactics, the role of information and communication, and the process of concession-making receive the most attention. Relationships between negotiators and their bureaucratic and public constituencies are deemphasized.[17]

Fourth, scholars who adopt a conflict resolution approach describe the process of negotiation as a rational convergence of the positions of the parties. In contrast to the trial and error conception offered by the traditionalists, these scholars characterize negotiation as a process of "concession-convergence."[18] Parties take initial positions on an issue and then converge on a jointly acceptable outcome based on a process of mutual concession. Not surprisingly, given this view of negotiation, these scholars devote much attention to factors influencing concession-making. Once this process is understood, strategies and tactics can be designed to encourage mutual concessions. These strategies and tactics can be taught, leading to the conclusion that effective negotiators are not necessarily born but also can be made.[19]

Finally, scientific approaches to understanding negotiation adopt a theoretical orientation to the subject. The primary aim of these scholars is not to derive lessons or maxims for policymakers but to develop a general theory of negotiation. Some scientifically inclined scholars who adopt a conflict resolution perspective are more likely to think in terms relevant to policymakers. Although most do not deliberately cast their research problems, analyses, and conclusions in terms that have a direct bearing on public policy, some scholars derive general principles or maxims to guide negotiators.

There are many strengths to this approach to understanding international negotiation. The parsimony that results from the scientific perspective aids theory development. The use of laboratory analysis, experimentation, and simulation forces scholars to cut through the complexity of historical reality and identify the critical factors influencing the success or failure of negotiations.

But there are weaknesses associated with the scientific approach as well. The conceptual simplicity of formal models and theories reduces their usefulness in explaining real world negotiating situations. The focus on unitary actors and negotiation as a concession-convergence process downplays the role of the environment or situational context within which real world negotiations occur. This may aid in the development of general theory, but it reduces the usefulness of this research to policymakers who confront negotiations with individual countries on specific issues in a particular historical context.

Bridging the Gap between Art and Science

Negotiation as art and negotiation as science represent ideal types. Each reflects a consensus among scholars and practitioners of negotiation about the most profitable approach to understanding how parties attempt to work out their differences. Both approaches have as their objective the explanation of negotiation. Negotiation as art emphasizes differences—the unique qualities of every negotiating situation. Negotiation as science emphasizes similarities—common factors and processes that recur in negotiating situations.

It is easy to exaggerate the differences between the two perspectives. Scholars who adopt each approach do tend to share certain assumptions about the nature of negotiation and the kinds of factors that influence the process and outcome of negotiating situations. At the same time, many scholars straddle the art-science divide in various ways.

Although most traditional writings on negotiation are highly descriptive, some scholars have attempted to derive generalizations about negotiating behavior from the examination of specific cases. Moreover, although most traditional writings on negotiation assume that successful negotiators are born, not made, some scholars suggest that certain negotiating skills can be taught. Monsieur DeCallieres, writing in the early eighteenth century, put it well: "The diplomatic genius is born, not made. But there are many qualities which may be developed with practice, and the greater part of the necessary knowledge can only be acquired by constant application to the subject."[20]

On the side of science, there are studies that focus on the role of culture in international negotiation—a topic that tends to be identified with the traditional approach to understanding negotiation.[21] And, as I have pointed out, other scholars who represent the mainstream of the scientific approach include social and political factors in their analyses of negotiating behavior.[22]

The most interesting and thought-provoking research on negotiation, in my view, draws from both perspectives. Negotiation as art places negotiation in the context of history, politics, and the broader relationship that exists between the parties. Negotiation as science offers important insights on the dynamics of the negotiating process, including concession-making and the convergence of positions. What is needed to aid American negotiators in the emerging security environment is a framework that builds on the strengths of each perspective and highlights the role of politics in international negotiation. Chapter 2 offers the elements of such a framework.

2. The Politics of Negotiation

Negotiating for strategic arms limitation is a far cry from labor or business negotiations to which many of us are accustomed. . . . Strategic arms negotiating is a form of politics—international politics. It is a facet of the constant interaction between the United States and the U.S.S.R.
—Gerard Smith [1]

Each scholarly or disciplinary approach to understanding negotiation offers a narrow and generally deterministic view of the nature and process of negotiation. Scholars from the negotiation as art school have contributed many intensive case studies of individual negotiating situations. Although descriptively elegant, these studies are not strictly comparable because they utilize different models of the negotiating process. This is evidenced in the uniqueness they ascribe to every negotiating situation. Thus the lessons that may be learned from the analysis of individual cases are limited.

In their efforts to develop comprehensive theories of negotiation, other scholars have sacrificed richness and complexity in favor of abstractness and simplicity. The result has been the development of theoretical constructs far removed from the reality of negotiation. Only when the strict assumptions underlying the scientific approach are relaxed and the historical, cultural, social, and political complexities of negotiation are addressed—in an admittedly often less than systematic way—does this approach to understanding negotiation lead to conclusions that address the needs of the policymaker.

What seems required is an approach that identifies factors influencing the process and outcome of different negotiating situations in a way that enables preliminary conclusions to be drawn across multiple cases.[2] This approach does not seek to explain a series of cases in terms of already existing theory. Instead, it involves the intensive examination of multiple cases as a way of theory-building. This is done not by posing formal hypotheses which are then tested in a rigorous way but rather by posing broader questions about the phenomenon under consideration. The same questions are asked of each case, thus allowing comparison across cases.[3] These comparisons may result in modification of the factors identified at the outset.

The advantages of this approach are clear. First, it is especially appropriate when investigating problems for which no definitive body of theory already exists. Theory development in international negotiation is in an early stage, and the diversity of approaches to the problem noted in chapter 1 illustrate the lack of consensus about the process and outcome of negotiations. Thus, international negotiation is a likely candidate for an approach based upon comparison across cases.

A second advantage of this approach is its potential for policy relevance. The factors that are selected for analysis are grounded in the real world of international negotiation, rather than in the laboratory. Building from multiple real-world cases to theory (rather than the reverse), the questions posed are likely to be those that policymakers ask themselves. Consequently, answers to these questions may emerge in a form which policymakers find useful.[4]

Of course, this approach has limitations as well. The factors that are identified for consideration may be labeled "soft" by the scientist because they are not susceptible to precise measurement. Moreover, the cases selected for analysis are not complete or even representative, in a statistical sense, of the universe of negotiations in which the United States has been involved. They are selected because they represent variety—that is, examples of negotiations that differ from each other in important respects. This means that it is inappropriate to draw statistically valid generalizations about the universe of cases from which the sample is drawn.[5] Thus, this approach does not contribute directly to the development of a general theory of negotiation.

The purposes of this chapter are, first, to identify the conditions or factors that influence the process and outcome of security negotiations in which the United States has been involved since World War II and, second, to formulate a set of general questions that will be asked of each case in subsequent chapters. Factors that represent critical influences on the process and outcome of negotiation include (1) background (history, culture, and the personal characteristics of negotiators and political leaders), (2) the context within which negotiations take place (defined as the prior relationship between negotiating partners), (3) substantive concerns (interests and objectives), (4) process considerations (bargaining and concession-making), and (5) political factors (the roles of international politics, regional politics, domestic politics, and bureaucratic politics). The general questions that will be asked of each case address relationships among the factors and relationships between the factors and the process and outcome of international negotiations in which the United States has been involved since World War II.

Background: History, Culture, and Personal Characteristics

The Germans aren't like anyone but the Germans and, in view of their history, can hardly expect to be.
—Gordon A. Craig[6]

Any statesman is in part the prisoner of necessity. He is confronted with an environment he did not create, and is shaped by a personal history he can no longer change.
—Henry Kissinger[7]

Background factors consist of constant or slowly changing conditions that diplomats bring to a negotiating situation which influence the process and outcome of negotiations. History, culture, and personal characteristics of negotiators and political leaders emerge as critical factors in much of the traditional literature on international negotiation, including the memoirs of negotiators themselves.

History affects negotiations in several ways. First, the parties to a negotiation bring with them attitudes and perceptions about each other that are based in part on prior experience or interactions between their nations. If previous contacts have been cordial, the present negotiation will more likely be viewed as a cooperative, problem-solving enterprise. On the other hand, if there is a history of conflict between the parties, both may view the present situation as primarily competitive. In a competitive environment it will be difficult to build trust between the parties because each will focus on conflicting interests, rather than common interests. The absence of trust and the inability to forge common objectives make successful negotiation difficult, if not impossible.

A second way in which history affects international negotiation is summarized by the concept of "lessons of history." Richard Neustadt and Ernest May have made a compelling case that policymakers draw conclusions from history and then apply those lessons to subsequent situations.[8] Negotiators may draw conclusions about the interests, objectives, intentions, and negotiating styles of their counterparts, based on their own experience or the diplomatic record, and apply these lessons to future negotiations. If these lessons become interpreted as narrow stereotypes, however, they may result in miscalculations and the application of inappropriate and ineffective negotiating strategies and tactics, leading to failure.

The role of culture in international negotiation has received a great deal of attention, particularly by diplomats and traditional scholars. Culture often is defined as a set of shared values that influence behavior. Some scholars have taken the concept further and suggest that nations exhibit different negotiating styles based upon their cultural traditions. This leads to conclusions about "the American diplomatic style" or "the Soviet approach to negotiation."[9]

Kenneth Young adopts this perspective in his description of differences in American and Chinese negotiating styles: "Aged in different histories and cultures, the negotiating styles of the Americans and Chinese Communists operate on utterly different conceptions of time. The Americans hurry, while the Chinese Communists wait. They contemplate historical cycles; the Americans watch the clock."[10] Moreover, the Chinese negotiate from a position of assumed cultural superiority in which all non-Chinese are considered inferior or "barbarians." This leads the Chinese to practice a form of "arm's length diplomacy."[11]

The latter perspective is shared by many of the Arab states. The love-hate relationship which characterizes interactions between the Arab states and the Europeans (and Americans, as well) has been linked to an Arab superiority complex grounded in their history and culture. This ambivalent relationship between the Arabs and the West is reflected in what has been called "the Arab diplomatic style." Writing about the Saudi style of diplomacy, William Quandt points out that they "still adhere to a more indirect mode of discourse. Elaborate rituals of hospitality are still required to set the stage for serious talk. Decisions cannot be made under the pressure of time. Yes and no answers are avoided if at all possible, but infinite variations of 'maybe' are available. Oral understandings are more important than written agreements. Secrecy is of the essence, and publicity is tantamount to a betrayal of trust." [12] These diplomatic practices, which are in many respects the product of Arab culture and historical experience, mean that Arab and Western negotiators often operate on completely different wavelengths, with negative consequences for the process and outcome of negotiations.

This national style or single factor approach to understanding the impact of culture on negotiation is limited, however, in its ability to explain changes in foreign policy or negotiating behavior. Because national style changes slowly, if at all, over time, variations in national style are inappropriate explanations of variations in foreign policy or negotiating behavior. However, national style, like other national attributes, provides the context within which negotiation takes place. It establishes limits within which negotiators operate. [13]

Another perspective is to view culture in terms of the social and political context and other situational factors that influence negotiating behavior. Robert Janosik refers to this as the "culture-in-context" approach. [14] History and culture are not independent factors but influence negotiation through the experiences and perceptions of negotiators. A negotiator's background, education and training in foreign affairs, involvement in previous negotiations, and general experience abroad and contact with other cultures will influence the process and outcome of negotiations.

Moreover, the effect of a negotiator's personal characteristics is likely to vary with the social and political context and other characteristics of the negotiating situation. Margaret Hermann, in her analysis of the impact of personal characteristics of political leaders on foreign policy, suggests that when a high level policymaker (perhaps an ambassador) has wide decision latitude (that is, a great deal of flexibility), personal characteristics are more likely to influence his or her behavior. [15]

In summary, history, culture, and the personal characteristics of negotiators and political leaders influence negotiating behavior only indirectly. These factors may generate certain views of the world and of negotiating partners. They may lead to different interpretations of the conduct of negotiations. And they may predispose negotiators and heads of state to particular styles of behavior. But the extent to which these factors influence the process and outcome of international negotiations varies with the social and political context and other characteristics of the negotiating situation.

Context: Dealing with Allies, Adversaries, and Friends

Through nearly 40 years, the North Atlantic Alliance has endured, even prospered, less as a military arrangement designed to counter a common threat than as a grouping of like-minded states united by a common heritage of freedom grounded on democratic principles and determined to stand together for the preservation of a just, democratic way of life.
—John A. Reed, Jr.[16]

The Soviets view the U.S.-Soviet relationship as adversarial, and they enter into arms negotiations as traders seeking to limit specific U.S. programs at minimum cost to their own, rather than as partners who share positive goals with us.
—Howard Stoertz, Jr.[17]

The situation or context within which international negotiations occur shapes the process and outcome of negotiations between the United States and its allies, adversaries, and friends. The context operates as a moderating influence on behaviors of individual negotiators and the bureaucracies and publics that sustain them. Context influences behavior through the concept of "relationship": "Negotiators experience a relationship as some sort of bond between the parties, a sense of interconnectedness. The experience bond is associated with how they define the relationship, what they see to be their specific role in it, and the time horizon they take into account when dealing with each other."[18]

Most international negotiations are not one-shot affairs but occur in the context of a preexisting relationship which will be maintained over a long period.[19] Thus, negotiations are influenced by the history of interaction between the parties and expectations about the nature and value of a continuing relationship. Negotiators make decisions about strategies and tactics—such as whether to adopt a hard or a soft bargaining style—based upon previous experience with their negotiating partner and whether the issue under consideration is but one of many the parties will be called upon to resolve. Negotiations not only lead to specific agreements but also function to shape attitudes and policies about relationships—roles, obligations, and privileges—between the negotiating parties.[20]

Three major factors comprise the negotiators' definition of their relationship: "how negotiators visualize their interdependence, the type of commitment the negotiator has made to the other party, and the degree of indebtedness he or she feels."[21] Abstracting from the relationship between individual negotiators to the relationship that exists between the nations they represent, I describe these factors as affect, commitment, and scope.[22]

Affect refers to the degree of positive or negative feeling evidenced in the relationship between the parties. All relationships include both cooperative and competitive elements, but they can be distinguished in terms of the relative amounts of cooperation and competition that have characterized the relationship over time.[23]

A second element in the relationship concerns the degree of commitment made to the other party. Commitment refers to the willingness to devote scarce resources to support the relationship. These resources may include money, manpower, and time. Commitment is independent of affect; nations can exhibit a high degree of commitment in the context of either primarily cooperative or primarily competitive relationships. And commitment generally establishes constraints on future behavior.[24]

Finally, scope describes the complexity of the relationship. Certain relationships are highly circumscribed, that is, narrow in scope, and govern only a small portion of the interactions between two countries. Other relationships are much broader in scope and extend over a wide range of cultural, economic, political, and military interactions between two or more countries.[25] Taken together, affect, commitment, and scope help define the relationship between the United States and its negotiating partner as ally, adversary, or friend.

Allies. Robert Osgood has defined an alliance as "a formal agreement that pledges states to co-operate in using their military resources against a specific state or states and usually obligates one or more of the signatories to use force, or to consider (unilaterally or in consultation with allies) the use of force, in specified circumstances."[26] In principle, then, an alliance is a relatively circumscribed relationship. In practice, however, a broader relationship generally exists between allies.

Alliance relationships are characterized by positive affect, high commitment, and broad scope. Although alliance relationships include both competitive and cooperative elements, cooperative elements predominate. Alliance members share a perception of the threat against which the alliance was created. But they also share a variety of interests that are left unspecified by the agreement.[27] Alliances generally entail a high degree of commitment by their members. Alliances are expensive propositions, both in terms of tangible resources and because they reduce the flexibility of their members' foreign policies. Finally, the relationships created by alliances generally are broad in scope. Members of an alliance often share similar cultural or historical experiences and political structures, which provide the foundation for cultural, economic, and political, as well as military, interaction.

These characteristics of allied relationships influence negotiations between allied nations. First, allies tend to view specific negotiations in the context of their overall relationship. Because the cooperative elements of the relationship predominate, allies view negotiations as a cooperative, problem-solving enterprise in which the objective is to arrive at an outcome that addresses the collective interests of the parties. Second, alliance relationships facilitate the identification of common interests. Membership in an alliance presumes a shared perception of the threat and the specification of joint or collective objectives. This suggests that allies are better able than non-allies to separate the interests of the parties from their formal negotiating positions. Third, the broad scope of alliance relationships gives the parties more room for maneuver during negotiations. Many side payments are available because negotiations occur in the context of a long-standing, continuing relationship. Finally, allies are more likely to trust each other because of a history of interaction in support of the collective interest. This means allies can devote less time to defining their relationship and more time to the specifics of the issue at hand.

Adversaries. Adversarial relationships involve very different political dynamics. These relationships are characterized by negative affect, high commitment, and broad scope. Competitive elements predominate in adversarial relationships. Although the parties share certain common interests (and recognition of these interests often leads them into negotiations), the overall relationship is viewed as primarily competitive.[28] Like allied relationships, relationships between adversaries generally involve the commitment of substantial resources—both tangible resources and reduced flexibility in foreign policy. Also similar to allied relationships, adversarial relationships are broad in scope. The history of conflict or competition between the parties generally permeates cultural, economic, political, and military interaction.

Adversarial relationships create special problems for negotiation. First, specific negotiations are viewed in the context of the overall relationship. But, unlike the situation with respect to negotiations between allies, the underlying competitive nature of the relationship means that negotiators view the process as primarily competitive, rather than cooperative. Thus, they are more likely to view negotiations as win-lose propositions, or zero-sum games. Second, adversaries experience difficulty in identifying the interests of the parties and in distinguishing those interests from formal negotiating positions. Moreover, the underlying competitive nature of the relationship makes it even more difficult to identify common interests—a process that is necessary for successful negotiations to occur. Third, there generally is less room for maneuver in negotiations between adversaries. The limited number of contacts that often exist between the parties makes side payments and exerting leverage less feasible.[29] And, fourth, trust develops very slowly, if at all, between adversaries. The negotiation of highly structured, formal arrangements and the experience of the parties with these arrangements over time may be the only way that trust can be developed.

Friends. Most of the literature on international negotiation has focused on relationships between adversaries and, secondarily, on relationships between allies. Few scholars or practitioners have focused on the problems encountered in negotiations between friends. "Friendly" relationships are characterized by positive affect, low or variable commitment, and limited scope. They are different in kind from either allied or adversarial relationships and present unique problems for negotiators.

In the first place, relationships between friends are less well defined than relationships between allies or adversaries. Although cooperative elements predominate in relationships between friends, just as they do in relationships between allies, the cooperation is less intense. Moreover, relationships between friends generally are characterized by low or variable levels of commitment, in contrast to the high commitment associated with relationships between allies and adversaries. Finally, relationships between friends are limited in scope. The interactions that occur between friends are generally more circumscribed than interactions between allies or adversaries.

Negotiations between friends are perhaps even more difficult than negotiations between allies or adversaries. First, the absence of a long-standing, continuing relationship between the parties means that specific negotiations tend to be approached on an ad hoc basis. This reinforces a "one-shot" mentality among the negotiators and encourages them to pursue individual, rather than common, interests. Second, and related to the first point, the absence of a continuing relationship makes it extremely difficult to identify common interests. Third, the narrowness of the relationship between friends means that few side payments are available—actually fewer than in negotiations between allies or adversaries. Finally, because of the absence of a long-standing relationship, friends are less likely to trust each other. Misperceptions and miscalculations are extremely likely in this negotiating environment.

In short, the situation or context within which international negotiations occur influences the process and outcome of those discussions. The prior relationship that two parties bring to the bargaining table—whether they are allies, adversaries, or friends—influences the identification of interests and negotiating strategies and tactics. However, negotiations also function to shape, and sometimes even transform, relationships.[30]

As demonstrated by international events during the late 1980s and early 1990s, relationships change over time: today's ally may be tomorrow's adversary, today's adversary may be tomorrow's friend, and today's friend may be tomorrow's ally. Understanding the dynamics of these relationships will help explain the process and outcome of international negotiations, both during and after the Cold War.

Substance: Interests and Objectives

We are unlikely to get what we want unless we know what that is.
—Roger Fisher[31]

It has long been agreed that the interests and objectives of nations influence the process and outcome of international negotiations. International negotiation is premised on the assumption that two kinds of interest must be present: "There must be both common interests and issues of conflict. Without common interest there is nothing to negotiate for, without conflict nothing to negotiate about."[32]

Harold Nicolson states the obvious when he says that "all diplomatists are bound to place the interests of their own countries in the forefront of their consciousness."[33] The issue for scholars and policymakers alike is how interests are defined. Although heads of state and other high-level policymakers often refer to the concept of the "national interest" in their public statements, by and large most scholars and practitioners recognize that governments pursue multiple, changing interests and objectives in international negotiations.[34]

One of the critical first steps in successful negotiation is identifying the interests of the parties, or determining what each has at stake in the situation. The definition of interests and objectives in the prenegotiation phase describes the problem or situation that will be addressed by the parties. Because situations are defined from the perspective of the negotiator, they reflect his or her values, personal goals, past experiences, and general images about international affairs. Differences may emerge in the perception of the situation from negotiator to negotiator. However, defining a common problem, or occasion for decision, in the prenegotiation phase is critical in moving the parties toward negotiation.[35] In other words, the parties must identify a common problem and determine that their shared interests in solving the problem through negotiation outweigh their competing or conflicting interests in allowing the problem to remain unsolved or in addressing the problem through other than peaceful means.

What are the sources of interests and objectives? In democratic societies, interests emerge from the continuing bargaining that occurs between bureaucratic and domestic actors. The so-called bureaucratic politics perspective likens the foreign policy process to a game in which executive and congressional decision makers are the major players.[36] Players' perceptions of problems and their positions on issues reflect their positions in the bureaucratic structure. In Graham Allison's often quoted phrase, "Where you stand depends on where you sit."[37] Players act to maximize their personal and organizational interests and, thereby, the national interest as they define it.

The pulling and hauling that occurs within the American political system in an effort to define interests and objectives has serious effects on the ability of the United States to successfully pursue international negotiations. Consider, for example, the American experience in dealing with the Soviet Union on arms control. Raymond Garthoff, a senior American foreign service officer who served on the SALT I delegation, says that "the greatest problem of the American side in the SALT negotiations has been the absence of consensus on our own negotiating objectives. Challenging as is the task of negotiating with the Russians, our greatest difficulties in doing so have arisen from the attendant burden of continual negotiating and maneuvering among various elements within the American government."[38]

Interests also are shaped by the activities of pressure groups and public opinion. The impact of U.S. public opinion on American policy in the Middle East and the Persian Gulf illustrates this point. The long-standing support of the American public for the state of Israel has closely identified American security interests with those of Israel. This definition of American interests has created problems for the United States in pursuing the negotiation of logistical support arrangements with other nations in that part of the world.

The American electoral process also influences the definition of interests and objectives. Every four years presidents generally run for reelection. Desire for foreign policy successes often leads an administration to reassess its view of the value of negotiations with adversaries. The shift in the Reagan administration's view of the Soviet Union, from an "evil empire" whose interests and foreign policy goals were in conflict with the United States to a government we could deal with, directly influenced the American negotiating position concerning intermediate-range nuclear forces in Europe.

The national interest serves less as a constant influence on negotiators than something that must be reassessed from situation to situation.[39] The existence of multiple, changing interests makes it difficult to pin down the stakes. As a result, parties often associate each other's interests with the formal positions that have been put forward. Defining interests as positions complicates the process of negotiation because it locks in the parties to stated positions and makes compromise extremely difficult.[40]

The interests and objectives that nations pursue through negotiation are, in part, a product of history, geography, and culture. To a greater extent, however, interests and objectives are created by the bureaucratic pulling and hauling that occurs within governments and the influence exerted by pressure groups and public opinion. So-called national interests and objectives that form the basis for negotiating positions thus reflect organizational, bureaucratic, social, political, and even personal interests.

If we are to believe Roger Fisher that the United States is unlikely to get what it wants through negotiation unless it knows what that is, then we should be very uncomfortable with this characterization of interests and objectives—what we have called the substance of negotiation. The interests and objectives that the United States and other governments pursue through negotiation are multiple and changing. Interests and objectives at any time are simply the result of an internal negotiation, a fragile consensus that must be maintained while American negotiators bargain with their counterparts across the table in Geneva or Bonn or Riyadh. This fact has serious consequences for the process and outcome of international negotiations in which the United States has been involved.

Process: Bargaining and Concession-making

Like the U.S. the Soviet Union enters negotiations with the object of maximizing the constraints on the adversary while minimizing the constraints on itself. In practice the bargaining pattern of successive waves of concessions by both sides leading to agreements means that the final treaty is usually a bargain in which both sides have made roughly comparable concessions.
—Michael J. Sheehan[41]

Once parties to a negotiation have made the decision to enter into discussions and have identified shared interests and a common problem, the process of bargaining and concession-making begins. Some scholars, primarily those who belong to the "negotiation as art" school, argue that the process of negotiation is incremental or trial and error. They place greater emphasis on understanding the substance of particular negotiations and are less concerned with the identification of common patterns across cases. Because they believe that substance drives process, the way in which a negotiation unfolds, and the interaction among the parties to that negotiation, cannot be separated from the specifics of the issue or problem that forms the subject of the negotiation.[42]

Other scholars, primarily those who belong to the "negotiation as science" school, argue that the process of negotiation can be described by a concession-convergence model.[43] As Michael Sheehan notes above with respect to Soviet-American arms control negotiations, the practice of negotiation follows a pattern that can be modeled, in which the parties make a series of concessions from their initial positions to reach agreement. Another example of this approach is the Zartman and Berman model of negotiation, which suggests that all negotiations follow the pattern of diagnosis, formula, and details. These scholars share the assumption that universal or near-universal bargaining strategies can be developed and applied across different negotiating situations. These strategies define the initial positions of the parties, their bargaining styles, and decisions about the timing of concessions.[44]

Both approaches to understanding the process of negotiation have merit, but each has limitations as well. Conceptualizing negotiation as trial and error makes it difficult to draw inferences from experience that can inform future negotiations. It is a truism to say that every negotiation is unique. Yet it is also clear that the United States may learn from its experience in dealing with a particular country, such as the Soviet Union, on a particular issue area, such as arms control, and apply those lessons to future negotiations.[45]

At the same time, efforts to model the process of bargaining and concession-making may be cast at a level of abstraction that makes the model of little use to policymakers. Telling American arms control negotiators that their best choice depends upon how they expect their Soviet counterparts to behave is of little help.[46] And the advice that "under high time pressure, a tough strategy produces concessions from an opponent while a soft strategy produces opponent toughness; a tough strategy used when time pressures are not severe is likely to evoke resistance and less yielding"[47] may be more or less relevant depending on whether the negotiator is dealing with an ally, an adversary, or a friend.

Moreover, the relevance of specific strategies depends on the interaction of the domestic politics of negotiating partners, a factor that tends to be neglected by scholars who adopt a concession-convergence approach to understanding the process of negotiation. The high level of abstraction that characterizes concession-convergence models generally assumes unitary actors on both sides. The unitary actor assumption simplifies the laboratory experimentation and simulation approaches often adopted by "negotiation as science" scholars.[48] In addition, models cast at a high level of abstraction permit scholars to "black box" environmental or situational factors as they focus exclusively on the structure of negotiation and the interaction of the parties.

The existence of multiple actors or multiple constituencies influences not only the definition of interests and negotiating objectives but also the selection of bargaining strategies and tactics. Decisions about whether or when to compromise are as much a product of politics as they are of the structure of the negotiation. And in some cases, political considerations may even override so-called rational decision making based on the structure of the negotiation. Viewed from this perspective, the process of bargaining and concession-making represents not only the convergence of positions but also the deliberate act of political compromise, both at home and abroad.

The United States generally has adopted a step by step or incremental approach to the negotiation of arms control agreements with the Soviet Union. Michael Sheehan argues that "frequent small steps are better than infrequent large ones because they are easier to negotiate and because they carry smaller political risks if problems arise."[49] At times, however, American presidents have departed from this sage advice, often for political reasons. The Carter administration proposed a radically different approach to SALT II in March 1977, designed to make a clear break with the Nixon-Ford experience. The proposal so surprised their Soviet counterparts that the negotiations were set back for many months and the ultimate agreement was delayed until it was defeated at home in the wake of the Soviet invasion of Afghanistan.

The experience of the Nixon administration in the negotiation of the Anti-Ballistic Missile (ABM) Treaty, signed by the United States and the Soviet Union in 1972, provides another example of the impact of politics on bargaining and concession-making. Concessions often will not be made in an international negotiation because they would have a negative effect on the process of building consensus at home for a negotiated solution to the problem. The ABM Treaty, which limits the United States and the Soviet Union to the deployment of fixed, land-based antiballistic missile launchers, would not have been ratified by the United States Senate without the support of the Joint Chiefs of Staff. In large part, this support was won by refusing to compromise with the Soviet Union on the issue of permitting research, development, and testing of fixed, land-based "exotic" ABM systems of the kind on which the U.S. military was then conducting experiments. The desire to protect this program and win the support of the military for the ABM Treaty shaped the bargaining and concession-making (or lack of concession-making) strategies adopted by American negotiators in Geneva. It also led to deliberately vague language on this point in the text of the ABM Treaty, a fact that was to come back to haunt the United States in the debate during the 1980s about the Strategic Defense Initiative.[50]

The process of negotiation involves both concession-convergence and politics. Decisions about whether and when to compromise in a negotiation are a product of the structure of the negotiation, contextual factors, and politics. The same may be said about the choice of a hard or soft bargaining strategy or of the decision to link concessions in one negotiation with desired behavior in another. The process and outcome of negotiation thus depends on understanding not only background factors, context, and substance, but also politics.

Politics: The Critical Dimension

Power is at the core of negotiations. A skillful blending of inducements and pressures is central. . . . Timing is of the essence.
—*William B. Quandt*[51]

The point missed by both strategic and processual models is that the participating parties to negotiations are people making decisions on how to change the others' stands and undergoing the effect of the others' decisions for the same purpose. . . . For this, more work is needed in the aspect of power that is most relevant to negotiations, that of political persuasion.
—*I. William Zartman*[52]

When it comes to international negotiation, politics does not stop at the water's edge. Politics is the glue that holds together international agreements. The negotiator or head of state who does not master the art of managing political relationships will not achieve his or her objectives. Steven Miller suggests that "the disappointing results of arms control seem to be a consequence of the effects of an imposing set of political impediments: policy formulation, the ratification process, electoral politics, congressional politics, bureaucratic politics, public opinion, even international politics have to be aligned properly or managed effectively if arms control is to be pursued successfully."[53] This conclusion applies not only to arms control but also to other types of international negotiations in which the United States is involved.

Every international negotiation actually involves two sets of negotiations: internal and external. Most of the literature on international negotiation has focused on the external negotiations—the bargaining that occurs between the representatives of nations. Less attention has been directed to the internal negotiations—the bargaining that occurs within governments and societies as they attempt to develop a unified position toward the negotiation. This is regrettable, believes Gilbert Winham, because "it is usually in the internal negotiation within government where the important decisions about change and accommodation are made."[54]

The struggles that occur during the internal negotiations, which continue throughout the course of the external negotiations, place tremendous pressure on the individual negotiators, who are torn between their responsibilities as representatives of their constituents and as principal bargainers.[55] Negotiators as bargainers see themselves as responsive primarily to their opposite numbers; negotiators as representatives see themselves as responsive primarily to their domestic constituents. Negotiators often are called upon to serve as arbitrators among diverse bureaucratic positions and must determine which among those positions they will push during the external negotiations.[56] At the same time, negotiators must avoid getting too far out in front of their constituents; if this happens, they may lose the domestic support needed to consummate an agreement. Negotiators thus face an extremely difficult task. They must maintain an internal consensus while engaging in a process of bargaining and concession-making with their opposite numbers.

Politics plays a critical role in defining interests and negotiating objectives. As I have already pointed out, nations pursue multiple, changing interests through negotiation, and these interests reflect personal, bureaucratic, and public agendas. Interests tend to be identified with formal negotiating positions, which are the product of bureaucratic pulling and hauling. As the bureaucratic and political rationales for a negotiating position are called into question, policy changes and a new rationale must be constructed. This happens often during an election year in the United States, when presidents determine that progress in international negotiations may aid their prospects for reelection.

Politics influences the definition of interests and negotiating objectives in yet another way. The interests of third parties often enter into the equation. For example, in formulating U.S. strategic arms control policy during the 1970s and the 1980s, American decision makers considered the interests and views of the European allies. Although the Europeans were not direct participants in the Soviet-American strategic arms control talks, their interests—and their security—were affected by the outcome of the negotiations. The politics of relationships between the United States and its European allies thus influenced the formulation of American negotiating objectives in SALT and START.

Successful negotiation requires political persuasion on several levels. The identification of common interests between the parties demands that political interests and effects be addressed, because the domestic politics of one party influences the policy-making process of the other. And "in the interaction of those politics often lie the real obstacles or opportunities in building or strengthening a relationship or changing a situation."[57]

Negotiators can take advantage of this phenomenon in two ways. First, smart negotiators will target or address the domestic constituencies of their opposite numbers who have a stake in the problem.[58] Bringing your opponent's constituencies into the process increases your leverage because it provides him or her with a domestic political rationale for reaching agreement. Second, smart negotiators may blame their own constituents for their inability to make concessions on a particular point. Responses such as "The Congress will not accept that" or "The interests of American allies will be damaged by that proposal" can take the place of a direct "No."

The politics of negotiation extend beyond the signing of international agreements. To quote Hedrick Smith, "One of the enduring lessons of the [negotiation] game is that agreement does not equal solution. It is merely a transition point to a new struggle, the winners trying to secure their gains, the losers trying to undo them."[59] The politics of negotiation continue in two ways. First, certain international agreements require ratification by the United States Senate. In the process of ratification, the Senate can amend international agreements in ways that change their scope and intent. At worst, and President Carter's experience with the SALT II Treaty is an example, the Senate can delay action until the political situation or international events make ratification impossible.[60] Second, other international agreements may require the appropriation of funds before they can be implemented. This requires action by both the House of Representatives and the Senate. The Congress can effectively "kill" an international program by delaying the appropriation of funds. Thus, opponents of an agreement can derail the negotiating process after the fact by targeting members of the House and Senate.

In short, politics is the critical dimension of international negotiation. Politics influences decisions to enter negotiations. Politics enters into the formulation of interests and objectives. Politics shapes negotiating positions. Politics influences the bargaining and concession-making process. And politics often influences outcomes after international agreements have been signed. International negotiation is fundamentally a political process. This conflicts with the assumption of the conflict resolution approach that negotiation entails problem solving. It also suggests different explanations of why the United States has been successful in certain negotiations and unsuccessful in others and offers valuable lessons for negotiation in the post–Cold War world.

Putting the Pieces Together

The purpose of this chapter has been to identify the factors or conditions that influence the course of international negotiations. Background factors (history, culture, and personal characteristics of negotiators and political leaders), context (whether the parties are allies, adversaries, or friends), substance (interests and objectives), process (bargaining and concession-making styles), and politics (international, regional, domestic, and bureaucratic) are the major elements. What remains is to put these pieces together in a series of questions that will be addressed in each case study.

These questions are general in nature. This is due, in part, to the early state of theory development about international negotiation. Collectively, the questions suggest a framework within which to understand the case studies that follow. Answers to the questions will not produce a formal model or theory of negotiation, but they will point in the right direction by allowing some conclusions about the elements that have been identified and suggesting whether other influences should be considered.

Question 1: What prompted the United States and its negotiating partner to enter into negotiations? In other words, what problem or situation brought the parties to the bargaining table?

Question 2: How did U.S. policymakers define their interests and objectives with respect to the negotiations? How did America's negotiating partner define their interests and objectives with respect to the negotiations? Were the parties able to define common interests and objectives?

Question 3: What factors influenced the formulation of negotiating positions? How did these positions change during the course of the negotiations? How did initial positions compare with negotiated outcomes?

Question 4: What strategies and tactics did the parties use during the negotiations? How did differences in bargaining style influence the process and outcome of the negotiations? What was the role of politics in the selection of strategies and tactics? If the negotiations resulted in the signing of a formal agreement, how did the process of concession-making occur?

Question 5: What additional action, if any, was required for implementation of the agreement? How did the implementation process reflect the role of background factors, context, substance, and politics?

Question 6: If the negotiations did not result in the signing of a formal agreement, to what extent can the framework account for failure?

The case studies that follow address each of these questions, as appropriate, to examples of security negotiations between the United States and selected allies, adversaries, and friends during the 1970s and the 1980s. All of these negotiations occurred in the context of the Cold War and its security arrangements—arrangements that are in flux in the early 1990s. However, the underlying dynamics of these negotiations, particularly the politics of the process in each case, offer useful lessons for American negotiators faced with the challenge of constructing a new international security order.

Part II

Bargaining with Allies

Bargaining with allies should be among the easiest tasks facing the United States in the international arena. The existence of an alliance relationship between the United States and its negotiating partners implies positive feelings, the willingness to devote extensive resources to the relationship, and a broad scope of interaction cutting across political, military, economic, social, and cultural issues.

These characteristics of an alliance relationship mean that cooperative elements should dominate negotiation. The parties are less likely to view problems in win-lose or zero-sum terms. The identification of common interests and objectives—a fundamental requirement for successful negotiation—should be facilitated by the existence of an allied relationship. Moreover, the presence of a highly complex set of interactions between the parties offers greater room for maneuver or the use of side payments as a way of moving the negotiation forward to a successful conclusion. Finally, because negotiating partners in an alliance relationship are more likely to trust each other, they should devote less time to defining the nature of their relationship and more time to the negotiation of specific arrangements designed to fulfill common interests and objectives.

Critical to the success of any negotiation—and the negotiation of agreements between allies is no exception—is consensus-building, both at home and abroad. Interallied consensus-building, that is, the building of consensus between or among parties to the negotiation, is a necessary condition for success. But interallied consensus-building is not a sufficient condition. Domestic consensus-building is required to sell agreements once they have been signed. This is particularly important if an agreement requires legislative ratification or the appropriation of funds for implementation.

The cases in Part II, selected to illustrate negotiations with allies, demonstrate problems in domestic and interallied consensus-building. The U.S.-German Wartime Host Nation Support Agreement, signed by the United States and the Federal Republic of Germany in April 1982, faced serious problems in implementation because the executive branch failed to build domestic consensus (especially by winning the critical support of the Congress) before the agreement was signed. The result was years of debate about the purpose of the agreement and cost-sharing arrangements. In contrast, the decision made by the United States and its European allies in December 1979 to deploy new theater nuclear forces in Europe was successful in large part because NATO designed a strategy to build domestic consensus within Western Europe in support of the deployments, a consensus that was able to withstand Soviet efforts to block implementation of the decision.

These cases also illustrate how negotiations between allies are influenced by the nature of the issue—that is, whether conventional or nuclear forces are the subject of discussion. Nuclear issues tend to be more visible to European and American publics—and thus are more politically sensitive—than conventional issues. The process of consensus-building, therefore, should be more difficult when nuclear forces are the subject of debate between allies. Despite this fact, inter-allied consensus-building succeeded in the intermediate-range nuclear forces case, while domestic consensus-building failed in the wartime host nation support case.

Finally, these cases demonstrate that consensus-building is more complicated in multilateral negotiations. Other things being equal, the greater the number of parties to the negotiation, the longer and more difficult is the process of consensus-building, both internally and externally. In the intermediate-range nuclear forces case, the governments of West Germany, the United Kingdom, Belgium, the Netherlands, and Italy faced widespread opposition to the deployment of new theater nuclear forces on their soil. The process of domestic consensus-building within each of these countries complicated joint alliance negotiation of a deployment package that made both military and political sense. Yet the United States was more successful in this case and less successful in bilateral negotiations with the Federal Republic of Germany on wartime host nation support.

3. The Failure of Domestic Consensus

Wartime Host Nation Support

The U.S.-German Agreement, signed in Bonn, April 15, 1982, is of critical importance to the sustainability in combat of the U.S. in place and reinforcing forces. The . . . Agreement is a major breakthrough in our continuing efforts to comply with Congressional guidance to obtain increased wartime host nation support.
– General Bernard Rogers
Supreme Allied Commander, Europe [1]

We had allegations last year that these pieces of equipment were to be provided to German reservists. They could take them home if they were farmers. They could take home jeeps and trucks. We were going to assist them in their economy. We have trouble with this.
– Senator Ted Stevens (R-Alaska) [2]

The transatlantic bargain struck by the United States, Canada, and Western Europe on April 4, 1949, established the parameters of U.S.-European relations in the postwar period. Consultation, persuasion, and negotiation were built into the North Atlantic Treaty Organization from the very beginning. Debates within the alliance from the 1950s to the 1980s about how best to defend Western interests, the role of theater nuclear forces in Europe, the strength of the U.S. strategic nuclear guarantee, and whether the Europeans carry their fair share of the defense burden occurred in the context of the consultative framework established by parties to the North Atlantic Treaty.

The debates of the 1990s—concerning the declining Warsaw Pact threat and the future role of the United States in Europe—will lead to the restructuring of NATO and the overall U.S.-European relationship. But even as this restructuring occurs, NATO will contribute to the maintenance of stability and the development of new security arrangements in Europe.[3]

While, in practice, primary responsibility under the terms of the North Atlantic Treaty devolved to the United States during the immediate postwar period, pressures for change in the original terms of the transatlantic bargain began to build up during the 1970s.[4] Debate about the relative roles of the United States and its European allies was the product of three trends. First, during the 1970s the Soviet Union continued to build up its conventional and nuclear forces. The achievement of strategic parity with the United States, which was formalized in the SALT I Treaty, raised questions on both sides of the Atlantic about the strength of extended deterrence—that is, whether the protection of the American nuclear umbrella extended to the European allies and Japan. Second, the relative capabilities of the United States and its European allies had changed rapidly by the 1970s. The economic recovery of Europe, one of the objectives spelled out in the Brussels Treaty, had by all measures been achieved. And, third, in part as a result of the first two trends, American public opinion expressed a desire for the Europeans to do more in support of their own defense.

By the late 1970s debates within NATO focused on the need to improve conventional and theater nuclear capabilities in response to the Soviet force modernization effort. The programmatic results of these debates occurred during the late 1970s and the early 1980s. On the conventional front, in conjunction with several other defense initiatives, the United States and the Federal Republic of Germany entered into negotiations on wartime host nation support.

The U.S.-German Wartime Host Nation Support Program

On April 15, 1982, Ambassador Arthur Burns, representing the United States, and Foreign Minister Hans-Dietrich Genscher, representing the Federal Republic of Germany, signed the Wartime Host Nation Support (WHNS) Agreement in Bonn, West Germany.[5] The agreement entails the provision of certain civilian support and the creation of new equipment-holding units in the Bundeswehr Reserve which, upon mobilization, will be dedicated to the support of U.S. combat forces in Germany. The approximately 93,000 West German troops that are dedicated to the support of U.S. forces in Germany in wartime will provide a variety of support, including security of U.S. Air Force and Army installations, transportation of materiel and fuel, evacuation of casualties, prisoner of war handling, and decontamination.

Traditionally, support has been considered a national responsibility within NATO, with each country expected to shoulder its own logistics burden. The WHNS Agreement represented a major breakthrough because, for the first time, a NATO ally agreed to pay a portion of the support costs of U.S. combat units dedicated to the defense of Western Europe.

On its face, the U.S.-German wartime host nation support program would seem to be a limited, technical, defense arrangement that served the security interests of both the United States and the Federal Republic of Germany. For the United States, the agreement offered some relief from the shortfall in airlift and sealift, enabling the United States to deploy more combat forces to Germany early in a crisis or war. For the Federal Republic of Germany, the agreement served to reinforce the American commitment to the defense of Europe and responded to American domestic criticism of Germany's willingness to do more in support of its own defense.

In practice, however, the WHNS Agreement was a political-level statement of intentions by the United States and the Federal Republic of Germany. The agreement established the basis for subsequent negotiations between the U.S. Department of Defense and the West German Ministry of Defense designed to specify the nature of the commitment entered into in 1982. The use of vague language in the WHNS Agreement as a way of papering over differences between the parties and postponing the settlement of major issues led to serious conflicts in the negotiation of implementing arrangements.

The U.S.-German wartime host nation support program illustrates the problems that arise when negotiators and political leaders fail to build a domestic consensus before signing an international agreement. Implementation of the WHNS Agreement required the appropriation of funds by the United States Congress and the West German Bundestag. The United States entered into an executive agreement with the Federal Republic of Germany to avoid a formal congressional vote on the program. But representatives of the Department of Defense had to appear before congressional committees to support the department's request for the U.S. share of funding for the program. By failing to build consensus on Capitol Hill in advance, the Department of Defense failed in the first years of the program to win congressional approval for the U.S. share of the costs. This, in turn, delayed the negotiation of implementing arrangements with the Federal Republic of Germany.

In short, despite shared perceptions of the problem and the identification of common interests and objectives, and despite the history of cooperation between the United States and the Federal Republic of Germany on security and defense issues, the process and outcome of WHNS was very much a product of near-term political interests and calculations.

The Decision to Negotiate

Question 1: What prompted the United States and its negotiating partner to enter into negotiations? In other words, what problem or situation brought the parties to the bargaining table?

The successful defense of Western Europe was premised on the strategy of mobilization. Neither the United States nor its European allies maintained large standing armies in peacetime. The economic costs and political constraints that influence decisions within democratic political systems led to a strategy based upon the ability to call up forces quickly upon warning of a Warsaw Pact attack. For the United States, which maintained approximately 300,000 troops in Western Europe, successful implementation of the mobilization strategy demanded the ability to move large numbers of American troops and equipment to the European theater in times of crisis or war.

Concepts developed by the United States in 1977 and 1978 became the core of the rapid reinforcement element of the NATO Long Term

Defense Program (LTDP). The Department of Defense reasoned that it could roughly double the level of U.S. Army combat troops in Europe within ten days, provided that the European allies supported the prepositioning of equipment for those troops, permitted the use of allied air bases as reception facilities for U.S. reinforcing aircraft, and pursued the development of bilateral logistical support arrangements.

The NATO Long Term Defense Program was formally ratified by NATO heads of government at the Washington summit in May 1978. The program represented a highest level political commitment to both short-term measures and longer-term efforts to enhance NATO's military capabilities across the board. The fundamental assumption underlying the LTDP was the need for greater coordination and integration of the defense policies and programs of the fourteen allies. In conjunction with approval of the Long Term Defense Program in 1978, the United States made a commitment to provide a ten-division force to NATO by D-Day (that is, by the day on which combat operations were expected to commence). This force would consist of four U.S. divisions forward deployed in the Federal Republic of Germany and an additional six reinforcing divisions.

The ability of the United States to fulfill this commitment was premised on NATO's agreement to permit the prepositioning of six division sets of equipment in the Federal Republic of Germany, Belgium, and the Netherlands.[6] In support of the U.S. commitment to provide a ten-division force by D-Day, NATO allies also agreed to provide increased host nation support, to increase their commitment of civil aircraft and sealift, and to provide other support and storage facilities. Of these additional NATO commitments, the one with the greatest potential for enhancing deterrence was increased host nation support.

The decisions taken by both parties to enter into negotiations were products of shared history, joint political and military commitments, and common perceptions of the threat, as well as economic and domestic political considerations. The United States and the Federal Republic of Germany are allies whose relationship has developed in the context of the North Atlantic Treaty Organization. This relationship is characterized by high positive affect, high levels of commitment, and broad scope. Cooperative elements predominate in the relationship. During the Cold War the parties shared a common definition of the threat—as defined by the North Atlantic Treaty—and viewed negotiations with each other as an appropriate means of addressing these commonly defined security problems.

By the late 1970s members of NATO expressed growing concerns about the sustained Soviet military buildup and the implications of strategic parity between the United States and the Soviet Union for extended deterrence. The programmatic result of this concern was agreement by NATO heads of state in 1978 to pursue the Long Term Defense Program. Wartime host nation support fit squarely with the need to improve NATO's conventional defense capabilities.

In addition, negotiations were prompted by domestic political and economic trends in the United States. The United States Congress had called for the allies to assume a greater share of the defense burden in Europe and argued that the economic resurgence of Europe made greater burdensharing not only possible but also appropriate. At the same time, the United States confronted economic problems of its own and was looking for a cost-effective way to bolster its rapid reinforcement capabilities. Increasing the host nation support provided to American troops in Europe offered a politically and economically viable solution.

Interests and Objectives

Question 2: How did U.S. policymakers define their interests and objectives with respect to the negotiations? How did America's negotiating partner define their interests and objectives with respect to the negotiations? Were the parties able to define common interests and objectives?

The interests and objectives of the United States and the Federal Republic of Germany in the wartime host nation support negotiations are reflected in the nature of the problem that brought them to the bargaining table. The United States faced tremendous shortfalls in both combat support structure—that is, the logistics support units needed for U.S. combat forces—and the airlift and fast sealift capability needed to rapidly reinforce Western Europe in the event of crisis or war. Because of these shortfalls, the United States could not guarantee a ten-division D-Day force without receiving host nation support from the European allies. Thus, the primary U.S. objective in these negotiations was to obtain critically needed wartime host nation support from West Germany.

But in order to sell the program at home, American officials needed to demonstrate that the WHNS program was cost-effective. This meant the negotiation of a cost-sharing arrangement that would allow U.S. officials to argue that WHNS was cheaper than the alternatives. Initial cost estimates associated with the program were approximately $580 million (in Fiscal Year 1983 dollars), to be shared equally by both countries over the five-year implementation period. During that period the Federal Republic of Germany would pay slightly more than 50 percent of the costs (approximately $300 million to a U.S. share of about $280 million). After the initial implementation period, the Federal Republic of Germany would pay about 60 percent of the steady-state annual recurring costs of the program.[7]

In addition to obtaining critically needed wartime host nation support under a defensible cost-sharing arrangement, American officials demanded assurances that the dedicated support would, in fact, be available in wartime. The United States had demonstrated its commitment to the defense of Western Europe yearly in the REFORGER (Return of Forces to Germany) exercises, which require the airlift of large numbers of American troops from the continental United States to Western Europe. The purpose of REFORGER is to demonstrate both America's intention and its ability to reinforce U.S. troops in Europe in the event of crisis or war. The United States was aiming for a WHNS equivalent to REFORGER from the Federal Republic of Germany— that is, a commitment to mobilize and exercise the equipment-holding units in the Bundeswehr Reserve that would comprise the bulk of the German host nation support provided to U.S. forces.

The Federal Republic of Germany had similar, although not identical, interests and objectives during the wartime host nation support negotiations. Germany was anxious to fulfill its commitments under the terms of the Long Term Defense Program. The quid pro quo for the American ten-division D-Day commitment was the provision of wartime host nation support. Mindful of the defense burden already shouldered by the German public, however, German officials were reluctant to enter into an agreement with the United States that required the commitment of substantial additional resources for defense. Moreover, German officials expressed concern that support dedicated to American troops in wartime should not detract from support of their own military forces.

Like the United States, the Federal Republic of Germany was interested in using the wartime host nation support discussions to pursue an agreement on reinforcement exercises. The objective for German officials was the creation of a joint U.S.-German committee to discuss problems that occurred from the use of German territory for military maneuvers. The Federal Republic of Germany was dissatisfied with the slow resolution of such issues as damage claims by German citizens against American troops on military maneuvers.[8] The WHNS negotiations offered Germany another opportunity to raise military maneuver subjects in conjunction with the American desire to build the exercise of WHNS units into an agreement.

At the aggregate level, American and German policymakers were able to identify roughly compatible if not entirely common interests and objectives. For the United States, the primary goal was to increase its ability to move troops to Europe quickly in times of crisis or war; the best way of achieving this given the shortfalls in American airlift and sealift was host nation support. For West Germany, the goal was to ensure that American combat troops would arrive in Europe as quickly as possible; German policymakers realized that the United States could supply more combat troops early in a crisis or war if West Germany provided logistic support. Both parties to the negotiations were acting to support the agreed upon NATO strategy of flexible response. Neither side could afford dramatic increases in defense spending, and host nation support offered a relatively cheap solution to their common problems.

This apparent national consensus on U.S. interests and objectives in the wartime host nation support negotiations hid significant differences within the U.S. government. The primary objectives supported by the White House and the Department of Defense were not shared by many in the Congress. The Department of Defense believed the WHNS program was a cost-effective way of providing badly needed support to U.S. forces in wartime. Defense officials, aware of the enormous cost of alternatives to host nation support, believed that a fifty-fifty split was a reasonable way to fund the program.[9] Moreover, the wartime host nation support program represented a breakthrough in American efforts to convince the Europeans to assume a larger share of the defense burden.

The Congress, on the other hand, viewed the issue from the broader political perspective of NATO burdensharing and pressed for 100 percent funding by West Germany. After all, as more than one senator or representative pointed out, these American troops were in Europe to defend their soil, not our own. In May 1982 Congressman Joseph Addabbo (D-N.Y.) expressed the sentiment of many on Capitol Hill when he commented: "We are paying them for their manpower to protect their turf. That is what we are doing. We are paying mercenaries."[10] Addabbo charged further that something was wrong with American priorities when, in the face of unemployment at home, "we are giving $300 million to the Germans to protect their own soil."[11] For these U.S. officials, opposition to wartime host nation support was grounded in the belief that the Europeans were not carrying their fair share of the defense burden. The WHNS negotiations provided yet another opportunity to pressure the Federal Republic of Germany to pay more of the cost of their defense.

There were other reasons for concern that the WHNS program was not in the best interests of the United States. Some members of Congress argued that it was inappropriate to procure equipment for storage in Europe and use by West German troops when American soldiers and airmen did not have sufficient equipment to train with in the United States.[12] On this issue Congress reflected the interests (and the lobbying efforts) of the U.S. reserves and National Guard.

In short, while the United States and the Federal Republic of Germany shared a number of security interests and objectives in the wartime host nation support negotiations, there were important divisions within the U.S. government and in the country at large. The absence of an American consensus at the outset was to have serious effects on the process and outcome of the WHNS negotiations.

Negotiating Positions

Question 3: What factors influenced the formulation of negotiating positions? How did these positions change during the course of the negotiations? How did initial positions compare with negotiated outcomes?

The wartime host nation support negotiations focused on four major issues: (1) nature of support to be provided; (2) cost-sharing arrangement; (3) whether equipment was to be procured in the United States or in the Federal Republic of Germany; and (4) schedule of WHNS unit activations.

Nature of Support. The first debate centered on the nature of the wartime host nation support model. The 1982 WHNS Agreement established the program, in principle, but specifics needed to be worked out by the defense establishments of the two sides. These specifics included the exact nature of support to be provided, where this support would be located, and how many spaces or positions in the German armed forces would be required to provide the support.

The negotiated model represented a compromise between the American desire for extensive support to fulfill its military requirements and the German desire to provide support to U.S. forces without detracting from the ability of the Bundeswehr to support its own forces in the event of war. The model indicated the number and types of German military units and both their peacetime and wartime personnel strengths. For example, the U.S. Army required support to locally secure thirty-nine of its installations in West Germany in wartime. The Federal Republic of Germany offered to satisfy that requirement with eleven security companies, twenty-eight security platoons, and a training center. These units would be manned in peacetime by a skeleton force of less than one hundred military and civilian personnel. The units would be filled out in wartime until they reached a wartime military strength of nearly 4,000 personnel.[13] The total support program for the U.S. Army consisted of fifty-one equipment storage sites, fifteen ammunition sites, and twelve headquarters and training centers.[14]

Cost-sharing Arrangement. Second, and related to the first debate, there was extensive discussion about the actual cost of the program. Although the United States pressed for cost-sharing from the beginning of the negotiations, there was no precedent for a host nation assuming a portion of the support costs of U.S. combat units dedicated to the defense of Western Europe. The Federal Republic of Germany was interested in minimizing the costs of the program as well. A fifty-fifty arrangement seemed like a reasonable compromise because it was clear that Congress would be unlikely to support the program if Germany paid less than half the cost. Moreover, the German commitment to pay the salaries of military personnel involved in the program and the American commitment to pay civilian salaries associated with the program may have been designed to anticipate objections later made by some in the Congress who argued that under the terms of the arrangement the United States was simply paying mercenaries.

A related issue concerned the construction of new facilities and whether new construction should be paid for by the U.S. and West German governments or through the NATO infrastructure program. The WHNS Agreement included a pledge by the parties to "strive for extensive cost limitation" through the use of available facilities, NATO infrastructure funding, or equitable cost-sharing where existing facilities and infrastructure funding were not available.[15] Existing facilities were identified by the two sides and made available for early unit activations in 1983 and 1984. But it became clear that additional construction would be necessary to support the program in later years. At this point the United States and the Federal Republic of Germany agreed to approach NATO to seek funding for construction associated with the WHNS program.

In November 1984 NATO determined that the wartime host nation support program was "in principle" eligible for NATO infrastructure program support under the category of reinforcement support. But NATO stated further that each project must be approved separately. The problem with relying on NATO infrastructure funding for WHNS facilities is that the slow NATO funding process could delay implementation of the program. In response to this concern, in February 1985 the Federal Republic of Germany offered a significant breakthrough solution to the infrastructure cost-sharing question and lack of facilities to support unit activations. Germany offered to prefinance construction projects if the United States agreed to share on a fifty-fifty basis those costs not covered by the NATO infrastructure program.[16] In March 1985, the United States accepted the German prefinancing offer subject to the availability of funds, joint U.S.-German review of individual facilities construction projects, and timely submission of all projects for NATO infrastructure funding.

Equipment Sourcing. A third major issue concerned whether equipment needed to support the program would be procured from American or German sources. The WHNS Agreement states that procurement will be handled on the basis of joint U.S. and West German decisions.[17] It was the American intention to procure the majority of equipment from U.S. sources, as had repeatedly been briefed to the Congress beginning in 1982. The Federal Republic of Germany, in contrast, argued for a largely German-produced equipment program.

The American argument was grounded in the political reality of the program and the need to win congressional support. In response to concerns expressed about the program by the Congress, defense officials indicated that nearly all the required equipment would be procured in the United States. However, these officials left open the option of acquiring some equipment from German sources as needed for operational or training reasons. This view was supported by the testimony of Department of Defense officials before subcommittees of the House Appropriations Committee in March and May 1982.[18]

Not all Americans involved in implementation of the program supported the political-level view that most if not all of the equipment should be purchased in the United States. Officers assigned to the headquarters of the U.S. Army Europe (USAREUR) and the U.S. Air Force Europe (USAFE) carried out joint studies on equipment sourcing with their German counterparts. These studies concluded that the equipment to be used by WHNS units should be similar to equipment being used by regular Bundeswehr units. From a military perspective, the argument made sense. German soldiers would be more effective when using equipment with which they already were familiar.

The Federal Republic of Germany offered a similar view. Although they recognized the political and economic aspects of the equipment sourcing issue, especially the need to make the "two-way street" a reality, German officials argued that decisions about equipment sourcing should be made on the basis of military requirements and cited the results of the studies conducted by joint U.S.-German military planning staffs that the majority of equipment to be used by WHNS units should be German equipment.

While some U.S. officials believed that support and interoperability would be enhanced if German sources were used, it was necessary for political reasons—namely, to win and maintain the support of the Congress for the WHNS program—to spend the majority of U.S. procurement funds on U.S. manufactured equipment. Following two years of intensive negotiations on this issue, a breakthrough occurred in February 1985, when Germany agreed with the American proposal that 60 percent of U.S. procured equipment for the WHNS program would be acquired from U.S. sources. That breakthrough was formalized in an equipment sourcing agreement which was signed in May 1985.

Unit Activations. Finally, there was much debate between the defense ministries about the activation of wartime host nation support units in the German Bundeswehr Reserve. The program was scheduled to be implemented between 1983 and 1987. In practice, units were still being activated in 1988,[19] in part because of financing considerations and procurement delays but also because the two sides disagreed about the order in which units should be activated.

For its part, the United States pressed for the activation of transportation and resupply units early on because of the significant U.S. shortfall in these areas of support. The Federal Republic of Germany, in contrast, was reluctant to agree to the activation of these types of units in the absence of strong support for the program in the United States Congress and given the lack of agreement on equipment sourcing issues.

On the basis of joint implementation and feasibility studies concluded by U.S. and German planning staffs, activation of the initial units—consisting of two security companies and nine security platoons—took place in 1983. The reasons for beginning with security units are clear. These units require minimal equipment and storage facilities. Actual appropriations, beginning with the Fiscal Year 1983 Supplemental Appropriations Bill, were much less than the Department of Defense requested for the WHNS program.[20] The absence of funding dictated the schedule of unit activations in the early years because the United States was unable to procure the items of heavy equipment associated with transportation and materiel handling units.

By 1984 and 1985, in large part because of the availability of funds, the identification of existing facilities, and resolution of the equipment sourcing issue, activations expanded to include transportation battalions, a nuclear, biological, and chemical defense battalion, airfield damage repair platoons, a casualty evacuation battalion, medical squadrons, personnel and materiel at collocated operating bases, and some civilian support. Here again, the debate was shaped by the availability of funds, equipment, and facilities. All units were activated by December 1988 and were planned to be fully equipped and operational by Fiscal Year 1993.[21]

Bargaining and Concession-making

Question 4: What strategies and tactics did the parties use during the negotiations? How did differences in bargaining style influence the process and outcome of the negotiations? What was the role of politics in the selection of strategies and tactics? If the negotiations resulted in the signing of a formal agreement, how did the process of concession-making occur?

The negotiations between the United States and the Federal Republic of Germany on wartime host nation support illustrate the use of multiple strategies, tactics, and bargaining styles. The impact of background, context, substance, and politics on the selection of strategies and tactics can be seen in the negotiation of both the 1982 agreement and the technical implementing arrangements on military and civilian support and reinforcement exercises.

Some aspects of the negotiations represent the concession-convergence model, where the parties make a series of concessions until they arrive at an agreement near the "middle" or center of their initial positions. In other words, they agree to "split the difference." The negotiations on cost-sharing and facilities construction illustrate the concession-convergence model. On cost-sharing, the Federal Republic of Germany would have preferred to maintain the NATO precedent of holding those countries with forces deployed in West Germany responsible for providing their own support—keeping with the motto "logistics is a national responsibility." For the United States, this position was untenable. U.S. negotiators anticipated congressional opposition to the wartime host nation support program, and outright objection unless Germany agreed to shoulder most of the cost. A reasonable compromise was the agreement to split the costs of the program fifty-fifty. The fifty-fifty cost-sharing provision in the WHNS Agreement then established a new precedent that was reflected in the 1985 agreement between the parties on facilities construction—the costs of new construction deemed not eligible for NATO infrastructure program funding would be shared equally by the United States and West Germany.

Other aspects of the wartime host nation support negotiations illustrate even more dramatically the impact of political considerations on bargaining between the United States and the Federal Republic of Germany. Both the American and German positions on equipment sourcing reflect the critical importance of domestic politics in these negotiations. The role of politics was perhaps most visible on the U.S. side, in the continuing conflict between the Department of Defense and the Congress.

Representatives of the Department of Defense won congressional funding for the program by pledging that a majority of the equipment would be procured from American sources. These unilateral commitments were made despite the fact that the WHNS Agreement states that "all procurements . . . shall be made on the basis of joint decisions, and in accordance with national laws and regulations of the Contracting Parties."[22] Once the secretary of defense had committed himself to procuring virtually all of the necessary equipment from U.S. sources, the result was a foregone conclusion. U.S. negotiators then used these political-level, public commitments to the Congress as leverage in equipment sourcing discussions with their West German counterparts. They argued, in effect, that the United States could not make concessions on this issue because it would interfere with the consensus-building process at home. This occurred despite the fact that lower level civilian bureaucrats (some in the Department of the Army) and component command military officers (especially from the staff of the headquarters of the U.S. Army Europe and the U.S. Air Force Europe) recognized the operational advantages of German soldiers using equipment with which they were already familiar.

For their part, West German officials linked the equipment sourcing issue to the broader political debate within NATO about the "two-way street." In 1982 Western Europe was confronted with a serious economic recession. Domestic demand was limited by government policies designed to control inflationary pressures. In this economic environment, West Germany was looking for foreign markets for its military equipment. Throughout the course of the wartime host nation support negotiations, West German officials had assumed that they would be able to sell the United States much of the required equipment.[23] Equipment sourcing, for Germany, was not simply an issue of military effectiveness and efficiency, but one of economics as well.

However, the West German defense minister was unwilling to place the WHNS program in jeopardy over the issue of the "two-way street" in NATO. If the WHNS program failed, the overall European financial contribution to NATO would drop. German defense ministry officials were well aware that although Germany had committed itself (along with other NATO allies) to an annual 3 percent increase in defense spending in real terms between 1979 and 1984, by 1982 the United States, Britain, Norway, and Luxembourg were the only NATO allies able to keep the pledge.[24] Growing criticism from the United States Congress about Germany's contribution to the common defense could lead the United States to renege on its commitment to provide ten divisions in Europe by D-Day. And this could have negative effects on other cooperative programs, such as POMCUS.

American supporters of the wartime host nation support program in the executive branch relied on linkage strategies in their dealings with the Congress as well as with West Germany. Wartime host nation support was not the only area in which the United States sought the cooperation of its German allies. The United States had pressed for some time for the construction of new troop facilities and the relocation of American forces in West Germany closer to their wartime defensive positions.[25] The relocation program, known as the Master Restationing Plan, was only one of several cooperative initiatives undertaken in support of the NATO strategy of forward defense. In numerous appearances before committees of the Congress, representatives of the Department of Defense argued that support of the wartime host nation support program would facilitate negotiations with Germany on the Master Restationing Plan, an issue of great concern to the Congress and the Department of Defense.[26]

The process of bargaining and concession-making that occurred throughout the negotiations on wartime host nation support thus illustrates the importance of both concession-convergence and politics. Even those issues that illustrate the concession-convergence model, such as cost-sharing and facilities construction, include elements of domestic politics. The political compromises that occurred on both sides shaped the nature of the WHNS Agreement as well as subsequent negotiations about the implementing arrangements.

Implementation

Question 5: What additional action, if any, was required for implementation of the agreement? How did the implementation process reflect the role of background factors, context, substance, and politics?

Responsibility for implementation of the wartime host nation support program, including the negotiation of technical arrangements, was delegated by the Office of the Secretary of Defense (representing the government of the United States) to the deputy commander in chief of the United States European Command, based in Stuttgart, West Germany. For the Federal Republic of Germany, responsibility was delegated to the deputy chief of staff of the German armed forces.

Negotiations on the military support technical arrangement began immediately following signature of the WHNS Agreement. The agreement, signed on June 13, 1986, specifies the details of German unit activations. The civilian support technical arrangement proved more difficult. By 1989 the two sides had not concluded these negotiations because they were unable to agree on a cost-sharing arrangement.[27]

In addition to technical arrangements on military and civilian support, the U.S. Department of Defense and the West German Ministry of Defense initiated discussions on a reinforcement exercises agreement, as provided for in Article 6 of the WHNS Agreement. Although it was not specifically mentioned in Article 6, the United States interpreted the purpose of this agreement as providing a means for ensuring that the host nation support units created under the program would be exercised in peacetime. The American military needed reassurance that the program would in fact work in wartime, and testing whether and how quickly these host nation support units would be called up in peacetime was one way to increase their confidence in the program. On January 21, 1983, the United States and the Federal Republic of Germany signed the "Agreement Concerning the Preparation for and Execution and Support of Reinforcement Exercises and Other Related Exercises."[28]

Under the terms of the Reinforcement Exercises Agreement, as it was called, West Germany will provide logistic support, supplies, and services from military and civilian sources to U.S. forces in Germany during exercises. The agreement addresses American concerns about the reliability of the host nation support program in Article 1: "Support may involve the employment of Federal Armed Forces units, including both active units and equipment-holding units."[29] The agreement also addresses German concerns about the resolution of disputes between the United States and West German citizens growing out of maneuver exercises. Article 7 creates a "Permanent Committee for Maneuver Subjects" designed to "discuss problems arising from the use of German territory for maneuvers held by U.S. Forces and will advise the U.S. commanders concerned and the Federal Minister of Defense of the Federal Republic of Germany on action to be taken with a view to lessening these problems."[30]

Conclusion: The Politics of Wartime Host Nation Support

The U.S.-German negotiations on wartime host nation support illustrate both the opportunities and the problems associated with dealing with allies. On the positive side, cooperative elements clearly dominated the discussions. The identification of compatible if not identical interests and objectives was facilitated by the existence of the alliance relationship and long history of interaction between the United States and the Federal Republic of Germany. The parties tended to view the negotiations not in win-lose or zero-sum terms but rather as a cooperative endeavor out of which both had much to gain.

If the United States and West Germany shared many common interests and objectives and were predisposed to see the negotiations succeed, what explains the many problems associated with the negotiation of the 1982 WHNS Agreement and subsequent implementing arrangements? Many elements are involved, but the common thread underlying these negotiations is politics.

The language of the 1982 agreement suggests that both the United States and West Germany were willing to leave resolution of some of the most difficult issues to subsequent discussion. On the one hand, this is not surprising given the nature of the U.S.-West German relationship. Allies could be trusted to work out the implementation of a political-level commitment. Undoubtedly neither country would have been satisfied with this approach if they had been dealing with an adversary. On the other hand, vague language on many critical issues provided easy targets for opponents of the agreement, particularly those in the United States Congress.

Perhaps the best example of this problem is the language on cost. Article 2 of the WHNS Agreement states that costs will be shared by the parties "subject to enabling legislation and the availability of funds."[31] American negotiators pressed for this stipulation because they had not yet received the approval of the Congress. But West German negotiators saw the situation differently; they assumed the executive branch had obtained the support of the Congress before entering into the agreement. In the view of the Federal Republic of Germany, failure of Congress to fund the program in the early years of its existence could be taken as repudiation of an international agreement.

The disagreement is grounded in differences between the American and German political systems: "In the German parliamentary system, failure of the Parliament (the German Bundestag) to ratify an agreement entered into by its Executive Branch would, in all likelihood, result in the fall of the government. Thus, from the German perspective, signature of the WHNS Agreement represented a national commitment." [32]

The wartime host nation support negotiations involved many bureaucratic actors or players. At the highest political level, actors included the respective heads of state and foreign and defense ministers. After the political-level WHNS Agreement was signed in April 1982, lower level bureaucratic players entered the game. Negotiations to flesh out the WHNS model and establish the technical arrangements necessary to implement the program were conducted by mid-level civilians and military officers in the U.S. and German ministries of defense and military command structures. Throughout this process, as we have seen, the United States Congress and the German Bundestag played critical roles because they controlled funding for the program.

The political problem for both sets of negotiators involved developing and maintaining domestic consensus in support of the program while making concessions to the other side. The signing of the WHNS Agreement in April 1982 represented not the end but the beginning of negotiations about the precise nature of the program, cost-sharing, and implementation. Negotiators developed first one consensus and then another internally, as they moved from one issue to the next. The relationships that existed among the issues that were the subject of these negotiations complicated the consensus-building process within each government and influenced the concession-making process that occurred between the parties. Cost-sharing arrangements could not be firmed up until the nature of the model became clear. The equipment-sourcing issue was tied to congressional decisions on funding. And unit activations—the goal of the program—could not begin in earnest until issues of equipment sourcing and funding were resolved.

Thus, the American negotiating experience on wartime host nation support demonstrates the extent to which negotiation is a political enterprise which does not end when a government-to-government agreement is signed. Perhaps the most difficult negotiations occur in debate about what an agreement means and how it should be implemented. This may explain why implementation of the program will take nearly twice as long as was intended when the agreement was signed in 1982. (Implementation was scheduled to conclude in 1988; by 1989 the Department of Defense had revised this date to 1993.)[33]

American negotiators would have faced difficult problems in dealing with their German counterparts even if they had first developed an internal consensus on the objectives of the WHNS negotiations. In fact, the United States used the absence of domestic consensus—namely, widespread opposition in the Congress—as an effective bargaining tool. However, the existence of greater internal consensus from the outset may have facilitated the negotiation of the technical implementing arrangements and the appropriation of funds to support the program. The failure of the United States to ensure domestic consensus complicated already difficult negotiations and fueled disputes between American and West German policymakers about implementation of an agreement that most on both sides of the Atlantic believed was in the security interests of the alliance.

The sea changes in the Soviet Union and Eastern Europe during the late 1980s and early 1990s will increase the complexity of negotiations between the United States and its European allies. Building interallied consensus, in particular, will become more difficult as the nature of the U.S.-European relationship changes. The decline of the Soviet threat, the democratization of Eastern Europe, the disintegration of the Warsaw Pact, and the unification of Germany signal the beginning of a redefinition of what it means to be allies.

The drawdown of U.S. and Soviet military forces will increase the political value of Germany's economic and geographic position.[34] In the near term, however, much of the NATO military structure will be maintained as a "safety net," able to receive U.S. reinforcements in the event of crisis or war.[35] Although a product of the Cold War, the U.S.-German wartime host nation support program is well positioned to support the transition to new security arrangements in Europe.

4. Building Interallied Consensus

Deploying Theater Nuclear Weapons in Europe

Deterrence is essentially political. Extended deterrence is essentially political, only more so. . . . There is no deductive way of arriving at a magic formula for extended deterrence.
— Michael Clarke [1]

We are not America's guinea pigs.
Help remove all nuclear weapons from the world— from the Netherlands to begin with.
— Slogans of the European Peace Movement [2]

Although nuclear weapons have been an integral part of NATO's defense posture for more than thirty years, debates about their role, missions, and deployment have at times threatened to tear apart the fabric of the U.S.–West European relationship. During the Cold War nuclear weapons represented the physical manifestation of the U.S. commitment to the security of Western Europe—the key to extended deterrence. The presence of U.S. nuclear forces in Europe demonstrated America's willingness to respond to Warsaw Pact aggression with nuclear retaliation. Theater nuclear weapons provided the link between U.S. conventional forces in Europe and the strategic nuclear guarantee. As such, they served to reassure the Europeans about the extent of the American commitment to the defense of Europe.

But theater nuclear forces also generated anxiety within political and public circles in Western Europe because if deterrence failed, many of these weapons would have exploded on West European soil. Moreover, the presence of theater nuclear forces in Europe was viewed by some Europeans as essentially provocative and likely to ensure that Western Europe would become the target of Soviet nuclear weapons in the event of war.[3] And by 1990 many argued that revolutionary changes in the Soviet Union and Eastern Europe had "undermined the military and political rationales for continued deployment of nuclear forces in Western Europe."[4]

The December 1979 decision by NATO to deploy new theater nuclear forces in Europe and to pursue arms control discussions with the Soviet Union designed to reduce and limit these weapons dramatically illustrates the continuing debate within the alliance about the role of nuclear weapons in Europe.

The December 1979 Dual Track Decision

On December 12, 1979, NATO foreign and defense ministers meeting in Brussels unanimously approved a two-track plan for deploying new long-range theater nuclear forces in Western Europe and pursuing arms control discussions with the Soviet Union. In the communiqué following the meeting, ministers pointed to their concerns about the sustained buildup of Warsaw Pact forces and, in particular, the Soviet Union's decision to modernize their long-range theater nuclear forces (LRTNF) and short-range nuclear weapons.[5]

The allies announced agreement to modernize NATO's LRTNF by the deployment of 108 Pershing II launchers (which would replace the U.S. Pershing I systems already deployed in Germany) and 464 ground-launched cruise missiles, all with single warheads. The communiqué indicated that all members of NATO's integrated defense structure would participate in the program and that the weapons would be based in "selected" countries. (After the fact, it became public knowledge that the weapons would be based in the Federal Republic of Germany, the United Kingdom, Belgium, the Netherlands, and Italy.)[6]

In conjunction with these new deployments, NATO ministers announced that the United States would withdraw 1,000 nuclear warheads from Europe "as soon as feasible."[7] NATO ministers agreed that an evolutionary upward adjustment in theater nuclear forces would occur within that reduced level. This implied that some adjustments would be made in other elements of NATO's nuclear arsenal.

With respect to arms control, NATO ministers endorsed the SALT

II Treaty, called on the United States and the Soviet Union to pursue limitations on long-range theater nuclear forces, and endorsed the U.S. decision to begin negotiations as soon as possible, within the framework of SALT III. Finally, NATO ministers established a special consultative body, known as the Special Consultative Group (SCG), "to support the U.S. negotiating effort." Although the allies would not be parties to negotiations with the Soviet Union on LRTNF, the SCG provided a mechanism for consultation with the United States and some assurances that their views would be taken into account as the United States formulated its negotiating position and engaged in bargaining with the Soviet Union.

Although the December 1979 dual track decision was unanimous, two allies expressed reservations.[8] The Netherlands delayed its final decision on whether to accept the ground-launched cruise missiles scheduled for deployment on their soil. Initially the decision was delayed for two years, but it was then extended. Belgium also reserved the right to reassess its decision to accept ground-launched cruise missiles in six months. That reservation also was extended to 1985. In both cases, these reservations were tied to a desire for the United States to explore prospects for arms control with the Soviet Union. Both countries envisaged an arms control agreement that would make any new deployments unnecessary.

The discussions between the United States and its West European allies about the deployment of new theater nuclear forces demanded consensus-building at two levels. First, each NATO government faced the task of building consensus internally in support of a response to the Soviet force modernization program. For some NATO governments, such as the United States and the United Kingdom, domestic consensus-building was easier than for others, such as the Federal Republic of Germany, Belgium, and the Netherlands. Internal consensus for several nations hinged on the development of an arms control track in support of force modernization. The strong domestic pressure for an arms control alternative, particularly in West Germany, Belgium, and the Netherlands, was a direct result of the political sensitivities historically associated with nuclear issues in Europe.

Building an international consensus, or an interallied consensus, demanded an outcome that all governments could accept. Each government had to balance multiple interests and objectives in assessing whether and how to participate in the NATO response. The special situation of West Germany meant, in practice, that the West German government exercised a veto over the outcome. For this reason, American officials probably devoted more time and effort to "the German problem" than to any other aspect of the negotiations.

A complicating factor in the design of an interallied consensus was an extensive propaganda campaign by the Soviet Union aimed at derailing the NATO decision-making process. Thus, this case also illustrates the impact of international politics and other external influences on the process and outcome of negotiations between allies.

The Decision to Negotiate

Question 1: What prompted the United States and its negotiating partners to enter into negotiations? In other words, what problem or situation brought the parties to the bargaining table?

By the mid-1970s, changes in the military balance raised concerns both in the United States and in Western Europe about the continued credibility of NATO's deterrent strategy. The Soviet Union had achieved strategic parity with the United States and had embarked on a sustained program of force modernization designed to improve its strategic, theater nuclear, and conventional forces across the board.

Of primary concern for the alliance were Soviet deployments of modernized theater nuclear forces—the SS-20 ballistic missile and the Backfire bomber. In the 1950s the Soviet Union had deployed SS-4 and SS-5 missiles against Western Europe. These weapons had the capability of striking Europe but not the United States. Although the United States deployed small numbers of similar weapons in Western Europe in the early 1960s—Thor and Jupiter missiles based in the United Kingdom, Italy, and Turkey—the Soviet Union maintained superiority in theater nuclear forces.

The SS-20 missile was viewed with increasing concern for several reasons. First, the missile was more accurate than the SS-4 and SS-5 and had greater range—and, therefore, greater target coverage. The

SS-20 was capable of striking targets not only in Europe, but also in the Middle East, Persian Gulf, and Asia. In addition, the SS-20 carried three independently targetable warheads, in contrast to the single-warhead SS-4 and SS-5. Finally, the SS-20 was a mobile missile. It could be moved from one location to another within the Soviet Union. Concerns also were raised about the capabilities of the Backfire bomber. The Backfire represented a new generation of Soviet aircraft, with an extended range capable of covering the European theater as well as the Middle East, Persian Gulf, and the Pacific.

European concerns were reflected in an address by West German chancellor Helmut Schmidt delivered to a meeting of the International Institute for Strategic Studies in London on October 28, 1977.[9] Schmidt argued that the advent of strategic parity between the United States and the Soviet Union had focused attention on the imbalances that existed at the theater nuclear and conventional levels in Europe. Theater nuclear forces were not being addressed in SALT II, and Schmidt felt that the United States was content to focus on its own security interests while ignoring those of its allies. Schmidt argued for a parallel approach to removing the disparities in the military balance that existed at the theater level. In large part, Schmidt's speech reflected European, and especially German, concerns about the reliability of the United States and doubts about the ability of President Jimmy Carter to take European interests into account in his dealings with the Soviet Union.

Thus, the decisions taken by the United States and its allies to enter into negotiations about the appropriate response to the Soviet buildup were prompted by somewhat different concerns. For the United States (and, in particular, for some American military officers), the problem was the Soviet deployment of new and modernized theater nuclear forces that placed the West at risk. While other American policymakers believed that no new military problem existed, the United States was drawn into negotiations by the Europeans, who saw the situation differently.

For the Europeans, the fundamental problem was growing concern about the reliability of the United States and whether American policymakers would take European interests into account in their dealings with the Soviet Union. The Soviets had deployed theater nuclear forces in Eastern Europe capable of threatening Western Europe since the late 1950s. What had changed by the mid- to late 1970s, however, was the nature of the strategic balance. Questions again were being raised about whether the United States would be willing to risk the security of Washington, D.C., in the defense of Bonn, West Germany.

Differences between the European and American views about the nature of the problem posed by Soviet force deployments were never completely reconciled during discussions leading to the December 1979 decision. The inability of the United States and its allies to fully resolve these differences is consistent with their varying interpretations of the NATO doctrine of flexible response and the way in which those interpretations colored policymakers' perceptions of interests and objectives.

Interests and Objectives

Question 2: How did U.S. policymakers define their interests and objectives with respect to the negotiations? How did America's negotiating partners define their interests and objectives with respect to the negotiations? Were the parties able to define common interests and objectives?

NATO strategy during the Cold War was premised on the concept of "flexible response," which was formally accepted by the alliance in 1967.[10] Under the terms of flexible response, NATO agreed first to mount a direct defense against Warsaw Pact aggression with conventional forces. In the event that direct defense failed, the alliance was prepared to be the first to escalate to the use of theater nuclear forces. And, if the adversary was not defeated at that level, the United States was prepared to respond with nuclear strikes against Soviet territory. The purpose of flexible response was to create uncertainty in the minds of Soviet decision makers about the nature of an allied response to aggression, thus prompting the aggressor to think twice about launching an attack against Western Europe.

Flexible response was tied to the NATO triad of forces. In order to implement the strategy, NATO relied on conventional forces, theater nuclear forces, and U.S. strategic nuclear forces, balanced at each level and linked (or "coupled") to facilitate alliance decisions to move from one level to the next.

Flexible response represented a compromise between the interests of the United States and Western Europe. For the Americans, the key to flexible response was the emphasis on conventional forces and controlling escalation to the use of nuclear weapons, especially U.S. strategic forces, as long as possible. For the Europeans, in contrast, the key to flexible response was the emphasis on avoiding a prolonged conventional or theater nuclear war in Europe and escalating to the use of U.S. strategic nuclear forces as quickly as possible.[11] These differences in interpretation were never fully resolved, and they influenced the definition of interests and objectives in the debate between 1977 and 1979 about the deployment of theater nuclear forces in Europe.

The discussion of interests and objectives crystallized around two major issues. First, what was the nature of "coupling," and did the modernization of Soviet forces represent a military problem or a political problem for the alliance? Second, what were the special concerns of the Federal Republic of Germany, and why was Germany critical in the formulation of an alliance response?

Coupling. Jonathan Dean, former U.S. arms control negotiator, has described the NATO experience with theater nuclear forces as "treating the coupling sickness."[12] Coupling is a product of the Soviet-American strategic relationship and the political relationship that exists between the United States and Western Europe. Soviet modernization of their theater nuclear forces during the 1970s created concern that the Soviet Union might achieve "escalation dominance"—that is, they had developed the capability to deter the alliance from escalating the conflict and thus confine any future conflict to the European theater. Moreover, many in the United States and in Europe were becoming increasingly concerned about the vulnerability of land-based intercontinental ballistic missiles (ICBMs). Would an American president be willing to use theater nuclear weapons if his Soviet counterpart had the capability of destroying much of the U.S. land-based ICBM force?

European concerns about the reliability of the United States have been raised when political relations between the United States and

Western Europe have been at low ebb.[13] The West German experience with the neutron bomb during the late 1970s confirmed their worst fears about the American understanding of the nuclear issue in Europe. Press leaks about the contents of Presidential Review Memorandum (PRM) 10 suggested that "given insufficient conventional forces in Europe, the United States would have to plan on the basis that in the event of an attack by the Warsaw Pact on Western Europe, NATO forces would have to adopt a strategy of falling back and trading space for time."[14] Neither of these events served to reassure Europeans about America's reliability.

Determining whether the Soviet deployment of the SS-20 and the Backfire bomber represented a political threat or a military threat, or both, and what kind of response was necessary thus became a test of alliance strength and the American commitment to the defense of Europe. Some, on both sides of the Atlantic, argued that there was a military problem, that a gap in the continuum of deterrence existed, and that a military response was required. In the United States, while there was no consistent support for the deployment of new long-range theater nuclear forces in Europe, some in the American military establishment favored new systems.[15] General Alexander Haig, then supreme allied commander, Europe, noted that "in the past ten years, the Soviet Union has undertaken improvements in its theatre nuclear forces whose cumulative effect has been to transform the former Western superiority into a current Soviet advantage, especially in longer range theatre nuclear systems."[16] Given these developments, Haig argued that theater nuclear force modernization was essential.[17]

In Europe, supporters of theater nuclear force modernization emerged from the ranks of the military and political leadership. Federal German defense minister Hans Apel was one of the strongest proponents. In an interview on West German radio, he argued that "the Soviet Union has achieved a great technological military lead with its SS-20 mobile missile, which is hard to detect in the terrain. We must do something, because our systems are outdated, and the Soviet Union's have been modernized. That is called closing the arms gap."[18] Perhaps of greatest influence was Chancellor Schmidt's October 1977 address, which argued for an unspecified response to support NATO's strategy of deterrence.[19]

Others suggested that the problem was purely political and that new deployments by the alliance were unnecessary. The United States adopted this position early in discussions within the High Level Group (HLG) of the NATO Nuclear Planning Group.[20] Many within the U.S. foreign affairs and defense bureaucracies argued that the Soviet Union would not distinguish between nuclear strikes launched against them from European bases and nuclear strikes launched from the continental United States. Their response could well be the same in either case—namely, strategic nuclear strikes on American soil. Moreover, U.S. strategic nuclear forces already possessed flexible command and control and targeting capability to cover additional Soviet targets and therefore "plug the gap in the continuum of deterrence."[21] In addition, the deployment of new long-range theater nuclear forces could be destabilizing, by encouraging the Soviet Union to launch a preemptive strike and therefore put pressure on the United States to "use them or lose them."

In Europe, the political interpretation of NATO's problem was articulated by Christoph Bertram, who suggested that "only political trust makes these tensions tolerable. To seek remedies for political strains in the Alliance through the nuclear route is, therefore, short-sighted. It is simply the wrong instrument."[22] Moreover, the deployment of new long-range nuclear forces was feared by others because the United States might believe that it could use nuclear weapons in Europe and limit the conflict to European soil. In return, Europe would become the target of an angry Soviet response. At best, from this perspective, new weapons were unnecessary; at worst, they served to put Europe at risk while decoupling the United States from Europe.[23]

The evolution of the debate about coupling suggests that the problem was both military and political, that it engaged both military and political interests, and that it demanded both military and political solutions. The High Level Group, whose members included senior military and defense officials, not surprisingly determined that a military response was required. The political leadership within NATO, represented by heads of state and government and foreign ministers, added the political dimension. Both the extent of the military response and the addition of an arms control track are products of this complex interpretation of European and American interests.

The Special Situation of Germany. The Federal Republic of Germany was critical to the theater nuclear forces program from the beginning. Whatever solution the alliance arrived at would have to address German concerns, be sensitive to Germany's political and military situation, and represent German interests and objectives.

Because of its geographical location, West Germany was perhaps the most vulnerable to Soviet military forces and political influence. In the event of war, Germany would bear the brunt of an initial Warsaw Pact offensive. The division of Germany into East and West during the Cold War further opened the Federal Republic to Soviet influence. Because West Germany attempted to balance its membership in NATO with a desire for improved relations with the Eastern bloc, arms control assumed a critical position in German security debates. Thus, it should not be surprising that West Germany pressed so hard for inclusion of an arms control track in the December 1979 decision.

Germany historically has endeavored to raise the nuclear threshold, because if nuclear weapons are used they are likely to be used on German soil. Germany has eschewed control over nuclear weapons, in large part for political reasons. But Germany also has been concerned about the possible use of nuclear weapons in Germany by its allies. The fear of "being defended with nuclear weapons against its will" appears frequently in the literature on German attitudes about nuclear weapons.[24]

Germany also historically has feared being branded a special zone, either in terms of force deployments or arms control. Therefore, any discussion of the deployment of nuclear weapons in Europe was bound to raise concerns within Germany about whether they were being singled out to carry more than their fair share of the defense burden. Hosting nuclear weapons meant, in the German view, that you were willing to be a target for Soviet nuclear weapons in the event of war.

The nuclear dilemma for NATO in the 1970s stemmed from both geographical and political concerns. The European members of the alliance were dependent on the United States for their security, yet the bulk of American strategic forces were on the other side of the Atlantic. This geographical imbalance could not be redressed for political reasons. Germany, the major European NATO military power, is a non-nuclear-weapons state, and there is little chance that this will change, because of domestic political opposition within Germany and long-standing concerns among the other allies about a nuclear-armed German state. NATO's nuclear dilemma thus concerned not only the technical capabilities of weapons but also the political adequacy or acceptability of nuclear weapons arrangements.

Negotiating Positions

Question 3: What factors influenced the formulation of negotiating positions? How did these positions change during the course of the negotiations? How did initial positions compare with the negotiated outcome?

Negotiations between the United States and its European allies about the deployment of long-range theater nuclear forces involved two major issues: (1) weapons configuration—the types of systems, their numbers, and basing arrangements; and (2) the role of arms control.

Weapons Configuration. The first issue confronting the alliance was the specific weapons configuration that would form the core of the December 1979 decision. The initial American position was that there were significant advantages associated with sea-based weapons. These weapons are mobile and therefore less vulnerable than many land-based systems, and they would enable the alliance to avoid the domestic political problems associated with basing new systems on European soil. Sea-launched cruise missiles (SLCMs), in particular, could provide coverage of the new Soviet systems.

There were at least two problems with a sea-based response, however. The first concern was that sea-launched cruise missiles "would not have the desired visibility and political impact"[25] of a land-based system. Visibility was a crucial issue for the Europeans. Chancellor Schmidt argued for a land-based response because it would send a signal to the Soviet Union about the strength of the American commitment to the defense of Western Europe. The second concern was that the deployment of SLCMs on surface ships belonging to the European members of NATO would require the presence of American naval officers on those ships to approve handling and use of the American weapons.

Although other options were considered, the High Level Group settled on the Pershing II ballistic missile (PII) and the ground-launched cruise missile (GLCM). The PII was an extended-range version of the Pershing I (PI) already deployed in West Germany. The PII had a range of approximately 1,000 miles (about twice the range of the PI), enhanced accuracy, and a short flight time to the target. In addition, PII "was to require less support equipment and personnel than the Pershing I and could be readied for firing more quickly, which improved its 'survivability' in a crisis."[26] Some U.S. Air Force officers preferred the medium-range ballistic missile (MRBM)—an air force program—but the PII won out, in part because it could be billed as the modernization of an existing system. Moreover, the MRBM was viewed by many as potentially provocative to the Soviet Union because of its longer range (approximately 1,500 miles), which could put Moscow at risk.[27]

The ground-launched cruise missile, the Tomahawk, had other advantages. The system was mobile and could be dispersed quickly in a crisis. It was a low-flying system that could home in on Soviet targets by approaching them under Soviet radar. Moreover, Tomahawk was a "slow flyer" (600 miles per hour), so that it could not be considered a first strike weapon. In addition, due to a Department of Defense decision in 1979 to reverse the research and development schedules of the GLCM and the SLCM, the GLCM would be available for deployment sooner.[28]

The decision to proceed with PII and GLCM had much to do with the fact that the United States had already made the decision to produce these systems. The programs were in train by 1977, so they were logical choices. There were bureaucratic rationales for these choices as well. PII was an army system and GLCM was an air force program. There existed built-in military and defense lobbies in favor of these systems, which assigned a portion of the long-range theater nuclear forces role to both services.

The issue of how many warheads were needed was related to basing arrangements. West Germany had said that they would not be the only continental European country to accept new weapons on their soil. If the program was to proceed, the weapons would have to be deployed in multiple countries. The purpose of this was to suggest that nations would share the risks associated with membership in the alliance as well as the benefits. Risks were shared to the extent that any country that based these weapons on their soil would open themselves up to Soviet nuclear attack in the event of war. The United States already had stationed 108 PI missiles in Germany; the alliance decision to replace those with PIIs enabled NATO to argue that the PII was simply a modernization of an existing system.

The High Level Group had determined that a response in the range of 200–600 additional warheads would be consistent with an evolutionary upward adjustment in NATO's long-range theater nuclear capabilities. Germany's unwillingness to be the only continental European country to accept new LRTNF on its soil and the alliance decision to deploy a mix of PII and GLCM prompted the search for additional basing countries. The basic unit of the GLCM was a "flight"—four launch vehicles with four missiles on each vehicle, for a total of sixteen missiles. The minimum logical deployment per area was three flights, or forty-eight missiles. Belgium and the Netherlands each received the minimum of forty-eight missiles. Raymond Garthoff reports the outcome: "The total number of GLCMs was set at 464, the next to highest multiple of sixteen that kept the LRTNF total (including the 108 Pershing IIs) under 600, the high side of the recommended range. Thus the figure of 572 missiles was reached."[29] In addition to the deployment of GLCMs in Belgium and the Netherlands, Germany accepted 96 missiles, the United Kingdom agreed to base 160 missiles, and Italy agreed to deploy 112 missiles.

Arms Control. The second issue confronting the alliance was the relationship between theater nuclear force modernization and arms control. Debate focused on whether arms control should be viewed as (1) an alternative to the deployment of new U.S. theater nuclear forces in Europe or (2) a complement to NATO force modernization.

By February 1978 the High Level Group had reached a consensus that new weapons deployments were needed in the context of an evolutionary upward adjustment in NATO's long-range theater nuclear forces. The consensus was fragile, however, because Belgium and the Netherlands still pressed for an arms control option that would obviate the need for new deployments. The consensus on security is tentative in both Belgium and the Netherlands, and it was sorely tested during the period leading up to the December 1979 decision. The Belgian and Dutch governments offered only qualified support for the NATO consensus on new deployments, tied to the active pursuit of arms control negotiations. Deployments were viewed as a last resort, to be implemented only if arms control talks failed. In short, for the Belgian and Dutch governments, arms control did not represent a second track, but an alternative. The growing peace movements in both countries were extremely influential and grounded in the organized Christian churches, and they placed inordinate pressure on their respective governments.[30]

The West German view of the relationship between arms control and force modernization was slightly different. Although antinuclear sentiment was growing in West Germany as well, Chancellor Schmidt argued for a parallel arms control track, not an arms control alternative. Schmidt believed that a NATO decision to deploy theater nuclear forces was required to bring the Soviet Union to the bargaining table. In January 1979, during meetings with British prime minister James Callaghan, French president Valéry Giscard d'Estaing, and President Jimmy Carter, Schmidt pressed for a parallel effort to negotiate limitations on theater nuclear forces, as a way of diffusing the growing antinuclear sentiment in the Federal Republic of Germany.[31]

In April 1979, in large part as a response to Chancellor Schmidt's concerns, NATO established the Special Group on Arms Control and Related Matters to develop an arms control proposal associated with the LRTNF deployment proposal being developed by the High Level Group.[32] The Special Group formulated what became known as the "arms control track" of the December 1979 decision. During the summer and fall of 1979 the Special Group developed terms of reference to guide the United States in negotiations with the Soviet Union. But it was clear to those involved that the arms control track was added as an afterthought, for primarily political, rather than military, reasons. By the late 1980s, however, the United States and the Soviet Union had taken a serious interest in theater nuclear arms control, and the treaty on intermediate-range nuclear forces, signed in December 1987, was the result.

Bargaining and Concession-making

Question 4: What strategies and tactics did the parties use during the negotiations? How did differences in bargaining style influence the process and outcome of the negotiations? What was the role of politics in the selection of strategies and tactics? If the negotiations resulted in the signing of an agreement, how did the process of concession-making occur?

From late 1977 to October 1979, the High Level Group debated the issue of theater nuclear force modernization, including whether modernization was needed and the political implications of alternative modernization programs. The course of this debate paralleled a similar debate within the U.S. government.[33] In October 1978 the High Level Group outlined weapons for consideration. The HLG made no specific recommendations at that time but identified ground-launched cruise missiles, submarine-launched cruise missiles, extended-range Pershing ballistic missiles, and a new mobile intermediate-range ballistic missile as possible options.

Between October 1978 and December 1979, the United States and its European allies assessed the military and political implications of alternative deployment packages and the role that arms control considerations should play in the decision. The bargaining process involved elements of concession-convergence and politics, although politics clearly dominated. With respect to weapons configuration, the negotiated outcome of 108 PIIs and 464 GLCMs represented the minimum deployment consistent with Chancellor Schmidt's demand that Germany not be the only continental European nation to base the new weapons. Schmidt's demand should not have surprised the United States and other allies, given Germany's aversion to being singled out as a special zone, whether for arms control or force modernization.

During these deliberations the United States made a serious mistake in expecting the Europeans, and particularly the Germans, to take the lead. The United States responded to Chancellor Schmidt's publicly expressed concerns by endeavoring to put the ball back in the European court—that is, by looking to the Europeans for specific solutions. Traditionally, however, the Europeans have not taken the lead on nuclear issues in NATO. Rather, they have expected the United States to do so. In cases where the United States has failed to act appropriately (in the view of the Europeans), the result has been crisis within the alliance.[34]

The addition of the arms control track also was dominated by political considerations. Under pressure from the Europeans (especially West Germany, Belgium, and the Netherlands, whose governments confronted strong peace and antinuclear movements), the United States agreed to pursue the arms control track late in the process. By the time the Special Group was established in April 1979, the High Level Group was far along in its work on LRTNF deployment. By late spring 1979, the HLG had agreed to support the deployment of a mix of PII and GLCM. Although the numbers were not yet firm, the HLG had accepted the U.S. proposal of between 200 and 600 weapons. The price of NATO consensus on the deployment track was U.S. agreement to pursue arms control negotiations with the Soviet Union.

By early fall 1979, the allies were moving toward closure on an agreement. In Washington, the interagency community drafted a single report which combined the recommendations of the High Level Group and the Special Group into a document which formed the basis of allied consideration in December. This report, known as the Integrated Decision Document (IDD), was shared with the allies in October 1979, through briefings conducted in European capitals by high level U.S. officials.[35]

Implementation

Question 5: What additional action, if any, was required for implementation of the agreement? How did the implementation process reflect the role of background factors, context, substance, and politics?

The period between the NATO decision to deploy new theater nuclear forces in Europe and the arrival of the first PII missiles in West Germany during December 1983 was characterized by tremendous political turmoil within the alliance. The controversy was due primarily to three related factors. In the first place, even before the NATO decision was made, the Soviet Union mounted an extensive propaganda campaign in Western Europe to discourage the decision. After the December 1979 decision, the Soviet Union redoubled its campaign in an effort to derail the LRTNF modernization program. A second factor was the perceived reluctance of the United States to enter into arms control negotiations with the Soviet Union. Failure to ratify SALT II set back the arms control process, and with the arrival of the Reagan administration in Washington in January 1981, arms control was placed on the back burner. And, related to the first two factors, a growing peace movement throughout Europe threatened the success of the LRTNF program.

As NATO moved toward a decision on theater nuclear force modernization in the fall of 1979, the Soviet Union mounted a propaganda campaign designed to drive a wedge between the United States and its European allies. On October 6, 1979, General Secretary Leonid Brezhnev delivered a speech in East Berlin in which he proposed to reduce medium-range nuclear weapons deployed in the western part of the Soviet Union if NATO agreed not to go ahead with the deployment of new LRTNF in Western Europe. Brezhnev argued that the deployment of new LRTNF by the West would upset the existing balance of these forces in Europe and that such deployments would necessitate a Soviet response. In the same speech, Brezhnev announced that the Soviet Union would withdraw 20,000 soldiers and 1,000 tanks from East Germany within one year. Finally, Brezhnev threatened those West European countries which permitted basing of the new LRTNF on their soil with massive nuclear attacks in the event of war and suggested that they would be spared if they refused to permit the stationing of the new American weapons.[36]

It should not be surprising that Brezhnev's speech was delivered in East Berlin nor that the troops and tanks subject to withdrawal within one year were from East Germany. Brezhnev's speech signaled the opening round of a propaganda barrage, directed first at West Germany but also toward the other European nations involved in the NATO decision on theater nuclear forces, in an effort to convince those nations to disapprove new deployments.

Following his speech, Brezhnev sent personal letters to Chancellor Schmidt and the governments of the United Kingdom, Italy, and Denmark, as a way of reinforcing the themes of the East Berlin speech.[37] Soviet officials engaged in a series of interviews with the European press, beginning in October 1979 but continuing long after the December 1979 decision was made, in an effort to, first, prevent the decision and, second, when that failed, derail the program before the first missiles were scheduled to arrive in Europe.[38] The Soviet Union also continued to press the United States and its European allies on the arms control front by unveiling a series of proposals designed to put the West on the defensive and raise questions about whether new deployments were necessary. This strategy culminated with the Soviet walkout of the Strategic Arms Reduction Talks (START) and the Negotiations on Intermediate-Range Nuclear Forces (INF) in Geneva in November 1983.[39]

European governments were especially vulnerable to these tactics because of a growing peace movement. The Federal Republic of Germany was in the most difficult position. Helmut Schmidt had narrowly won the support of his Social Democratic party (SPD) for the dual track decision at its Party Congress in Berlin in December 1979. Schmidt placed his personal prestige on the line, and some observers have suggested that the SPD went along with Schmidt only because they knew they could not win the next national election (scheduled for October 6, 1980) without him.[40] The SPD began to shift leftward, with many of its youngest members supporting the Green party on the issue of nuclear weapons. Protests began in earnest in January 1981. Although arms control could have provided a solution, the Reagan administration had other priorities. By August 1981 the protests reflected growing anti-Americanism. The result for Schmidt was tragic, and the government fell in August 1982. The political situation in Germany had been so transformed that the new chancellor—Helmut Kohl of the Christian Democratic Union (CDU)—argued for a move away from the "zero option" then supported by the United States and toward cancellation of the Pershing II deployment in exchange for a reduction in Soviet SS-20s targeted against Western Europe.[41]

The situation in the United Kingdom was somewhat different. In May 1979 the Conservative party under Margaret Thatcher assumed power. Prime Minister Thatcher strongly supported the December 1979 decision. Opposition to the program centered in the left wing of the Labour party and the Campaign for Nuclear Disarmament (CND), a peace group formed in the 1960s. Announcement that ground-launched cruise missiles were to be deployed at two Royal Air Force bases (Molesworth and Greenham Common) inflamed public opinion and resulted in protests at both locations throughout 1980. Only six months after the December 1979 decision, a protest in London drew 20,000 people, and by 1983 more than 200,000 individuals turned out to demonstrate.[42] The Labour party, like the SPD in Germany, shifted left and adopted resolutions calling for unilateral nuclear disarmament, reductions in conventional forces, and cuts in defense spending. Despite these events, the Thatcher government remained firm in its support of the deployments. Opposition to deployments peaked at 61 percent in January 1983 but had declined to 39 percent by June 1983, at the time of the general election.[43]

Like the Federal Republic of Germany and the United Kingdom, Italy agreed to accept new theater nuclear forces on its soil. As Jeff McCausland has pointed out, "Italy's support for INF was principally based on a complex mix: Italian desire for a more active role in Alliance decision making, the selection of a site that would not inflame public opinion, and an effort by the Socialist party to assume a leadership role in Italian politics."[44] The Italian Parliament voted in favor of basing in October 1979. Prime Minister Francesco Cossiga, a Christian Democrat, won the support of Republicans, Liberals, Social Democrats, Social Movement party members, and even some Socialists. The Communist party in Italy attempted to distance itself from Moscow and, arguing that both Soviet and NATO deployments threatened to upset the balance of forces in Europe, called for negotiations between the two sides designed to stabilize the military balance at lower levels. By 1983 the Communist party had rejected the plan to begin deploying the missiles in December 1983 if no progress was made on the arms control front. The peace movement was slow in getting off the ground in Italy, although by 1981 protests became common. The situation in Italy was influenced by the relatively isolated basing site for the ground-launched cruise missiles—in southeastern Sicily—which managed to keep protesters at a distance.[45]

The consensus on security in Belgium and the Netherlands was tested both during the period leading up to the December 1979 decision and between the decision and the beginning of new deployments. The qualified support offered by the Belgian and Dutch governments for the NATO decision presented an opportunity for Soviet influence. During 1980 and 1981 organized protests occurred throughout Belgium and the Netherlands, placing pressure on the governments and resulting in further delays in their decisions to accept basing of ground-launched cruise missiles.[46]

By December 1983, however, missiles began arriving in Europe. The Federal Republic of Germany and the United Kingdom were the first to accept new missiles on their soil. By 1987 all five countries—including Italy, Belgium, and the Netherlands—had begun to deploy new American theater nuclear forces. The NATO decision had been implemented, but at no small cost to alliance unity.

Conclusion: The Politics of Deploying Theater Nuclear Forces

The debate between the United States and its European allies about the deployment of theater nuclear forces was fundamentally a debate between parties with very different perspectives on the political and strategic situation in the late 1970s. The problem was a political one for the Europeans. Growing concerns about the reliability of the United States and whether American policymakers would take European interests into account in their dealings with the Soviet Union were raised throughout Europe. The theater nuclear force threat was not new. What had changed by the mid- to late 1970s, however, was the nature of the strategic military balance between the United States and the Soviet Union.

The military argument contended that the absence of a NATO response to Soviet force modernization had resulted in a gap in the continuum of deterrence, leaving NATO without a balanced force structure across the NATO triad of conventional, theater nuclear, and strategic nuclear forces. But there was also a political gap in the continuum of deterrence, reflected in European concerns about the reliability of the United States and, as the negotiations proceeded, in American concerns about the reliability of the Europeans.

The United States viewed the modernization of NATO's theater nuclear forces in conjunction with the improvement of NATO's conventional force capabilities; the objective was to strengthen deterrence by improving NATO's ability to counter aggression at the theater level. The Europeans, in contrast, viewed the modernization of NATO's theater nuclear forces in conjunction with the strengthening of the American strategic nuclear guarantee. For the Americans, the objective (albeit unspoken) was to place greater emphasis on the European theater. For the Europeans, the objective was to reinforce a quick American decision to use strategic nuclear forces against the Soviet Union in defense of Europe. The Europeans, then, placed emphasis on theater nuclear force modernization to reinforce linkage. Thus, American and European interests and objectives in these negotiations were overlapping, but not identical.

The process and outcome of these negotiations was also influenced by the fact that the United States was dealing with multiple negotiating partners. Although Germany was central to the debate, the United Kingdom, Belgium, the Netherlands, and Italy—the other basing countries—also played critical roles. Unlike the U.S.-German wartime host nation support negotiations, which occurred bilaterally and outside the formal NATO arena, the discussions about theater nuclear forces took place in the context of the formal NATO structure—the High Level Group of the Nuclear Planning Group. NATO decision-making bodies operate on the basis of consensus. Thus, the United States had to balance German, British, Dutch, Belgian, and Italian concerns, among others, in moving the alliance toward a consensus about the deployment of theater nuclear forces.

Moreover, the domestic politics of the European countries strongly influenced the course of negotiations. The creation of the Special Group in April 1979 was due in large part to the growing public opposition within Europe to the deployment of new theater nuclear forces on European soil and the implications of this opposition for the stability of European governments. Strong opposition within Belgium and the Netherlands led to less than total support by the governments of those countries for the December 1979 decision. But the situation would have been even worse had the United States not agreed to accept the arms control track of NATO's response.

In addition, the configuration of weapons agreed to by the alliance was strongly influenced by Germany's condition that the Federal Republic not be the only continental European country to accept new weapons on its soil. The search for additional basing countries thus was prompted primarily by political, rather than military, considerations.

The Soviet Union also played a critical role in the NATO debate about deploying theater nuclear forces. Domestic public opinion was especially significant in influencing the debate in Europe. Political differences within and between the NATO allies offered the Soviet Union an opportunity to undercut the alliance by attempting to influence European leaders and European public opinion directly. Brezhnev's speech in East Berlin on October 6, 1979, clearly was designed as a last ditch effort to drive a wedge between the United States and its European allies. In addition, Brezhnev's personal letters to heads of government in the Federal Republic of Germany, the United Kingdom, Italy, and Denmark represented an effort to convince those nations to reassess the NATO decision. The Soviet Union's public posture on arms control from December 1979 to December 1983 was designed to appeal directly to European publics as a way of putting additional pressure on their governments to withdraw support for the December 1979 decision.

In summary, the NATO debate about deploying new U.S. theater nuclear forces in Europe during the late 1970s was largely a product of political considerations. Unlike the U.S.-German wartime host nation support case, in which there was a common perception of the nature of the problem and the objectives of the negotiations, in this case differences between the United States and its negotiating partners (and even within those partners) emerged from the very beginning and never were completely reconciled. The inability of the parties to agree on the nature of the problem complicated the discussions and opened the door to public and Soviet pressure on the participating governments. Moreover, the fact that the debate concerned nuclear weapons, rather than conventional forces, reinforced the role of domestic publics and the Soviet Union. But by defining the December 1979 decision and its implementation as a test of the alliance, the United States and its European allies were able to build the interallied consensus necessary to offset Soviet pressures.

As we enter the 1990s, the future of nuclear weapons in Europe is uncertain. The conventional arms control agreement signed by the United States, the Soviet Union, and twenty other nations in November 1990 will lead to deep cuts in Soviet forces in Eastern Europe, thus removing a central element of the military rationale for the continued presence of U.S. nuclear forces in Europe. President Bush's decision in spring 1990 to scale back U.S. plans for modernizing short-range nuclear forces in Europe and to move toward negotiations with the Soviet Union on these weapons was greeted with relief by most of America's NATO allies. The democratization of the potential targets for these weapons—Eastern European countries—and the unification of Germany have transformed the political context within which members of the alliance address nuclear issues. Thus, reaching consensus on the future of theater nuclear forces in Europe may not present as much of a challenge to the alliance in the 1990s as the issue posed during the 1970s and the 1980s.

Part III

Negotiating with Adversaries

Negotiating with adversaries, by its very nature, is more difficult than negotiating with allies. An adversarial relationship is characterized by negative feelings that pervade the broad range of political, military, economic, social, and cultural interaction between nations. Moreover, parties in an adversarial relationship (particularly if that relationship is long-standing) generally are willing to devote extensive resources to denying the adversary its foreign policy objectives.

These characteristics of an adversarial relationship mean that competitive elements tend to dominate negotiation. The parties are likely to view problems in win-lose or zero-sum terms. The identification of common interests and objectives will be more difficult for adversaries than for allies. This leads both parties to equate interests and objectives with negotiating positions, which reduces bargaining flexibility. Adversarial relationships generally mean less room for maneuver, fewer side payments, and limited leverage in negotiations. Finally, adversaries are less likely to trust each other when negotiations begin; because trust develops slowly, if at all, the parties are likely to demand highly structured, formal arrangements that offer protection against violations.

Critical to the success of negotiations between adversaries is the identification of common interests and objectives. Because this is more difficult for adversaries than for allies, negotiations between adversaries are likely to be more time-consuming and—other things being equal—less successful than negotiations between allies.

The cases in Part III have been selected to illustrate negotiations with adversaries. These cases, one representing failure and the other success, highlight the importance of the identification of common interests and objectives in explaining the process and outcome of negotiations between adversaries. The Negotiations on Mutual and Balanced Force Reductions (MBFR) between members of NATO and the Warsaw Pact illustrate how problems in identifying common interests and objectives can derail negotiations between adversaries. In the case of MBFR, neither side really wanted an agreement when the negotiations began in Vienna in 1973; by 1989, when both sides seemed willing to pursue conventional arms control in a serious way, structural problems with the MBFR forum brought those negotiations to a close.

In contrast, the Negotiations on Intermediate-Range Nuclear Forces (INF) between the United States and the Soviet Union ended successfully in December 1987, when President Ronald Reagan and General Secretary Mikhail Gorbachev signed a treaty eliminating an entire class of weapons. Like MBFR, the INF talks began slowly in 1980; neither party seriously wanted an agreement. By 1985, however, both sides had identified a "mutuality of interests" on intermediate-range nuclear weapons.

These cases, like those in Part II, illustrate how negotiations between adversaries are influenced by the nature of the issue, that is, whether conventional or nuclear forces are the subject of discussion. Because nuclear issues are more visible to European and American publics, they are more politically sensitive. This is as true for arms control negotiations with the Soviet Union and the Warsaw Pact as it is for negotiations between the United States and its NATO allies on force improvement efforts. One would expect negotiations on nuclear arms control to be more difficult than negotiations on conventional arms control. However, the visibility of the nuclear issue may provide greater incentives on both sides to reach agreement; that seems to be true for the INF case.

Finally, the MBFR and INF cases demonstrate that identifying common interests and objectives may be more difficult in multilateral negotiations. The United States was only one of many Western negotiators in the MBFR talks. The allies had to arrive at a consensus internally before presenting a negotiating position to their Eastern counterparts. The multiple interests and objectives of participating nations undoubtedly complicated the process of identifying common interests and objectives with the East. In the INF case, in contrast, the United States and the Soviet Union were the sole participants. The interests of the Europeans—both West and East—were important considerations for both parties. However, success depended upon the ability of the United States and the Soviet Union to design an agreement that satisfied their common interests and objectives, not those of their allies.

5. Conventional Arms Control

The Negotiations on Mutual and Balanced Force Reductions

The MBFR talks are an example of a round of negotiations conceived in sin. . . . The fact that neither side really wants a deal contributes to the extraordinary difficulty negotiators face in trying to reach agreement.
— *Paul C. Warnke* [1]

The principal problem in the Vienna negotiations has been neither too many players nor the absence of context. The central obstacle has been the lack of a strong mutuality of interest between NATO and the Warsaw Pact.
— *Coit D. Blacker* [2]

On February 2, 1989, at the 493d plenary session, the long-standing negotiations between members of NATO and the Warsaw Pact on the reduction of conventional forces in Central Europe came to an unsuccessful conclusion. The Negotiations on Mutual and Balanced Force Reductions (MBFR), as they were called, began nearly sixteen years earlier in Vienna, Austria. Despite the strong incentives on both sides to enter into these negotiations in 1973, the parties left Vienna without reaching an agreement.

The demise of MBFR received no more notice in the press than had the negotiations themselves. Throughout its history, MBFR had been eclipsed by the more visible and politically sensitive negotiations on nuclear weapons. Beginning with the signing of the SALT I Treaty in 1972, extending to the SALT II Treaty in 1979, and culminating with the treaty on intermediate-range nuclear forces in December 1987, nuclear arms control captured the attention of the public, while announcements of the beginning and end of MBFR negotiating rounds in Vienna received at most a one or two paragraph reference in major newspapers.

The lack of public attention paid to conventional arms control during the 1970s and the 1980s is ironic because the negotiations concerned the political future of Europe. As noted by Robert Blackwill, a former U.S. ambassador to MBFR, "Conventional arms control is sharply distinct from its nuclear counterpart in its potentially historic influence on the political geography of Europe."[3] The renewed attention given conventional arms control in the 1990s, in the form of the Negotiations on Conventional Forces in Europe (CFE), was tied to the political and economic transformation of Eastern Europe and the Soviet Union and the reassessment of the roles of NATO and the Warsaw Pact in the new security environment.[4] On November 19, 1990, the United States, the Soviet Union, and twenty other members of NATO and the Warsaw Pact signed what has been called "the most ambitious arms control treaty in history," in which they agreed to destroy thousands of tanks, artillery pieces, and other items of conventional military equipment in Europe.[5] This diplomatic success, coming on the heels of sixteen years of fruitless discussions in MBFR, was inextricably linked to the end of the Cold War and the transformation of East-West relations.

There has always been a close relationship between conventional arms control and "the German problem." Negotiations on conventional forces in Central Europe focus on Germany because that country bears the brunt of what has been called "the largest peacetime military concentration in human history."[6] The deployment of hundreds of thousands of NATO and Warsaw Pact troops and their equipment, the staging of military maneuvers that disrupt the lives of German citizens, and the reality that until 1990 the inter-German border reflected a postwar political division all suggest the special position of Germany in negotiations on conventional forces in Central Europe. The inability of both sides to address the German problem during the 1970s and the 1980s, in its political and military dimensions, helps explain the failure of the MBFR negotiations. In contrast, resolution of the German problem in 1990 enabled East and West to bring the CFE talks to a successful conclusion.

Much of the literature on the MBFR negotiations has focused on technical aspects of the discussions—analysis of the nature of the military balance in Central Europe and the impact of proposals and counterproposals offered by NATO and the Warsaw Pact on the military balance. Less attention has been paid to the impact of political considerations on the process and outcome of MBFR, yet political considerations facilitated both the birth and death of the MBFR negotiations as well as the resurrection of conventional arms control in the Negotiations on Conventional Forces in Europe and the signing of an agreement in November 1990.

The Negotiations on Mutual and Balanced Force Reductions

On October 30, 1973, representatives of seven NATO nations and four Warsaw Pact countries met in Vienna, Austria, for the first substantive round of negotiations designed to reduce conventional forces and armaments in Central Europe. The agreed area of reductions, or the NATO Guidelines Area (NGA) in MBFR parlance, consisted of the Federal Republic of Germany, the Netherlands, Belgium, Luxembourg, the German Democratic Republic, Czechoslovakia, and Poland. Soviet territory was excluded from the area of reductions—a fact that was to create both political and military obstacles to an agreement.

The United States and the Soviet Union served as informal heads of the Western and Eastern blocs. For the West, other "direct" participants (those with armed forces deployed in the agreed area of reductions) included Belgium, Canada, the Federal Republic of Germany, Luxembourg, the Netherlands, and the United Kingdom. "Indirect" participants (those without armed forces deployed in the agreed area of reductions) were Denmark, Greece, Italy, Norway, and Turkey. For the East, other direct participants included Czechoslovakia, the German Democratic Republic, and Poland. Indirect participants were Bulgaria, Hungary, and Romania.

The stated objective of MBFR, as agreed in the final communiqué of the preparatory consultations leading to the opening of the negotiations, was "to contribute to a more stable relationship and to the strengthening of peace and security in Europe."[7] Both sides agreed to consider the mutual reduction of armed forces and armaments and associated measures in Central Europe during the course of the negotiations.

The formal negotiating mechanism was the weekly plenary session, in which a representative of the East or the West offered a prepared statement. The plenary allowed questions but no discussion of the delivered statement. The cumbersome nature of the plenary prompted East and West to hold weekly supplementary informal sessions, during which representatives from both sides discussed the plenary statements and tested new ideas before introducing them as formal proposals. These "informals," as they were called, soon replaced the plenaries as the locus of serious negotiation.[8]

The MBFR negotiations were structured as bloc-to-bloc discussions, rather than as truly multilateral negotiations. Each side had to develop an internal consensus around a negotiating position before that position could be offered formally to the other side. The problem of internal consensus-building was more difficult for the West than for the East. The United States, the United Kingdom, and the Federal Republic of Germany took the lead in developing illustrative positions, which were then submitted to the other Western participants for discussion.[9] The multiple interests and objectives of the various NATO participants complicated the consensus-building process in the West. Each Western participant had to balance multiple interests and objectives in assessing the merits of alternative Western proposals. The situation also presented an opportunity for the East to play off one NATO ally against another. As was the case during the NATO negotiations concerning the deployment of theater nuclear forces in Europe, the Soviet Union targeted West Germany because the West German government exercised a veto power over Western proposals.

Building an East-West consensus around an acceptable negotiating outcome in MBFR was complicated by the intra-NATO consensus-building process. Although East and West agreed with the general objective of the negotiations, as expressed in the preparatory consultations, the history of MBFR demonstrates that the parties entered into the talks for different purposes. The failure to identify a "mutuality of interests" in the MBFR negotiations and the absence of sufficient "political will," as noted by participants and observers on both sides, doomed these negotiations from the beginning.[10]

The inability of East and West to agree on the title of the negotiations should have indicated that problems lay ahead. The West preferred MBFR because it supported the NATO argument that the overwhelming conventional military superiority of the Warsaw Pact demanded large, asymmetrical reductions. The East, in contrast, preferred "Reduction of Armed Forces and Armaments in Central Europe" because it supported the Warsaw Pact argument that there was parity or approximate equality in conventional forces in Central Europe. The compromise solution was to formally call the talks "Mutual Reduction of Forces and Armaments and Associated Measures in Central Europe," although most in the West continued to use "MBFR" throughout the history of the negotiations.[11]

The Decision to Negotiate

Question 1: What prompted the United States and its negotiating partners to enter into negotiations? In other words, what problem or situation brought the parties to the bargaining table?

For the West, and particularly for the United States, domestic political and economic pressures to enter into negotiations were paramount. Beginning in the mid-1960s, Senator Mike Mansfield (D-Mont.) had introduced a series of resolutions calling for the unilateral withdrawal of U.S. troops from Europe. Arguing that the Cold War was beginning to thaw and pointing to the high cost of stationing American troops in Western Europe, the amendment that Senator Mansfield introduced in 1966 called for the reduction of 50,000 American troops. Mansfield introduced similar resolutions in every session of Congress from 1966 until 1974, when the United States had entered the MBFR negotiations.

Presidents Johnson and Nixon argued strongly against unilateral American troop reductions. In June 1968 NATO foreign ministers had issued a communiqué calling for negotiations designed to reduce the conventional military confrontation in Central Europe. In the face of Soviet calls for improved East-West relations, NATO leaders believed that public support for conventional force improvements in the West depended upon NATO's support of an arms control initiative. President Nixon, supported by his national security adviser, Henry Kissinger, believed that the unilateral withdrawal of American troops would weaken Soviet incentives to participate in arms control discussions with the West.[12]

Like the United States, West Germany was opposed to the unilateral withdrawal of American troops from Western Europe. At the same time, West Germany wanted to engage the Soviet Union (and East Germany) across a range of political and economic issues—not only arms control, but also the flow of people, goods, and services between East and West. Conventional arms control, if it contributed to a lessening of tensions between NATO and the Warsaw Pact, would support these broader West German objectives, which were tied to the opening of the Conference on Security and Cooperation in Europe (CSCE) in 1972. Moreover, West Germany's historical concerns about the creation of a special German arms control zone prompted the Federal Republic to participate in MBFR to ensure that its interests in this regard were well represented.

The East, and particularly the Soviet Union, expressed less interest in MBFR than in the Conference on Security and Cooperation in Europe. For the Soviet Union, agreement to participate in MBFR represented the price for the agreement of the United States to participate in CSCE: "Since 1966, Soviet leaders had spoken of the need to undertake a general relaxation of tensions in Europe so as to confirm postwar 'territorial and political realities' and to 'eliminate completely the vestiges of World War II.' They looked in particular to a multilateral security conference to impart legitimacy to that process and to provide an institutional mechanism to anchor and sustain it."[13] Thus, for the Soviet Union, desire for the ratification of postwar boundaries in Europe and the improvement of Soviet–West German relations were the primary factors that brought the East to the bargaining table.

The deal was struck at the May 1972 summit meeting when President Nixon and General Secretary Brezhnev agreed to endorse the Conference on Security and Cooperation in Europe in exchange for

Warsaw Pact agreement to participate in negotiations designed to reduce conventional forces and armaments in Central Europe.[14]

Interests and Objectives

Question 2: How did U.S. and West European policymakers define their interests and objectives with respect to the negotiations? How did the West's negotiating partners define their interests and objectives with respect to the negotiations? Were the parties able to define common interests and objectives?

The interests and objectives of Western and Eastern participants in MBFR are contained in the rationales that brought them to the bargaining table. Western, and particularly U.S., objectives changed over time. In the period 1968–73, before the MBFR negotiations began, the primary American objective was to prevent congressionally imposed unilateral reductions of American troops in Western Europe. Beginning in 1973 the stated objectives of the United States changed.

In military terms, the objectives were threefold. First, the West was determined to redress the conventional force imbalance that placed NATO at a military disadvantage. Second, the West aimed to reduce the surprise attack options available to the Warsaw Pact. And, third, the West aimed—through achievement of the first two objectives—to enhance the mobilization time available for NATO in the event of crisis or war in Central Europe.[15]

These military objectives, which were accepted by the other Western participants in MBFR, emerged from an analysis of the conventional balance in Central Europe that revealed Warsaw Pact superiority.[16] The major concerns expressed at the time were that (1) the East maintained more ground forces than the West, (2) the East had an advantage of two-and-one-half to one in tanks, and (3) the West suffered a major disadvantage because the United States was eight times as far from Central Europe as the Soviet Union.[17] Taken together, these disparities represented a threat to stability in Central Europe because they created Warsaw Pact incentives to use, or threaten to use, military force to achieve political objectives.

Of particular concern to military officers and defense officials in the West was the impact of geographical asymmetries on the stability of the military balance. Because the Atlantic Ocean separates the United States from its European allies, NATO strategy was premised on obtaining early warning of aggression and the rapid mobilization and reinforcement of deployed forces in the theater. Significant reductions in Warsaw Pact forces could enhance warning and buy time for NATO decisions on mobilization and reinforcement. Thus, the West argued for approximate parity in the military manpower of the two sides in the area of reductions.

At the same time, the West expressed concern that the reduction of conventional forces in Central Europe should not diminish the security of flank states. The interests of Italy, Greece, and Turkey, on the southern flank of NATO, and Denmark and Norway, on the northern flank, demanded an MBFR agreement that did not reduce Warsaw Pact forces in Central Europe only to redirect the threat to the flanks. Italy and Turkey strongly argued that they should be included in MBFR, if only as indirect participants, to ensure that the negotiations did not produce an agreement that decreased the military confrontation in Central Europe only to increase the threat to their security.[18]

West German interests in MBFR reflected both political and military considerations. Perhaps more than any other NATO member, West Germany—led by a Social Democratic government with a long-standing commitment to conventional force reductions in Europe—supported the military objectives as enunciated by the United States. In addition, West Germany saw MBFR as an element in its overall policy of détente with the Soviet Union and the improvement of relations with East Germany.[19] But West Germany did not want MBFR to lead to an outcome that would single out the Federal Republic as a special arms control zone. For this reason, West Germany opposed the imposition of national limits on the military forces of any single participant in the negotiations.[20]

France refused to participate in the MBFR negotiations, believing that resolution of the political sources of tension in Europe was a precondition for successful arms control negotiations with the East. MBFR, with its bloc-to-bloc format, would simply reinforce existing differences between East and West.[21] Thus, it should not be surprising that France was one of the early supporters of the Conference on Security and Cooperation in Europe and argued throughout the course of the MBFR negotiations that CSCE represented a more appropriate forum for the negotiation of European arms control. (The French were proven right, in a sense, when MBFR was dissolved early in 1989 and was replaced by the Conventional Forces in Europe talks, which produced an agreement in November 1990.)

The Soviet Union, mirroring the interests of the East, placed the objective of political normalization of East-West relations ahead of progress in conventional arms control. The Soviet Union did not accept the Western premise that the military balance in Central Europe was skewed in favor of the East. When French forces and theater nuclear forces were included in a net assessment of the military balance, the Soviet Union argued, the capabilities of East and West were roughly equal. This explains the Soviet push for inclusion of the language on "equal security" in the final communiqué of the preparatory consultations and their commitment to equal as opposed to asymmetrical reductions.[22] In addition, the Soviet overriding security concern in the late 1960s and the early 1970s seemed to be U.S. strategic nuclear forces. There is some evidence to suggest that the Soviet leadership simply could not pay sufficient attention to the U.S. nuclear threat and address conventional arms control issues as well.[23]

Why, then, did the Soviet Union agree to participate in MBFR, and in support of what interests and objectives? For the Soviets, the primary objective was to pursue conventional arms control as an illustration of the general relaxation of tensions between East and West and as a means of improving relations with West Germany. Secondary Soviet objectives may have been to offset pressures for the unilateral reduction of American troops, which might have encouraged greater European defense cooperation, and to exert some influence over the size and composition of the West German military establishment.[24]

Thus, the decisions taken by members of NATO and the Warsaw Pact to enter into negotiations about the reduction of conventional forces in Central Europe reflected very different interests and objectives. The inability of both sides to identify common interests and objectives, illustrated by debates about whether stability should be defined in political or military terms, set the stage for fifteen years of difficult negotiations.

Negotiating Positions

Question 3: What factors influenced the formulation of negotiating positions? How did these positions change during the course of the negotiations?

The Negotiations on Mutual and Balanced Force Reductions focused on four major issues: (1) the size and nature of reductions to be taken by East and West, (2) limitations on residual forces, (3) data on the military forces of the participants, and (4) associated measures.

Reductions. Western and Eastern negotiating positions on the size and composition of force reductions were directly related to each side's view of the prevailing military balance. When the MBFR talks opened in fall 1973, both sides came prepared with early proposals. On November 8, 1973, the East introduced their proposal for an agreement that called for three stages of reductions. In Stage 1, which would be implemented by 1975, East and West would each withdraw 20,000 troops from the area of reductions. In Stage 2, to be carried out by 1976, each direct participant in the negotiations would further reduce their military forces by 5 percent. An additional 10 percent reduction would be taken by each direct participant in Stage 3, which would be implemented by 1977.[25] A critical element of the Eastern proposal was the inclusion of equipment, extending to nuclear weapons, in the reductions proposal. In addition, all participants would be required to agree to the three-stage procedure in a single, initial agreement.

The West quickly tabled a response to the Eastern initiative during the first round of the negotiations. On November 22, 1973, the West proposed reductions be taken in two phases. In Phase 1, the Soviets would withdraw a five-division tank army, including 68,000 troops and 1,700 tanks, from the area of reductions. The United States would withdraw 29,000 individual soldiers. In Phase 2, East and West would reduce their ground forces to a common ceiling of 700,000 in the area of reductions.[26] The precise nature of the reductions to be taken by each participant in Phase 2 would be negotiated in a separate agreement, after a Phase 1 accord had been signed.

There were major differences between Eastern and Western approaches to reductions early in the negotiations. The Eastern approach, calling for percentage reductions, was a logical extension of their view that the military forces of both sides were approximately equal. The inclusion of equipment, particularly nuclear weapons, was designed to place restrictions on U.S. nuclear capabilities and the pre-positioning of equipment in the area of reductions.[27] For the West, the call for a common ceiling on military forces and asymmetrical reductions supported the Western view that the Warsaw Pact maintained an overwhelming military superiority in the area of reductions. Equal percentage reductions, while drawing down the forces of both sides, would not eliminate this fundamental asymmetry. In addition, requiring the Soviet Union to withdraw a complete tank army would cut more deeply into Soviet military capabilities than would an option that allowed the Warsaw Pact to thin out the personnel of multiple units while leaving their infrastructure intact.

The first substantive change in the West's position on reductions came on December 16, 1975, when the West offered to add U.S. nuclear weapons to the reductions package. Known as "Option 3," because of the label accorded this alternative in government working papers, this proposal offered to reduce 1,000 U.S. nuclear warheads, 54 F-4 aircraft, and 36 Pershing I ballistic missile launchers, in addition to the 29,000 individual soldiers offered in November 1973.[28] The Western shift was designed to appeal to the Soviet Union's desire for limits on U.S. aircraft and nuclear forces in Europe. Option 3 was conditional, however, on the withdrawal of a Soviet tank army.

The next major move was Eastern acceptance of the Option 3 offer and modification of their proposed reductions in manpower. On February 19, 1976, the East scaled back their three-stage proposal to two stages, calling for 2–3 percent reductions in U.S. and Soviet personnel in units with their equipment in Stage 1. The East also offered to match U.S. nuclear and aircraft reductions in Stage 1 with similar Soviet reductions. In Stage 2, the East called for 15 percent reductions in the manpower of all direct participants, taken in units and including their equipment.[29] Although the East pocketed the West's Option 3 offer, they failed to meet the Western demand for reduction of a Soviet tank army in exchange for U.S. nuclear weapons and aircraft.

The last major reductions proposal in MBFR was introduced by the West on December 17, 1979. There were three major elements in the Western initiative. First, the West withdrew Option 3 from the negotiating table, arguing that the East had not met the Western demand for reduction of 68,000 Soviet troops. Second, in conjunction with the withdrawal of Option 3, the West scaled back its demands on Soviet reductions in Phase 1 from 68,000 to 30,000 troops taken in three divisions; for the West, U.S. reductions would also be scaled back from 29,000 to 13,000 troops, two-thirds of which would be taken in units and one-third as individuals. And, third, the West introduced a package of associated measures designed to be put in place before Phase 1 reductions occurred.[30] The major reason for the Western initiative was the December 1979 NATO decision to deploy ground-launched cruise missiles and Pershing II ballistic missiles in Europe. Western representatives expressed concern that leaving Option 3 on the table could interfere with implementation of the December 1979 decision.

In summary, by December 1979 the two sides were beginning to converge on a reductions package. The West had dropped its insistence on Soviet reductions in the form of a tank army. The East had accepted, at least in principle, the Western proposal for reductions to a common collective ceiling in the context of a two-phase agreement. But agreement on reductions was not enough. The other major issues separating the two sides were limitations on residual forces, the data discrepancy, and associated measures.

Limitations on Residual Forces. Eastern and Western positions on the issue of limitations on residual forces in the area of reductions focused implicitly, if not explicitly, on the status of Germany. From the very beginning, the East, led by Soviet representatives, pressed for national limitations on forces in the NATO Guidelines Area following reductions. The Eastern objective was clear—obtain limits on the size of the West German Bundeswehr.

The Western view, in contrast, argued for collective ceilings or limitations on residual forces, rather than national ceilings. The concept of national ceilings was unacceptable to the West for two major reasons. First, acceptance of national ceilings suggested the West was willing to give the East a *droit de regard* over NATO military planning and force structure. National ceilings would interfere with NATO's ability to adjust the composition of its forces in the area of reductions. Second, and perhaps even more important, the concept of national ceilings was directed squarely at the Federal Republic of Germany. Given the expressed opposition of the Federal Republic to creation of a special arms control zone in Germany, national ceilings were clearly unacceptable to the West.

The positions of East and West on residual limitations changed less dramatically during the course of the negotiations than their positions on reductions. The West remained steadfast in their opposition to national limits in a Phase 2 agreement. In their opening initiative, the West called for residual ceilings on U.S. and Soviet manpower and Soviet tanks following a Phase 1 agreement. Phase 2 reductions would produce a common collective ceiling of 700,000 ground forces, with no national ceilings for other direct participants.[31] This position was supplemented in December 1975, when the West implicitly, if not explicitly, accepted residual limits on U.S. nuclear warheads, F-4 aircraft, and Pershing ballistic missiles in the area of reductions, following a Phase 1 agreement. This initiative also expanded the scope of residual limitations to include air forces as well as ground forces. Beginning in December 1975, Western proposals called for a common collective ceiling of 700,000 ground forces and 900,000 combined ground *and* air forces in the area of reductions.

Beginning with their proposal of November 1973, the East argued for ceilings on the residual personnel and equipment of all direct participants in the negotiations. The East did not modify their position on residual limitations until June 8, 1978, when they proposed "modified national ceilings" on manpower within the common collective ceiling.[32] This represented a major concession because it was the first time that the East formally accepted the West's position on the common collective ceiling and suggested a willingness to budge on the issue of national ceilings. However, the concession, as I have pointed out, was tied to Western acceptance of Eastern data—a major issue that was not resolved.

Data Discrepancy. The MBFR negotiations eventually turned into negotiations on data, rather than on reductions. Jonathan Dean, a former U.S. ambassador to MBFR, has argued that the data dispute was the "primary practical obstacle" to an agreement.[33] The data discrepancy was related to differing perceptions of East and West about the nature of the military balance in Central Europe. The West charged that the East maintained a preponderance of force in the area of reductions, while the East argued that the military capabilities of the two sides were approximately equal.

The implications of these different perceptions became clear once East and West agreed that the objective of the negotiations was a common collective ceiling of 700,000 ground forces and 900,000 combined ground and air forces. If parity existed (the Eastern view), approximately equal reductions would bring both sides down to the required level of forces. On the other hand, if the East was superior (the Western view), large asymmetrical reductions by the East would be required.

In November 1973 the West introduced their estimates of NATO and Warsaw Pact ground forces in the area of reductions. These figures revealed that there were 925,000 Warsaw Pact ground forces and 777,000 NATO ground forces in the area. The East did not present comparable figures until June 1976, when they estimated 987,300 Warsaw Pact ground and air forces in the area. The East did not dispute Western estimates of NATO forces in the area. The West revised its earlier estimates of NATO ground forces and included data on air forces in December 1976, estimating 1,162,000 Warsaw Pact and 984,000 NATO forces total in the NATO Guidelines Area.[34]

The relationship between data and reductions is obvious. Based on Western figures, the East would be required to reduce 262,000 forces to reach the 900,000 common collective ceiling; the West would be required to reduce only 84,000 forces. In contrast, based on Eastern figures, the East would be required to reduce 87,300 forces and the West 84,000 to reach the 900,000 ceiling.

Beginning in March 1978, East and West presented disaggregated data on their forces in order to determine the source of the data discrepancy. The two sides concluded that the major problems lay in estimates of Soviet and Polish forces.[35] Despite efforts by the West to engage the East on the data issue and obtain their cooperation in resolving the problem, a solution was not found.

The West continued to insist on prior agreement on data before reductions could occur, until December 5, 1985. In what proved to be the last major proposal by the West in MBFR, Western representatives dropped their demand for prior agreement on data in exchange for Eastern agreement to accept associated measures, including on-site inspection. The December 5 proposal argued that the two sides should attempt to solve the data dispute through on-site inspection based on the exchange of figures after the reduction of U.S. and Soviet forces in a Phase 1 agreement. The West proposed a quota of thirty inspections per year for a three-year period, after which the agreement would expire if the two sides were unable to resolve the data issue.[36]

In effect, this proposal represented a shift in the Western position, from favoring prior agreement on data *and* verification as independent conditions for an MBFR accord to agreement on data *through* verification as the basis for an accord. The idea of conceding the data issue originated in Western Europe, not in the United States. West German chancellor Helmut Kohl and British prime minister Margaret Thatcher argued strongly for the concession, citing repeated Soviet statements that once the data issue was resolved to their satisfaction an MBFR agreement would quickly follow.[37]

Unfortunately, for reasons that are as yet unclear, the East failed to respond to this major concession by the West. By early 1986, General Secretary Gorbachev had announced a major nuclear arms control initiative, which shifted the spotlight away from conventional arms control. In addition, the West's insistence on ninety on-site inspections over a three-year period probably was rejected by Eastern military advisers and defense officials on the grounds that they would reveal sensitive information about Warsaw Pact military forces.[38]

Associated Measures. Associated measures in MBFR, known as confidence-building measures in other arms control forums, were supported by the West from the outset of the negotiations. These measures, to be implemented in conjunction with force reductions, are designed to aid verification of reductions and residual limitations, provide warning of military buildups and preparations for surprise attacks, and enhance confidence by increasing the transparency of military activities on both sides.

Both sides agreed during the preparatory consultations that associated measures could be considered during the negotiations.[39] However, the West did not formally put a package of associated measures on the table until December 17, 1979. These measures included (1) advance notification of out-of-garrison activity; (2) the right to send observers to these preannounced activities; (3) prior notification of major military movements into the area of reductions; (4) the right to conduct up to eighteen inspections during a year on the territory of the other side in the reductions area; (5) establishment of permanent entry/exit points for forces moving into or out of the area of reductions; (6) exchange of information about the forces to be withdrawn, and the organization of forces remaining in the area of reductions; (7) prohibition of interference with national technical means of verification; and (8) the creation of a joint consultative body to aid implementation of the agreement.[40]

Perhaps the most significant element of the Western proposal was that the first two measures—prior notification and observers—would have applied not only within the area of reductions, but also throughout Europe, including a significant portion of the western part of the Soviet Union. For the first time, one of the parties to the negotiations had introduced a proposal that went beyond the geographical boundaries of MBFR as had been agreed during the preparatory consultations.[41] The West argued that geographical asymmetries demanded restrictions on the movements of Soviet forces in the western military districts in order to increase warning of surprise attack preparations.

The East argued in their proposals of November 1973 that national technical means of verification (widely interpreted as satellite photography) were sufficient to verify an MBFR agreement. To the East, associated measures were simply an excuse for spying by the West.[42] It was not until December 1980 that the East softened their position on associated measures, when they presented a package of thirteen measures that would be applied within the area of reductions. Although the Eastern package included provisions concerning the prior notification of large exercises, the prior notification of large military movements within the area, and notification of entry into and departure from the reductions area, these measures lacked "bite" (from the West's perspective) because they did not extend to the western Soviet Union.[43]

The next major Eastern statement on associated measures came outside of the MBFR forum on April 18, 1986, in the context of a speech by Soviet general secretary Gorbachev to the East German Communist Party Congress. Gorbachev proposed the reduction of large numbers of Eastern and Western forces (including those of the United States and Canada) in Europe and expanded the area to be covered to all of Europe, "from the Atlantic to the Urals." Gorbachev also stated that both national technical means and other international forms of verification, including on-site inspection, should be considered.[44]

The Gorbachev speech signaled the beginning of the end of MBFR. During 1986 and 1987 MBFR rounds continued, but the major work in developing a mandate for new talks on conventional arms control "from the Atlantic to the Urals" occurred during informal discussions among the participants (and, at times, representatives of France). The mandate was finally agreed to and signed by twenty-three nations on January 10, 1989.[45]

Bargaining and Concession-making

Question 4: What strategies and tactics did the parties use during the negotiations? How did differences in bargaining style influence the process and outcome of the negotiations? What was the role of politics in the selection of strategies and tactics?

Bargaining and concession-making during the Negotiations on Mutual and Balanced Force Reductions contained elements of both concession-convergence and politics. On some issues, such as the size and nature of manpower reductions, a concession-convergence model operated. On other issues, such as data and associated measures, political considerations dominated the proposals made by East and West.

The problem of consensus-building in the negotiations operated on two levels for the West. First, NATO faced the task of building an intra-alliance consensus in support of Western proposals. The alliance evolved several mechanisms to build consensus. The institution of "trilaterals" between the United States, the United Kingdom, and the Federal Republic of Germany provided a forum for the development of new proposals for presentation to other members of the alliance. Within NATO circles, the Senior Political Committee (an arm of the North Atlantic Council) and the MBFR Working Group served as consensus-building mechanisms. And in Vienna, the NATO Ad Hoc Group—composed of the heads of the Western delegations—met on a weekly basis to forge consensus on new proposals and the language of plenary and informal statements.[46]

At a second level, consensus had to be forged with Eastern participants in the negotiations. In practice, this meant consensus with the Soviet Union. Although the United States and the Soviet Union were viewed as the leaders of their respective sides, Germany (and especially the Federal Republic of Germany) played a critical role. The proposals of both East and West tended to match or pair the reduction of Soviet forces with the reduction of American forces in Europe. The primary objective of the Soviet Union, however, was not the withdrawal of U.S. forces from Europe but reductions and limitations on the size of the West German Bundeswehr.[47] Thus, the unspoken comparison was between the Soviet armed forces and the German Bundeswehr. However, because of West Germany's aversion to being singled out for special consideration in the negotiations, the Soviet–West German tradeoff was always implicit, rather than explicit.

A second element of the bargaining and concession-making process was linkage. Throughout the course of the negotiations, MBFR was linked with other issues and concerns, generally to the detriment of MBFR. The opening of MBFR was delayed by the Conference on Security and Cooperation in Europe, as the Soviet Union refused to participate in MBFR until CSCE was under way. Later, the MBFR negotiations were held hostage to intermediate-range nuclear forces.

In December 1979 Western participants removed Option 3 from the bargaining table so that it would not interfere with the alliance's decision on intermediate-range nuclear forces. And in December 1983 Eastern participants refused to set a date for the resumption of the MBFR negotiations in response to the arrival in Western Europe of the first U.S. Pershing II ballistic missiles and ground-launched cruise missiles.

MBFR also was held hostage to politics, during both the Carter and the Reagan administrations. During most of 1980, as the election approached, the Carter administration seemed to adopt a "less-is-better" approach to arms control. Within the administration, interagency study groups shifted the focus away from force reductions and toward confidence-building measures. In part, this shift was a natural response to growing interest in confidence-building measures in Europe. But it also suggested that the administration was attempting to develop a new approach that the East would "buy," to produce an MBFR agreement before the election. During 1981, the first year of the Reagan administration, the MBFR negotiations were suspended while the administration emphasized the modernization of U.S. conventional and nuclear forces. The idea, in principle, was to place the United States (and, ultimately, the West) in the position of negotiating from strength. In fact, however, the delay reflected the anti–arms control bias of many new political appointees in the Reagan administration.

Bargaining and concession-making that occurred within the context of the negotiations also reflected political considerations. The major bargain struck in the MBFR negotiations undoubtedly was the tradeoff between data and associated measures. The Western offer in December 1985 to drop the requirement of prior agreement on data in exchange for Eastern acceptance of associated measures, including a rigorous on-site inspection regime, was controversial within the alliance as well as with the East.

During 1979 the Federal Republic of Germany expressed serious concerns about the associated measures package under review within the alliance. These concerns were directed at two measures in particular: observers at out-of-garrison activities, and ground and aerial inspection. West German representatives to MBFR noted the obvious advantages of enhanced transparency in obtaining information about Eastern forces; these measures would contribute to the objectives of verification and stability in Central Europe. On the other hand, the measures cut both ways. They would be applied to the West as well as to the East. The acceptance of aerial inspection, in particular, seemed to many in the Federal Republic to single out Germany for special treatment. Despite these objections, however, the Federal Republic ultimately accepted the American argument that these measures were essential for an effective and militarily significant package of associated measures.

Political considerations also help explain changing Soviet and Warsaw Pact views about on-site inspection. The traditional Soviet objection to on-site inspection began to shift in June 1983, when the Warsaw Pact proposed a draft treaty in MBFR that included a complete set of verification measures. Implicitly, the Soviet Union linked progress in MBFR, and their acceptance of associated measures, with NATO's refusal to implement the December 1979 decision on intermediate-range nuclear forces. The Eastern MBFR initiative came in the middle of an extensive propaganda campaign in Europe designed to derail implementation of NATO's December 1979 decision to deploy new theater nuclear forces in Europe.[48] By 1986, Gorbachev had proposed unilateral reductions of Soviet forces in Eastern Europe, and the Warsaw Pact had picked up on his suggestion that international means of verification, including inspection, should be considered. The idea of major reductions by East and West, accompanied by international means of verification, was expressed in the Budapest Appeal of the Warsaw Pact on June 11, 1986.

Explaining Failure

Question 6: If the negotiations did not result in the signing of a formal agreement, to what extent can the framework account for failure?

To say that the Negotiations on Mutual and Balanced Force Reductions failed may seem like an overstatement. By the mid-1980s, the positions of East and West were closer on a number of issues than they had been at any time since the negotiations began. Despite this apparent convergence in negotiating positions, Eastern and Western representatives left Vienna in February 1989 without an agreement. What explains this outcome, and to what extent do background factors, context, substantive issues, and politics contribute to the explanation?

In the first place, structural characteristics of MBFR certainly contributed to the failure of the negotiations. The agreed area of reductions did not include the western military districts of the Soviet Union. This meant that the West would have no control over the redeployment or readiness status of Soviet forces after they were withdrawn from Eastern Europe. American troops would be withdrawn to the continental United States (CONUS), with all that implies for the ability of the United States to reinforce Europe rapidly in a crisis. The geographical asymmetry placed the West at a military disadvantage; some analysts argued, in fact, that any substantial reduction of U.S. and Soviet troops would put the West at an even greater disadvantage.[49]

A second structural issue concerned the nature of direct and indirect participants in the negotiations. France was conspicuous in its absence from the Western side. The French expressed understandable reasons for not participating in MBFR, but it was difficult for the West to justify the French absence to the East. The East insisted that the 60,000 French forces deployed in the Federal Republic of Germany be included in the NATO totals. So although France was not involved, Western participants were held accountable for the presence of French troops in the area of reductions. This affected the size of the reductions required for the West to reach the 700,000–900,000 common collective ceiling. In effect, Western participants had to absorb additional reductions to make up for the French refusal to participate in the negotiations.[50]

The third structural issue that may have contributed to the failure of MBFR was the primary focus on military personnel, rather than equipment. The West initially pressed for a focus on personnel because they believed that a focus on equipment would be detrimental to their interests. West European participants in the negotiations expressed particular concern about including equipment in MBFR.[51] But the Western focus on personnel may have been misguided. Personnel represent less effective measures of military capabilities than equipment. Reductions in Soviet military equipment would have contributed to the Western objective of reducing the ability of the Warsaw Pact to launch a short-warning attack.[52] On the other hand, given the nature of the area of reductions and the requirement for the United States to withdraw its equipment to CONUS, including equipment in MBFR could have placed an unacceptable burden on the West's ability to rapidly reinforce Central Europe in the event of crisis or war.

In addition to structural factors, some observers have pointed to substantive differences between East and West on major issues in the negotiations that made agreement unlikely. The two issues identified most frequently are data and associated measures, especially on-site inspection. The data discrepancy clearly delayed agreement during the first twelve years of the negotiations. But the West conceded their position on data in December 1985, when they proposed an interim Phase 1 agreement and associated measures in exchange for dropping the requirement for prior agreement on data. And while the East argued for many years that national technical means of verification were sufficient and on-site inspection not required, this obstacle began to dissolve in 1986 as first Gorbachev and then the Warsaw Pact called for major force reductions accompanied by international means of verification, including inspection. Thus, although major differences separated the parties throughout the negotiations, by the mid-1980s their positions on many critical issues were beginning to converge.

Another explanation may simply be that other arms control issues, especially those dealing with intermediate-range nuclear forces, strategic nuclear weapons, and the U.S. Strategic Defense Initiative, captured the public interest and the policy-making agenda on both sides, leaving little time for the consideration of conventional arms control in Europe.[53] During the 1970s and the 1980s the United States and the Soviet Union were consumed with the negotiation of the Anti-Ballistic Missile Treaty, the Interim Accord on Offensive Weapons, the Vladivostok Accord, SALT II, and the treaty on intermediate-range nuclear forces. What linkage existed between MBFR and other issues seemed to place MBFR in a secondary position. Related to the lack of public interest and crowded policy-making agendas is the often cited absence of "political will." Put differently, as suggested by Paul Warnke at the beginning of this chapter, during the 1970s and the 1980s neither side really wanted an agreement.

Finally, the MBFR negotiations ended with a whimper and not a bang because the participants anticipated the opening of a new and in many ways more attractive forum in which to discuss conventional arms control in Europe—the CFE negotiations, which opened in Vienna one month after the closing MBFR plenary session. MBFR faced stiff competition all along in the "security basket" of the Conference on Security and Cooperation in Europe. When the CSCE process produced the Stockholm Accord on confidence and security-building measures on September 22, 1986, CSCE began to be viewed as a logical alternative to MBFR—a position that the French had argued from the beginning.[54]

The structural characteristics of CSCE—French participation and measures negotiated in this forum applicable "from the Atlantic to the Urals"—made CSCE an attractive alternative to the long-suffering MBFR negotiations. Moreover, the mandate for new discussions of conventional forces in Europe has led to a focus on military equipment in CFE. In short, CSCE and the CFE negotiations seemed to address some of the structural problems associated with MBFR.

Finally, to many observers, MBFR symbolized the institutionalization of the Cold War in arms control. The bloc-to-bloc structure of the forum and its focus on the military confrontation in Central Europe were overtaken by events in the late 1980s and early 1990s. Political and economic changes in Eastern Europe and the Soviet Union, the disintegration of the Warsaw Pact, and the unification of Germany made MBFR irrelevant to the challenge of building a new structure for European security.

In summary, many factors help to explain why MBFR failed to reach an agreement during more than fifteen years of negotiations. Structural characteristics of the talks, substantive differences between the parties, competition with other arms control issues for space on the policy-making agenda, the lack of political will on both sides, the emergence of new, more attractive forums for the discussion of European security issues, and the rapid transformation of the political and economic environment in Europe all played a part in the demise of MBFR. The common thread running through all of these explanations is politics.

Conclusion: The Politics of Conventional Arms Control in Europe

The Mutual and Balanced Force Reductions negotiations were a product of political considerations from the beginning. Politics influenced the decisions of Eastern and Western participants to enter into the negotiations. The two sides shared little in the way of common interests or objectives: only the abstract visions of "a more stable relationship" and "the strengthening of peace and security in Europe" that were expressed in the final communiqué of the preparatory consultations.

In addition, political considerations influenced the debates between East and West about many of the specific issues, such as limitations on residual forces in the area of reductions. Western participants understood the political sensitivities of the Federal Republic of Germany and developed negotiating positions accordingly. This explains the West's hard line on national limits. It was not until Chancellor Helmut Schmidt proposed in March 1979 that no state should supply more than 50 percent of the armed forces of its alliance in Central Europe that the East saw an opening on the issue of limitations on residual forces.[55] This suggestion was taken up by the East in the draft treaty of February 18, 1982, when they proposed that at the end of Phase 2 reductions no single direct participant would have more than 50 percent of the combined ground and air force manpower in the area.[56] The Federal Republic obviously was the political target of this proposal.

The data discrepancy and on-site inspection were not simply technical issues, but political issues as well. Once the East had tabled data on its forces in the area of reductions, it was publicly committed to the numbers. To withdraw those figures in the face of Western criticism would have suggested that the East had tabled false data in 1976. Thus, East and West were locked into the data discrepancy from the moment differences between Eastern and Western estimates of Eastern forces became public knowledge. And on-site inspection raised political concerns in both the Federal Republic of Germany and the Soviet Union.

Throughout the history of MBFR, when political considerations were right, breakthroughs or major concessions occurred in the negotiations. Political pressures often elicited new proposals from both East and West. In July 1982 the West introduced a draft treaty that called for a single comprehensive agreement—a shift from the long-standing Western position that reductions should be taken in two phases. The stated rationale for the shift in position was to encourage the East to be more forthcoming on the data issue. However, some observers have suggested that another purpose was to draw public attention away from the antinuclear movements in Europe.[57]

Changes in Soviet political leadership in the mid-1980s and Gorbachev's efforts to restructure the Soviet economy undoubtedly influenced Eastern positions in the MBFR negotiations. Gorbachev's willingness to accept conventional force reductions from the Atlantic to the Urals, while excluding the territory of the United States, represented a step-level change in the debate about conventional arms control in Europe. The impetus for this shift was embedded in dramatic economic and political changes in the Soviet Union and Eastern Europe.

Until 1990, the fundamental issue in MBFR—the postwar status of Germany—was not resolved. The participants debated reductions, residual limitations, data, and associated measures but avoided explicit discussion of the future of Germany in Europe. But the postwar status of Germany was the key to successful conventional arms control in Europe. When East and West found a way to address this political problem, progress in conventional arms control followed. The result was an ambitious agreement designed to dramatically reduce the conventional military confrontation in Europe.

6. Nuclear Arms Control

The Negotiations on Intermediate-Range Nuclear Forces

Arms control is essentially a political, rather than a military, exercise and it cannot be isolated from the political realities of the prevailing domestic and international context.
—*Michael J. Sheehan* [1]

NATO's principal problem during the debate over INF was its inability to agree on a consistent set of strategic and arms control objectives.
—*Lynn E. Davis* [2]

During the Washington summit in December 1987, President Ronald Reagan and General Secretary Mikhail Gorbachev signed the first U.S.-Soviet arms control agreement designed to eliminate an entire class of nuclear weapons. The "Treaty between the United States of America and the Union of Soviet Socialist Republics on the Elimination of Their Intermediate-Range and Shorter-Range Missiles" emerged after seven years of on-again, off-again negotiations between the United States and the Soviet Union. The INF Treaty represented the first major arms control success for the superpowers since the signing of SALT I in 1972.

The INF negotiations can be separated into two phases. The first phase began one month before the 1980 presidential election, as the Carter administration moved to implement the arms control track of NATO's December 1979 "dual track" decision on theater nuclear forces. When he assumed office in January 1981, President Reagan decided to emphasize the rearming of America—to ensure that the United States could negotiate from strength when they entered into arms control negotiations with the Soviet Union. Those negotiations opened in Geneva in November 1981. The Soviet Union walked away from the bargaining table in November 1983, one day after the West German Bundestag voted to approve the stationing of Pershing II ballistic missiles in the Federal Republic. The Soviet walkout represented the end of the first phase of negotiations.

The INF negotiations did not resume until March 1985, when they opened in conjunction with talks in Geneva on strategic offensive and defensive forces. From March 1985 until November 1987, when the final concessions on INF were made, the negotiators made slow but steady progress toward an agreement. Unlike the first phase of INF, which resulted in deadlock, the second phase produced a treaty.

Political considerations—both domestic and international—help explain why the first phase of INF ended in stalemate and the second phase ended in agreement. Reaching an agreement on intermediate-range nuclear forces was not a primary objective of either the United States or the Soviet Union during the first phase of the negotiations. The United States was anxious to maintain allied support for the force modernization track of the December 1979 decision. The Soviet Union was determined to use the arms control process to pressure America's NATO allies to renege on their agreement to accept Pershing II ballistic missiles and ground-launched cruise missiles on European soil. Failure to achieve this objective prompted the Soviet walkout in November 1983.

By March 1985, when the INF negotiations resumed, both sides viewed arms control in a different light. The Reagan administration faced strong pressures to reduce the federal deficit and defense spending. President Reagan had reassessed his "evil empire" characterization of the Soviet Union and was prepared to deal with Mikhail Gorbachev. For his part, Gorbachev had an ambitious domestic political and economic agenda in glasnost and perestroika and also wanted relief from the burden of Soviet defense expenditures. Agreement was in the interests of both sides by 1987.

The Treaty on the Elimination of Intermediate-Range and Shorter-Range Missiles

On December 8, 1987, in Washington, D.C., President Reagan and General Secretary Gorbachev signed an agreement to eliminate all of their ground-launched ballistic and cruise missile systems with ranges between 500 and 5,500 kilometers (between roughly 300 and 3,400 miles). The treaty also gives both sides the right to carry out verification measures to monitor compliance with its provisions.[3]

For the United States, the missiles affected by the treaty are the Pershing II ballistic missile and the ground-launched cruise missile (GLCM). The shorter-range U.S. Pershing Ia is also eliminated by the treaty. For the Soviet Union, the affected missiles are the intermediate-range SS-20, SS-4, and SS-5 and the shorter-range SS-12 and SS-23.

The INF Treaty consists of four principal documents. First, the Treaty Articles require both sides to eliminate all their intermediate-range and shorter-range missile systems within three years and ban them thereafter. They also require the United States and the Soviet Union to put into force measures to facilitate effective verification of the terms of the treaty. A second element of the treaty is the Memorandum of Understanding (MOU). This document includes data valid as of November 1, 1987, exchanged by the United States and the Soviet Union prior to signature, regarding the numbers, characteristics, and locations of each side's intermediate-range and shorter-range missile systems.

Third, and perhaps most significant, the treaty includes an Inspection Protocol, which sets forth the procedures for conducting agreed on-site inspections, including short-notice inspections and continuous portal monitoring. The Inspection Protocol is twenty-one pages long (actually longer than the Treaty Articles, which run nineteen pages in the original text) and includes intrusive verification provisions that go far beyond anything the two sides have agreed to in previous arms control arrangements. The final element of the INF Treaty is the Elimination Protocol, which describes the detailed procedures for elimination of missiles, launchers, support facilities, support structures, and support equipment covered by the Treaty Articles.

The INF Treaty is one of unlimited duration. Either party may withdraw if it decides that extraordinary events related to the subject matter of the treaty have jeopardized its supreme national interests. If one party decides to withdraw from the treaty, it must notify the other party six months prior to withdrawal.

All of the treaty documents, including the Memorandum of Understanding and the Inspection and Elimination Protocols, were subject to ratification by the United States Senate and the Supreme Soviet. The Senate approved the resolution of ratification by a vote of 93–5 on May 27, 1988. The Supreme Soviet ratified the treaty the following day, and it entered into effect on June 1, 1988, when President Reagan and General Secretary Gorbachev exchanged the instruments of ratification during the Moscow summit.

There has been much debate about the military significance of the INF Treaty. For the first time, the United States and the Soviet Union signed an arms control agreement that eliminated an entire class of nuclear weapons. But the treaty clearly did not result in major changes in the military balance. The missiles destroyed by the two sides represented only about 3 percent of their nuclear arsenals. The United States and the Soviet Union retained thousands of battlefield nuclear weapons (with ranges less than 500 kilometers) and strategic nuclear weapons (with ranges greater than 5,500 kilometers) that were not covered by the treaty.[4] Moreover, British and French nuclear systems were left out entirely. The INF Treaty did require the Soviet Union to eliminate those systems deemed most threatening by the NATO alliance in December 1979—namely, the SS-20. In this respect, the treaty addressed one of the problems that drew the United States to the negotiating table in October 1980.

The Decision to Negotiate

Question 1: What prompted the United States and its negotiating partner to enter into negotiations? In other words, what problem or situation brought the parties to the bargaining table?

The initial decision by the United States to enter into negotiations with the Soviet Union in October 1980 was a direct outgrowth of NATO's December 1979 decision to deploy new theater nuclear forces in Europe, which assumed that force modernization and arms control were closely linked. The final communiqué issued by NATO foreign and defense ministers meeting in Brussels on December 12, 1979, set the stage for the negotiations. NATO foreign and defense ministers supported ratification of the SALT II Treaty, supported the inclusion of Soviet and American long-range theater nuclear forces in future negotiations, and supported the decision of the United States to negotiate limitations on long-range theater nuclear forces with the Soviet Union.[5]

The decision of the Carter administration to begin negotiations with the Soviet Union just one month before the 1980 presidential election was based on two considerations. First, the administration hoped for progress in at least one arms control forum to bolster President Carter's prospects for reelection. The ratification debate on the SALT II Treaty was stalled in the Senate, and there had been little progress in the Mutual and Balanced Force Reductions negotiations. And, second, President Carter recognized that initiating arms control discussions with the Soviet Union on intermediate-range nuclear forces was needed to hold the European allies firm on implementation of the force modernization track of the December 1979 decision. European governments had won public support for new deployments by committing themselves to the arms control track in 1979. The absence of any U.S.-Soviet discussions fueled already strong peace movements in Western Europe, particularly in West Germany, Belgium, and the Netherlands, and placed those governments in jeopardy.

The Soviet Union approached negotiations on intermediate-range nuclear forces from a different perspective. Following the Soviet invasion of Afghanistan in December 1979, General Secretary Brezhnev made the ratification of SALT II a precondition for negotiations on theater nuclear forces.[6] And, in the aftermath of NATO's December 1979 dual track decision, Brezhnev made revocation of that decision another precondition.[7] During the early part of 1980 the Soviet Union was not predisposed to open negotiations with the United States, choosing instead to adopt a hard line in an effort to divide the United States from its allies and derail the December 1979 decision.

Soviet views had changed by June 1980, when Brezhnev—during a visit by West German chancellor Helmut Schmidt to Moscow—removed these conditions and declared the Soviet Union's readiness to enter into negotiations.[8] Undoubtedly Brezhnev's move was directed to the relationship between arms control and force modernization that NATO had established in the dual track decision. If progress in arms control could be demonstrated, the NATO consensus around the deployment of new theater nuclear forces might dissolve.[9]

The election of Ronald Reagan as president of the United States put a damper on the theater nuclear forces negotiations in Geneva during November 1980, as the Soviet Union waited to see what arms control proposals the new administration would offer. When it became clear that the Reagan administration had decided implementation of the force modernization track of the December 1979 decision was a precondition for arms control negotiations, the Soviet Union adopted another strategy for bringing the United States back to the negotiating table.

In February 1981, in a report to the 26th Soviet Party Congress, Brezhnev proposed a Soviet-American moratorium on the deployment of new theater nuclear missile launchers in Europe and the European parts of the Soviet Union. In addition, Brezhnev called for the resumption of arms control discussions as soon as possible. The moratorium would remain in force while negotiations proceeded, with the objective a treaty that reduced and limited these nuclear forces.[10]

By late 1981 tensions had increased within the NATO alliance, and the focus was the deployment of theater nuclear forces in Europe. Membership in the British Campaign for Nuclear Disarmament had risen to 30,000, and on October 24 the organization sponsored an antinuclear demonstration in Hyde Park, London, that drew more than 250,000 people. Massive protests occurred in Amsterdam, Paris, Brussels, Rome, and Bonn as well.[11]

In addition to the Soviet arms control offensive and the growing antinuclear movement in Western Europe, tensions were fueled by statements made by American leaders concerning the use of nuclear weapons in Europe. President Reagan had indicated that a limited nuclear war could be fought in Europe. Secretary of State Alexander Haig had made his famous "shot across the bow" statement—that is, the willingness of the United States to resort to "nuclear demonstration shots" in support of NATO strategy. These statements, coming on the heels of the announcement that the United States intended to produce the neutron bomb, increased anxieties in Western Europe.[12]

The situation was ripe for arms control initiatives. For the United

States, it was clear that allied governments could not maintain public support for the force modernization track of the December 1979 decision without at least the appearance of progress in arms control. For the Soviet Union, arms control supported their objectives of dividing the United States from the Europeans, fueling antinuclear sentiment in Western Europe and, ultimately, undermining support for NATO's December 1979 decision. Thus, neither the United States nor the Soviet Union, in 1980 or in 1981, entered into negotiations on intermediate-range nuclear forces with the serious intention of reaching an agreement to reduce and limit those weapons.

In a situation that mirrored the opening of the MBFR negotiations in 1973, the United States and the Soviet Union were unable to agree on the title of the talks. The United States preferred "Talks in Geneva on Intermediate-Range Nuclear Forces" or "INF Talks," to signal their interest in focusing on weapons in the 1,000–3,000-mile range. The Soviet Union argued for "Soviet–United States Negotiations on the Limitation of Nuclear Arms in Europe," suggesting their interest in the European theater.[13] This disagreement highlights major differences in Soviet and American interests and objectives during the INF negotiations—differences that were reflected in negotiating positions adopted by the two sides during the INF marathon.

Interests and Objectives

Question 2: How did U.S. policymakers define their interests and objectives with respect to the negotiations? How did America's negotiating partners define their interests and objectives with respect to the negotiations? Were the parties able to define common interests and objectives?

In 1980–81 the United States faced a problem that was both military and political in nature. The military problem was an assessment of the balance of intermediate-range nuclear forces in Europe that showed a growing Soviet superiority. This situation raised serious questions about coupling and extended deterrence. The political problem was twofold: first, to maintain alliance support for implementation of the

December 1979 decision in the face of Soviet efforts to convince the allies to renege on that decision and, second, to reassure the allies about the American commitment to their defense.

Assessments of the military balance that had formed the basis for the December 1979 decision were reflected in U.S. statements about their interests and objectives in the INF negotiations. Based on U.S. counting rules, in late 1981 the Soviet Union held a six to one advantage in intermediate-range nuclear weapons in Europe.[14] U.S. officials expressed concern that the growing imbalance at this level could lead the Soviet Union to believe that they could break the strategic link between the United States and Europe while threatening the European members of the alliance with their theater nuclear forces.[15]

Between 1981 and 1983, however, political interests and objectives dominated the American agenda. The primary U.S. objective during this period was to maintain support within the alliance for implementation of the force modernization track of the December 1979 decision. By entering into arms control negotiations with the Soviet Union, the United States hoped to take the steam out of the antinuclear movements in Western Europe and thus take some of the public pressure off allied governments to renege on the December 1979 decision. Moreover, in the aftermath of the withdrawal of the SALT II Treaty from Senate consideration, statements by American officials concerning the use of nuclear weapons in Europe, and the announcement that the United States would begin producing the neutron bomb, the United States believed that resuming the nuclear arms control dialogue would reassure the allies about America's commitment to their defense.

Beginning in late 1984 and early 1985, however, a new assessment of U.S. interests began to coalesce within the government. The Soviet Union had walked out of the INF talks in November 1983, following a vote by the West German Bundestag approving the deployment of Pershing IIs in the Federal Republic. Several Soviet leaders had briefly appeared and then disappeared from the scene.[16] President Reagan had been reelected by a large margin. The Reagan administration program to rearm America, if not a complete success, had run out of political support in the face of the federal deficit and charges of waste and mismanagement in the Pentagon.[17] And President Reagan had begun to reassess his perception of the Soviet Union as an "evil empire" and "the focus of evil in the modern world." [18] Arms control was once more winning a place on the American foreign policy agenda.

Although not direct parties to the INF negotiations, America's European allies had important interests in the outcome of the talks. The Federal Republic of Germany wanted to avoid an arms control solution that would create a "Euro-strategic balance" that would isolate Germany for special treatment and play to the fears of those who argued that a balance of forces at the theater level would be decoupling. For this reason, German officials pressed the United States in 1978 and 1979 for arms control discussions between the superpowers in the context of SALT III.[19] The demise of the SALT II Treaty in December 1979 eliminated this option, at least for the near term. The shift in NATO and U.S. terminology from "theater nuclear forces" to "intermediate-range nuclear forces" in 1981 signaled the alliance's sensitivity to German concerns "that the United States considered Europe just another theater of operations, one where there might be a limited nuclear conflict." [20]

Great Britain and France remained firm in refusing to include their nuclear weapons in negotiations between the United States and the Soviet Union on intermediate-range nuclear forces, either directly or indirectly through compensation to the Soviets. The British and French governments viewed these weapons as strategic, designed for the defense of their homelands, rather than theater forces. France, although not a participant in the NATO deliberations leading to the December 1979 decision, welcomed the NATO decision to pursue modernization of their theater nuclear forces; French support for the arms control track of the decision was lukewarm at best. Only if the superpowers agreed to substantial cuts in their nuclear forces in Europe would either Great Britain or France consider putting their forces on the negotiating table.[21]

Belgium and the Netherlands had pressed for inclusion of the arms control track in the December 1979 decision. Moreover, both countries had reserved judgment on the deployment track pending the outcome of arms control negotiations between the United States and the Soviet Union. Each hoped that successful arms control negotiations would make deployments of ground-launched cruise missiles in their countries unnecessary. Thus, Belgium and the Netherlands saw the Pershing II and GLCM as bargaining chips and arms control as an alternative to, rather than a complement of, force modernization.[22]

Soviet interests and objectives in the negotiations, like American interests and objectives, changed between 1981–83 and 1985–87. During the first phase of the negotiations, which ended with the Soviet walkout in November 1983, the primary Soviet objective was to stop the deployment of Pershing II and GLCM in Western Europe. Based on Soviet counting rules, which included British and French forces and U.S. forward-based systems, the balance of theater nuclear forces in Europe was approximately equal.[23] NATO's decision to deploy 572 additional warheads in the theater represented an attempt by the West to gain superiority in this class of weapons. This theme was to be reflected in many of the early Soviet arms control proposals, which called for a moratorium on any new deployments by either side.

Of particular concern to the Soviet Union was NATO's plan to deploy the Pershing II ballistic missile. The Pershing II, with a flight time to Soviet targets of minutes, not hours, as was the case for the GLCM, shifted the burden of decision making for initiating a nuclear war to the Soviet Union. In addition, the ability of the PII to threaten Soviet command and control facilities, as well as the SS-20 and intercontinental ballistic missile bases, made the weapons destabilizing in a crisis—for many of the same reasons that the SS-20 was viewed by the United States as being destabilizing in a crisis.[24]

The Soviet Union also was interested in protecting its deployments of SS-4s, SS-5s, and SS-20s in the Far East. These weapons were deployed against China, although during the course of the INF negotiations the Soviet Union rarely referred to the Chinese threat directly. Soviet negotiators preferred to raise the specter of "other security concerns" that must be met by the deployment of theater nuclear forces in support of their argument that reductions to zero were unacceptable.

By late 1984 and early 1985 Soviet interests and objectives had changed. The Soviet effort to derail implementation of the December 1979 decision had failed when the first Pershing IIs and GLCMs began arriving in Western Europe in late 1983. With the emergence of Mikhail Gorbachev in the Soviet Union, domestic problems came to the forefront of the Soviet policy agenda. Like the United States, the Soviet Union seemed to view arms control as a means of building domestic support for reductions in defense spending. By 1984 concerns had arisen about a new component of the arms race, prompted in part by the United States' Strategic Defense Initiative (SDI) program. These domestic considerations, in conjunction with the Soviet desire to avoid another round in arms competition with the United States, may have brought the Soviet Union back to the bargaining table early in 1985.[25]

Negotiating Positions

Question 3: What factors influenced the formulation of negotiating positions? How did these positions change during the course of the negotiations? How did initial positions compare with the negotiated outcomes?

The Negotiations on Intermediate-Range Nuclear Forces focused on three major sets of issues: (1) nature and scope of the reductions, (2) the problem of shorter-range systems, and (3) verification. While debate about the nature and scope of the reductions occurred throughout the negotiations, debate about how to handle shorter-range systems and verification dominated the second phase of the talks, between 1985 and 1987.

Nature and Scope of Reductions. The initial positions offered by the United States and the Soviet Union in the INF negotiations reflected different views of the military balance. In October 1980, during the first, brief encounter between the two sides in Geneva, the United States proposed the establishment of equal ceilings on long-range, land-based, theater nuclear missiles. The weapons to be included in the ceilings were Pershing II, GLCM, and the Soviet SS-4, SS-5, and SS-20. Under the terms of this proposal, the Soviet Union would be required to take asymmetrical cuts because of their superiority in this category of weapons. For their part, the Soviet Union continued the call for a freeze on the deployment of theater nuclear forces by the two sides. The Soviet proposal was based on the assumption that approximate equality existed and included U.S. forward-based systems as well as British and French systems in the category of weapons to be affected.[26]

When the United States and the Soviet Union next met in Geneva in January 1982, both came prepared with new, more specific proposals. The U.S. proposal, announced by President Reagan in a televised address on November 18, 1981, was tabled in Geneva on February 2, 1982, in the form of a draft treaty. Known as the "zero option," the proposal said that the United States was prepared to cancel the deployment of the Pershing II and GLCM if the Soviet Union agreed to dismantle their SS-20s, SS-4s, and SS-5s.[27]

The zero option was based on several principles that had won agreement within the alliance: (1) negotiations should focus on the most threatening systems, namely, land-based missiles; (2) negotiations should result in global limits, rather than "European" limits; and (3) negotiations should exclude allied systems. The focus on land-based missiles was designed to avoid including U.S. forward-based systems—especially nuclear-capable aircraft based in Europe—in the negotiations. The American rationale was grounded in their assessment of the conventional military balance in Europe. American negotiators argued that including aircraft in the negotiations would weaken NATO's conventional capabilities at a time when the United States was trying to convince the allies to improve NATO's conventional force posture. The focus on global limits reflected both political and military considerations. In political terms, the emphasis on global limits was designed to respond to West German concerns that an arms control solution not lead to the creation of a Eurostrategic balance. On the military side, the United States argued that global limits were essential because the mobility of the SS-20 would allow the Soviet Union to redeploy SS-20s from the east, thus bringing them within range of European targets. Finally, the exclusion of allied systems was in response to the firm objection of the British and French to including their strategic nuclear forces in the negotiations.[28]

The Soviet Union responded quickly to the zero option. On February 3, 1982, Brezhnev proposed a freeze on the deployment of new INF systems, to be followed by reductions in medium-range missiles and aircraft to 600 systems by 1985 and 300 systems by 1990.[29] The Soviet proposal focused on weapons "intended for use" in Europe—

that is, only those Soviet systems located west of the Ural Mountains—
in contrast to the American proposal which argued that limits should
be global in scope. Moreover, the Soviet proposal argued for the inclusion of British and French nuclear forces in the reductions and
limitations.

The next shift in the positions of the two sides occurred during the
informal "walk in the woods" in July 1982.[30] During July 1982 U.S.
ambassador Paul Nitze and Soviet ambassador Yuli Kvitsinsky engaged
in a series of informal discussions on the major issues separating the
two sides. The result of these talks was a compromise formula, under
the terms of which the United States and the Soviet Union would each
be limited to 225 intermediate-range missile launchers and aircraft in
Europe. The United States would agree to deploy only GLCMs within
its limit, which would extend also to F-111 and FB-111 aircraft. Limits
on Soviet aircraft would include the Backfire, Badger, and Blinder.
Moreover, the Soviet Union would be limited to 90 intermediate-range
missile launchers in the eastern Soviet Union, outside range of West
European targets. Although the "walk in the woods" formula resolved
several of the major issues separating the two sides, neither government accepted the concept.

The last major proposal before the Soviet Union walked out of the
INF negotiations in November 1983 was the U.S. proposal for an "interim agreement" announced by President Reagan on March 31, 1983.
During late 1982 and early 1983 the United States was under a great
deal of pressure from the allies to move off the zero option because
it had proved to be nonnegotiable with the Soviet Union. In response
to European concerns, and in order to maintain allied support for
implementation of the December 1979 decision, the Reagan administration offered to reduce substantially the planned deployment of
Pershing IIs and ground-launched cruise missiles if the Soviet Union
reduced the number of warheads deployed on its intermediate-range
nuclear forces to an equal level. The ultimate American objective was
still zero, but "zero plus" was viewed as an acceptable interim solution.[31] The Soviet Union quickly rejected the American proposal for
an interim agreement, which continued to call for global ceilings on
intermediate-range nuclear missiles. The Soviet decision to walk out of

the INF negotiations on November 23, 1983, brought the first phase of negotiations to a close.

When the INF negotiations resumed in March 1985, the political context had changed dramatically. Mikhail Gorbachev had assumed office on March 11, 1985. The opening of the new INF discussions (the Soviet Union insisted that these talks were not linked to the discussions in 1980–83) linked INF to negotiations on strategic offensive forces and strategic defensive forces. When the Negotiations on Nuclear and Space Weapons opened in Geneva on March 14, 1985, the Soviet Union insisted that progress on intermediate-range nuclear forces and strategic offensive forces was linked to progress on strategic defensive forces—in other words, to the Strategic Defense Initiative.[32]

Little progress occurred in the discussions about the nature and scope of INF reductions until January 15, 1986, when Gorbachev proposed a three-stage plan to remove all nuclear weapons from the earth by the year 2000. One element of this proposal included the elimination of intermediate-range nuclear missiles in Europe by 1990. The Soviet Union seemed to have accepted the idea of a "zero option," at least in Europe. Moreover, the Soviet proposal dropped the requirement of formal compensation for British and French nuclear forces.[33] The United States welcomed this proposal but insisted that Soviet missiles in Asia be included.

During the Reagan-Gorbachev summit held in Reykjavik, Iceland, on October 11–12, 1986, the Soviet Union made several concessions on the INF issue that eliminated the last of the major differences between the parties concerning the nature and scope of reductions.[34] The Soviet Union proposed the elimination of all intermediate-range nuclear missiles in Europe and a global limit of 100 intermediate-range nuclear missiles for each side outside Europe. In addition, the Soviet proposal included a freeze on short-range missiles, with subsequent negotiations to reduce and limit those missiles. Finally, the Soviet Union indicated its willingness to discuss on-site verification measures.[35]

The Soviet Union made the final concession on the nature and scope of reductions on July 23, 1987, when they proposed removing all medium-range nuclear missiles from Asia as well as Europe if the

United States agreed to include the Pershing Ia (PIa) in any INF deal. By early in 1987 agreement on the nature and scope of reductions had all but been achieved. The major remaining issues separating the parties were how to handle the problem of shorter-range systems and verification. These issues were to consume American and Soviet negotiators until the treaty was signed on December 8, 1987. And the verification issue was to reemerge to complicate the Senate debate on ratification of the treaty during the spring of 1988.

Shorter-Range Systems. The deployment of Soviet SS-20s, SS-4s, and SS-5s in Eastern Europe and the European Soviet Union was not the only problem facing the alliance in the late 1970s and early 1980s. The Soviet Union had also deployed shorter-range nuclear missiles in Eastern Europe capable of targeting Western Europe. These missiles had ranges between 500 and 1,000 kilometers and included the SS-12 and SS-22. Both were single-warhead mobile missiles; the SS-22 was just entering the inventory.

The shorter-range missile threat was noted by NATO in the December 1979 decision. These missiles represented a threat because they could reach targets in West Germany from bases in Eastern Europe. An arms control outcome that focused on weapons with ranges between 1,000 and 5,500 kilometers would leave Soviet shorter-range missiles unconstrained; the threat would not be eliminated but simply redirected. The Federal Republic of Germany was especially concerned about the shorter-range missile threat because those missiles would fall on German soil. An often-heard German comment during the INF negotiations was "the shorter the range, the deader the Germans."[36]

The zero option tabled by the United States on February 2, 1982, addressed the problem of shorter-range systems by "collateral constraints."[37] While Soviet SS-20s, SS-4s, and SS-5s would be eliminated under the terms of the proposed treaty, SS-12s and SS-22s would be limited at existing levels. (Approximately 100 were deployed at that time.) In this way, additional shorter-range missiles could not be deployed in Eastern Europe to make up for the loss in target coverage created by the elimination of the medium-range missiles. The United States did not raise the U.S. Pershing Ia ballistic missile in the context of this proposal, but later—in May 1983—American negotiators indicated a willingness to discuss limits on the PIa, a system comparable to the SS-12 and SS-22.[38] In their early assessments of the military balance in Europe, the Soviet Union had included the Pershing I in Western totals, while they excluded the SS-12 and SS-22 from Soviet totals. The logic behind this practice confused American negotiators because the ranges of the SS-12 and the SS-22 were greater than the range of the PI.[39]

The issue of shorter-range systems did not become a "show-stopper" in the INF negotiations until April 14, 1987, when Gorbachev publicly proposed the so-called double zero option, which would eliminate all shorter-range nuclear missiles from Europe along with the medium-range missiles that had been the primary subject of discussion. This public offer repeated a proposal that had been made during the Reykjavik summit in October 1986.[40]

The double zero option put the United States and the European allies on the defensive. In the United States, the elimination of shorter-range missiles was opposed by many in military and defense circles who had planned to dispose of the PIIs by converting them to the shorter-range PI.[41] In Britain and France, opposition emerged because the elimination of the entire category of Soviet and American shorter-range missiles would increase pressure on these governments to dedicate their independent nuclear forces to the defense of Western Europe. Moreover, some French officials also believed that the elimination of shorter-range missiles would leave the West vulnerable to a Soviet decision to increase their conventional forces.[42]

In Germany, there were multiple concerns. First, the elimination of shorter-range missiles raised the specter of decoupling. And, second, including this provision in a Soviet-American treaty would increase the pressure on the Federal Republic to give up their Pershing Ia missiles.[43] The German government was divided on the issue. Chancellor Helmut Kohl favored the deployment of a new American shorter-range missile in West Germany in conjunction with an INF treaty. In the absence of new shorter-range weapons on the NATO side, Germany would remain vulnerable to the battlefield missiles of Warsaw Pact forces with ranges less than 300 kilometers. Other German leaders argued for the "right" to deploy shorter-range missiles to match Soviet numbers without committing the alliance to stationing those missiles. And still others supported the double-zero option because prospects for an INF treaty seemed to portend a dramatic improvement in German-Soviet relations.[44]

The debate within the alliance on the merits of the double zero option continued throughout the spring of 1987. On June 11, 1987, NATO foreign ministers meeting in Reykjavik accepted the double zero proposal. On July 23, 1987, the Soviet Union formally proposed removing all medium-range nuclear missiles from Asia as well as Europe, if the PI was included in an INF agreement.[45] This "global double zero" option raised the issue of how to deal with West Germany's Pershing Ia missiles, which they had acquired from the United States in 1964.[46] The U.S. position was that these Pershings could not be included in the bilateral U.S.-Soviet INF negotiations because they belonged to the Federal Republic of Germany. On August 26, 1987, Chancellor Kohl pledged that Germany would dismantle their Pershing Ia missiles as soon as the United States and the Soviet Union signed the INF Treaty, thus removing what had been called the key obstacle to an agreement.[47]

Verification. Arms control verification traditionally has served two functions. First, verification provisions allow the parties to detect violations of an agreement that may place their security interests in jeopardy. Second, verification provisions help promote public confidence in the agreement.[48] The second function is especially critical for the United States because of the requirement that arms control treaties be ratified by the United States Senate.

During the first phase of the negotiations, between 1981 and 1983, the United States and the Soviet Union said little in public about verification. When the United States tabled the zero option in February 1982, American negotiators and policymakers indicated that any agreement reached in the negotiations must be verifiable and that verification measures proposed by the parties must be "effective."[49] There is no public record of Soviet statements about verification during the early phase of the INF negotiations. It seems reasonable to assume that the Soviet position at that time mirrored their position in other arms control forums, such as the Negotiations on Mutual and

Balanced Force Reductions, where they argued that national technical means of verification were sufficient.

During the second phase of INF talks, between 1985 and 1987, both sides expressed greater concern about verification. In December 1985, President Reagan issued a report to Congress accusing the Soviet Union of a pattern of noncompliance with arms control agreements.[50] Although this statement focused primarily on alleged Soviet violations of the unratified SALT II Treaty, which was due to expire on December 31, 1985, the implications for INF were clear. Strict verification provisions would be necessary to win domestic support for an INF agreement.

The first major concession on verification came during the Reykjavik summit in October 1986, when Gorbachev agreed in principle to three major U.S. verification requirements for an INF treaty: data exchange on the numbers of affected missile systems before and after reductions; on-site monitoring of missile destruction; and monitoring of missile production facilities.[51] Gorbachev indicated that he wanted the details of verification to be worked out between the two delegations in Geneva. This significant Soviet move allowed the delegations to focus seriously on verification during the early months of 1987.

The debate about on-site inspection was at least as heated within the U.S. government as it was in Geneva. On-site inspection cuts both ways. The price of access to Soviet missile bases and missile production facilities is Soviet access to their American counterparts. There was much concern within the Department of Defense and in the defense industry about permitting Soviets access to U.S. military bases and missile production facilities. The concern was twofold. First, Soviet inspectors might take advantage of their access to sensitive U.S. facilities to reap important intelligence information. And, second, acceptance of on-site inspection in the INF treaty would set a precedent for future arms control arrangements that would be difficult to break.[52]

The negotiations on verification were facilitated by Gorbachev's July 23, 1987, proposal to eliminate all medium-range nuclear missiles from Asia as well as Europe if the United States agreed to include the Pershing Ia in the deal. The Reagan administration argued that verification could be simplified under the global double zero solution and softened its demands concerning surprise inspections and the inspection of nuclear missile production facilities. The United States also announced concessions on the makeup and operation of inspection teams and the timetable for dismantling missiles.[53]

By mid-November 1987 the two sides had failed to agree on procedures for exchanging data on the location of their missiles and on measures for inspecting "suspect" sites—that is, sites suspected of concealing missiles that were outlawed by the treaty.[54] These issues were resolved during meetings in Geneva between Secretary of State George Shultz and Soviet foreign minister Eduard Shevardnadze during the last week in November. Shultz said he was reassured by the exchange of verification-related information because it was consistent with U.S. intelligence estimates of Soviet capabilities.[55]

Although the issue was resolved for the moment, questions about verification provisions contained in the INF Treaty were to be raised again in 1988 during the debate in the United States Senate over the resolution of ratification.

Bargaining and Concession-making

Question 4: What strategies and tactics did the parties use during the negotiations? How did differences in bargaining style influence the process and outcome of the negotiations? What was the role of politics in the selection of strategies and tactics? If the negotiations resulted in the signing of a formal agreement, how did the process of concession-making occur?

Consistent with their changing interests and objectives in the negotiations on intermediate-range nuclear forces, the United States and the Soviet Union adopted very different bargaining strategies in the early phase of the talks than in the later phase. Between November 1980 and December 1983 neither side seriously pursued an agreement. As a result, the proposals offered by both sides from 1980 to 1983 were not meant to be taken seriously. Some U.S. officials privately indicated that the zero option was an ideal negotiating position because the Soviet Union would never agree to it—thus, the United States would get credit for pursuing arms control, but the allies would have no alternative but to accept the new American missiles in the fall of 1983.[56] For their part, the Soviet Union tabled a series of nonnegotiable proposals in Geneva, while announcing a unilateral freeze on the deployment of any new medium-range missiles in the European part of the Soviet Union and threatening "retaliatory steps" if NATO proceeded with plans to deploy the new missiles.[57] The carrot and stick approach failed, and Soviet negotiators walked out of the talks in November 1983 as the first missiles began arriving in Western Europe.

When the negotiations resumed in March 1985, in the context of new negotiations on nuclear and space weapons in Geneva, the United States seemed prepared to deal while the Soviet Union insisted that there could be no progress on the reduction of offensive weapons unless the United States agreed to limit space arms. Both the decision to resume arms control discussions and the bargaining and concession-making on major issues that occurred between March 1985 and the signing of the treaty in December 1987 were motivated primarily by political considerations in Washington and Moscow.

In Washington, President Reagan had been reelected by a landslide and was beginning to think in terms of his foreign policy legacy. Moreover, support for the high levels of defense spending that characterized the first four years of the Reagan administration was declining, both in the Congress and in the public at large. The administration undoubtedly believed that returning to the arms control table would help strengthen wavering support for major nuclear weapons programs.[58]

In Moscow, Mikhail Gorbachev had assumed office and faced serious domestic economic problems. Shifting public attention to foreign affairs and going on the arms control offensive, much as the Soviet Union had done during 1982 and 1983, was an attractive strategy for the new Soviet leader. Concern about the implications of the U.S. Strategic Defense Initiative for the security of the Soviet Union also prompted Gorbachev to return to the negotiating table, although SDI has been given more credit than it probably deserves for bringing the Soviet Union back to the talks.[59]

The major concession offered during the latter phase of the INF negotiations came on February 28, 1987, when Gorbachev proposed separate negotiations on medium-range missiles in Europe, dropping Soviet insistence on a link between those negotiations and restrictions on SDI. The Reykjavik summit had ended in deadlock the previous October because President Reagan had refused to accept constraints on the development of strategic defenses. By February, it became clear to Gorbachev that there was little chance for progress on strategic defenses. President Reagan was not going to abandon SDI, and continued insistence on that condition for progress on other arms control issues would rule out any agreement.[60]

On the nature and scope of reductions, the Soviet Union seems to have made most of the concessions, finally coming around to the Reagan administration's zero option (much to the dismay of some within U.S. and allied defense circles who supported the proposal only because they believed the Soviets would never agree). In 1985 the Soviet Union stopped calling for the reduction of nuclear-capable aircraft along with missiles. And in 1987 Gorbachev dropped his insistence on formal compensation for British and French nuclear systems. Finally, Gorbachev proposed the double zero option in April 1987 and expanded that to global double zero in July 1987, thus responding to the American demand for worldwide limits.

The United States conceded on the issue of shorter-range missiles, when they agreed to the elimination of those systems. The preferred outcome in defense circles would have been to allow the conversion of Pershing II missiles to the shorter-range Pershing Ib.

Both sides made important concessions on verification. The Soviet Union took the first step at the Reykjavik summit, when Gorbachev agreed in principle to data exchange on existing forces, on-site monitoring of missile destruction, and monitoring of missile production facilities. The United States also made politically difficult concessions on the makeup and operation of inspection teams and the timetable for missile destruction during the summer and fall of 1987.

Beginning in 1981 the Reagan administration argued that the NATO decision to deploy new theater nuclear forces in Western Europe would enable the United States to negotiate from a position of strength and eventually bring the Soviet Union to the bargaining table. The concept of "negotiating from strength" is not new in arms control circles. Some observers argue that ongoing defense programs provide the United States with needed bargaining leverage in dealing with the Soviet Union; that is, they increase the likelihood of Soviet concessions and the negotiation of arms control agreements that support the security interests of the United States. Others have suggested that U.S. weapons programs strengthen Soviet resolve and encourage them to initiate or accelerate programs to avoid falling behind; the result is new competition in the arms race.[61]

During the early phase of the negotiations, between 1981 and 1983, the Soviet Union's primary objective was to derail the force deployment track of NATO's December 1979 decision. When that strategy failed, the Soviet Union walked out of the negotiations. When the talks resumed in March 1985, the Soviet Union focused on the linkage between INF and SDI. Gorbachev did not drop the linkage requirement until February 1987. From that point, the Soviet Union seriously pursued the negotiation of an INF treaty, and both sides focused specifically on technical issues, such as the modalities of reductions and the verification regime. The Soviet Union's decision to resume the negotiations in March 1985 may have resulted in part from their recognition that the earlier strategy had failed; U.S. Pershing II ballistic missiles and ground-launched cruise missiles were on the ground in Western Europe. By 1985 the specter of SDI offered new incentives to return to the bargaining table. And NATO's plans to modernize their shorter-range nuclear forces (including the conversion of PII to PIb) may have influenced Gorbachev's proposal for a double zero option in April 1987.

In short, although it is difficult to draw direct linkages between U.S. and NATO force deployment, weapons development, and modernization decisions and Soviet concessions in the INF negotiations, these decisions probably did influence Soviet calculations. But other factors, especially domestic political and economic conditions, probably exerted equal influence on Soviet concessions during the negotiations.

Implementation

Question 5: What additional action, if any, was required for implementation of the agreement? How did the implementation process reflect the role of background factors, context, substance, and politics?

The period between December 8, 1987, when President Reagan and General Secretary Gorbachev signed the INF Treaty in Washington, D.C., and June 1, 1988, when Reagan and Gorbachev exchanged formal instruments of ratification in Moscow, was characterized by much debate in the United States.[62] The debate stemmed from the constitutional requirement of Senate ratification. On January 25, 1988, President Reagan transmitted the INF Treaty to the United States Senate for their consideration. The Senate Foreign Relations Committee, chaired by Claiborne Pell (D-R.I.), had primary responsibility for the treaty, although the Armed Services Committee, chaired by Sam Nunn (D-Ga.), also held public hearings. The Senate Select Committee on Intelligence, chaired by David Boren (D-Okla.), conducted a closed review of the treaty that focused on the verification regime and reported its findings to the Foreign Relations Committee to assist in their deliberations.

The Reagan administration marshaled important witnesses to testify in support of the INF Treaty. Secretary of State Shultz, the Senate Foreign Relations Committee's first witness, cited the treaty as a historic example of the value of "hanging tough" in negotiations with the Soviet Union. Ambassador Max Kampelman, head of the nuclear and space arms talks in Geneva, denied that the agreement would weaken NATO's strategy of flexible response but admitted concern about Soviet compliance with past arms control treaties.[63] Admiral William Crowe, chairman of the Joint Chiefs of Staff, testified on February 4 that "the JCS have unanimously concluded that, on balance, this treaty is militarily sufficient and effectively verifiable. In turn, they believe that this accord is in the best interests of the United States and its allies and strongly recommend its ratification by the U.S. Senate."[64]

On February 11, 1988, during a NATO meeting in Brussels, General John Galvin, supreme allied commander, Europe, reaffirmed his support for the INF Treaty, which he termed "worth the risks" because of the precedent-setting agreement by the Soviet Union to accept asymmetrical reductions and on-site verification.[65] The administration mobilized European support as well. During a visit to Washington, D.C., in mid-February, West German chancellor Kohl went to Capitol Hill and lobbied for quick Senate ratification of the treaty.[66]

Two major issues were raised during the Senate debate on the resolution of ratification: (1) verification and (2) whether conditions or amendments should be attached to the treaty. Concerns about verification of the INF Treaty were raised before the Senate Foreign Relations Committee and during the Senate floor debate on the treaty, which began on May 17, 1988—less than two weeks before the scheduled Moscow summit.

During testimony before the Senate Foreign Relations Committee, administration witnesses characterized the treaty's verification provisions as "effective." As explained by Paul Nitze, special adviser to the president on arms control, this meant that the United States would be able to detect any militarily significant violation of the treaty in time to respond effectively and thereby deny the Soviet Union any benefits from the violation. Verifiability was enhanced by the double zero outcome and by the fact that neither side would be permitted to maintain essential infrastructure for the banned missiles or conduct test flights.[67]

During March and April 1988 Soviet and American officials held a series of technical discussions to work out the details of on-site inspection provisions associated with the INF Treaty. These meetings focused on such questions as how personnel and equipment would be moved between sites, routes for inspector aircraft, and what types of cameras and other equipment could be used during inspections.[68] Serious differences emerged between the United States and the Soviet Union over ten points related to the implementation of inspection and elimination procedures. When these differences became public knowledge in late April, they threatened prospects for ratification before the Moscow summit.[69] It took a final high-level meeting between Secretary of State Shultz and Foreign Minister Shevardnadze on May 11–12, 1988, to resolve the issue and open the way for Senate ratification.[70]

The second major issue that was raised during Senate debate concerned whether "conditions" should be attached to the Senate's resolution of ratification. Conservative opponents of the INF Treaty, led by Senator Jesse Helms (R-N.C.), offered a series of amendments which others labeled "killer amendments" because they would require renegotiation of the treaty with the Soviet Union, thus "killing" any chance of ratification. Helms argued that the Soviet Union could circumvent the treaty because it did not require them to destroy the warheads associated with their missiles. Moreover, Helms questioned the accuracy of data supplied by the Soviets in the Memorandum of Understanding.[71] The last three of these challenges were defeated on May 23, 1988, just four days before the Senate voted to approve the resolution of ratification.[72]

The debate about conditions or amendments to the treaty was also a political debate between the president and the Senate over the Senate's constitutional role in the treaty ratification process. The debate was an outgrowth of the conflict between the Reagan administration and the Senate about interpretation of the Anti-Ballistic Missile (ABM) Treaty. The Reagan administration argued for a "broad" interpretation of the treaty, one that would allow the United States to proceed with the development, testing, and ultimate deployment of SDI. Many in the Congress objected to the administration's effort to reinterpret the treaty. Senator Nunn had held hearings on the issue and after examining the negotiating record of SALT I determined that the "narrow" interpretation of the treaty advocated by most U.S. officials who had been involved in the treaty's negotiation was the correct reading. Nunn's concern was that the Reagan administration had attempted to change the meaning of the already ratified ABM Treaty without Senate consent.[73]

Early in 1988 Senator Nunn again raised the issue of treaty interpretation with the Reagan administration, but this time the INF Treaty was the focus of Nunn's attention. Senator Nunn and Majority Leader Robert Byrd sought reassurances from Secretary of State Shultz that testimony provided by administration witnesses in support of the INF Treaty was authoritative, that the meaning of the treaty as presented by those witnesses was legally binding, and that Senate approval would be required for any other interpretation of the treaty.[74] Nunn and Byrd threatened to delay hearings on the treaty until these assurances were given. After debate within the administration and between the administration and conservative critics of the INF Treaty who were concerned that such a statement would undercut Reagan's position on the ABM Treaty, Shultz acknowledged that administration testimony on the INF Treaty was authoritative. Nunn and Byrd then agreed to drop their effort to delay hearings on the treaty.[75]

The issue was not resolved, however, until March 29, 1988, when the Senate Foreign Relations Committee appended to the resolution of ratification a condition that stipulated the Senate's role in treaty interpretation. The condition stated that the treaty would be interpreted in accordance with the understanding shared by the president and the Senate at the time of Senate consent to ratification, that the testimony of administration witnesses formed the basis for this common understanding, and that no other interpretation could be adopted without the advice and consent of the Senate.[76] This condition was attached to the Senate's May 27, 1988, resolution for advice and consent to the ratification of the INF Treaty, which was passed by a vote of 93–5. The Senate's action came just in time for the Reagan-Gorbachev summit meeting in Moscow, where the instruments of ratification were exchanged.

Conclusion: The Politics of Nuclear Arms Control in Europe

What for years had been a political debate between the United States and the Soviet Union, with neither side seriously interested in an agreement, had become by 1987 a determined push for a treaty on intermediate-range nuclear forces. Much of the credit for the INF Treaty goes to Ronald Reagan and Mikhail Gorbachev, who wanted an arms control agreement in 1987. Each had his own reasons. Reagan was beginning to consider his political legacy and saw an arms control agreement with the Soviet Union as the crowning achievement of his administration. Gorbachev faced an ambitious domestic political and economic agenda and saw an arms control agreement with the United States as providing "breathing space" abroad.[77]

But it took six years to get there. The early years of the INF negotiations were driven primarily by political considerations. Positions adopted by both sides between 1980 and 1983 were chosen as much for their political impact as for their military rationale or negotiability. The American zero option won the support of many defense civilians, such as Assistant Secretary of Defense Richard Perle, precisely because it was nonnegotiable. The proposal was designed primarily to buy time until the arrival of Pershing II ballistic missiles and ground-launched cruise missiles in Europe. Similarly, the moratorium proposals made by Brezhnev and Andropov were directed at the European members of NATO in an effort to derail those deployments.

Even after the negotiations resumed in March 1985, the United States and the Soviet Union continued to focus on the political benefits of arms control. Reagan used the ongoing Nuclear and Space Talks to maintain domestic support for the Strategic Defense Initiative and ICBM modernization. And Gorbachev's proposal to eliminate nuclear weapons from the face of the earth by the year 2000 was directed at least as much to world public opinion as to the United States.

Politics influenced the negotiations on intermediate-range nuclear forces at several levels. First, bureaucratic politics within the U.S. government helped to shape both American initiatives and responses to Soviet proposals. The failure of the "walk in the woods" formula to win approval in Washington (and in Moscow, for that matter) can be explained by bureaucratic opposition to the compromise. In Washington, civilians in the Department of Defense were opposed to the sacrifice of the Pershing II and the inclusion of aircraft, both essential elements in the deal. And in Moscow, although the evidence is less clear, there were some who argued that a better use of the INF issue was to drive a wedge between the United States and its European allies and postpone U.S.-Soviet arms control until the 1990s.[78]

Second, domestic politics influenced not only the negotiations but also implementation of the INF Treaty. By 1985 the Reagan administration faced strong domestic pressures to slow down the defense buildup and deal with waste, fraud, and abuse in the Pentagon. Prospects of an agreement on strategic arms were dim, but the chances of an agreement on intermediate-range nuclear forces seemed much better. Some in the Reagan administration supported an INF agreement because they hoped it would take the pressure off President Reagan to make ill-advised concessions on strategic offensive forces or SDI.[79] Gorbachev also was in need of a foreign policy success; for him, INF represented an opportunity to demonstrate his ability to extract concessions from the Americans during a period in which he had been unable to convince the Reagan administration to back down on SDI.

The treaty ratification debate illustrates both the politics of arms control verification and the impact of congressional-executive relations on the ratification process. Verification was as much an issue of domestic politics as it was an issue for negotiation with the Soviet Union. By the mid-1980s the issue had won broad public attention in the midst of charges by the Reagan administration that the Soviet Union had violated previous arms control agreements. In this political environment only the most stringent verification provisions could win support for an INF Treaty. Previous disagreements between members of the Senate and the Reagan administration about interpretation of the ABM Treaty established a confrontational atmosphere for consideration of the INF Treaty. Neither side was predisposed to trust the other, and three Senate conditions on the INF Treaty are the result.

Third, the negotiations on intermediate-range nuclear forces were influenced as well by international politics. The United States pursued consensus-building first with their European allies, in the formulation of initial negotiating positions, and then with the Soviet Union. Views of the Europeans on the nature and scope of reductions, shorter-range systems, and even verification (as it pertained to on-site inspections on European soil) had to be taken into account. The linkage of arms control and force deployments in the December 1979 decision made political consultation imperative. Changes of leadership in the Soviet Union complicated consensus-building and undoubtedly extended the negotiations. The arrival of Gorbachev on the Soviet political scene clearly represented a major opportunity for progress in arms control, and the Reagan administration took advantage of it.

The negotiations on intermediate-range nuclear forces also illustrate the public dimension of nuclear arms control. Unlike the MBFR negotiations, which continued unnoticed except by the experts for fifteen years, the INF negotiations captured front-page headlines. The Soviet effort to target Western European publics on the INF arms control issue parallels their efforts to target those same publics on the INF deployment issue. The "politicization" of nuclear arms control makes already technically difficult negotiations nearly impossible—except, that is, when the political conditions on both sides are right, as they were in 1987.

Part IV **Dealing with Friends and "Mixed" Relationships**

Dealing with friends and the problem of "mixed" relationships presents even more of a challenge for the United States than dealing with allies or adversaries. Relationships between friends are similar to relationships between allies, in that they are characterized by positive feelings. Unlike relationships between allies, however, relationships between friends exhibit low or variable commitment and limited scope. Friends do not share the broad, pervasive relationships of allies—relationships that cut across political, military, economic, social, and cultural issues.

With the end of the Cold War, American policymakers will be confronted increasingly with mixed relationships. These are relationships between allies where the issue under discussion falls outside the scope of narrowly defined alliance commitments. Mixed relationships share some of the characteristics of relationships between allies; however, the focus on nontraditional issues means that they may resemble relationships between friends.

Negotiations between friends and negotiations between allies on nontraditional issues are even more difficult than negotiations with allies or adversaries. Negotiations between friends are characterized by the pursuit of individual, rather than common, interests. The absence of a long-standing relationship between the parties reinforces a one-shot mentality. The parties consider negotiations in isolation from the broader relationship—because no broader relationship exists. The parties also find it difficult to identify common interests and objectives. There are few opportunities for side payments and leverage because of the limited scope of the relationship. Moreover, the absence of trust leads to misperceptions in negotiations between friends.

Dealing with allies on nontraditional issues raises other problems. Negotiations that move the debate outside the limits of alliance responsibilities, as they have been defined historically, threaten the consensus that holds the alliance together. It is more difficult to identify common interests and objectives when dealing with nontraditional issues than when dealing with mainstream alliance concerns. Differences between allies on nontraditional issues are likely to raise concerns at home about the reliability of allies and the costs of the commitment to their security.

The cases in Part IV illustrate the difficulties in dealing with friends and mixed relationships. The absence of a long-standing relationship, in the case of negotiating with friends, or the focus on a nontraditional issue, in the case of negotiations with allies, complicates the identification of common interests and objectives. Negotiations between the United States and the Arab states and Israel about logistical support for a U.S. deployment to the Persian Gulf and Southwest Asia in the early 1980s illustrate the problem of negotiating with friends. While the United States viewed the Soviet Union as the major threat to the stability of the region, many of the Arab states viewed Israel as the major external threat and domestic instability as the major internal threat. The inability of the parties to agree on the nature of the threat and the extent of the American commitment to their security contributed to the limited success of these negotiations.

The negotiations between the United States and its European allies about logistical support for a U.S. deployment to the Persian Gulf and Southwest Asia in the early 1980s illustrate the problem of negotiating with allies on nontraditional issues. This was known as the "out-of-area" problem because the United States attempted to extend the scope of alliance responsibilities outside of the area defined by the North Atlantic Treaty. Here, again, the United States and the European allies differed on the nature and source of the threat to the flow of oil from the Persian Gulf. The inability of the parties to agree on the nature of the threat and the allies' uncertainty about the impact of their support for U.S. strategy in the Gulf on East-West relations contributed to the limited success of these negotiations.

The Iraqi invasion of Kuwait in August 1990 tested American strategy in the Persian Gulf and the results of its negotiating efforts with friends and allies during the 1980s. The first crisis of the post–Cold War world was met by a Saudi invitation to the United States to deploy thousands of American troops on their soil. Other American friends in the region, including Bahrain, Oman, and Egypt, contributed military forces or other support to deal with the Iraqi threat. For their part, America's European allies also responded with individual contributions to the multinational effort. The absence of critical access and prepositioning agreements in the region, in this case, did not unduly constrain the American response to the Iraqi threat. Negotiations between the United States and the Arab states and Israel and with the European allies during the 1980s, in combination with the end of the Cold War and relaxation of the Soviet threat, undoubtedly created the climate in which a cooperative response was made possible.

7. The Arab States and Israel

Negotiating

Logistical

Support for the

Persian Gulf

The task of deploying a large number of U.S. troops to Southwest Asia presented an unprecedented challenge to American military planners. The distances involved in transporting men and equipment from the United States were enormous; the theater lacked a sufficient military infrastructure; the climate in the region was extremely harsh; and any operation depended on the elusive political cooperation of regional states.

— Charles A. Kupchan [1]

Access is still needed in several key nations within our geographical area of responsibility to significantly increase the amount of POL, ammunition, and supplies/equipment. While our pre-positioning program has been partly successful, and our initiatives promising, some critical gaps remain in terms of location, quantity, and types of material stored.

— General H. Norman Schwarzkopf
   Commander-in-Chief, U.S. Central Command [2]

The United States has confronted major challenges to its diplomatic skills in the Persian Gulf and Southwest Asia. Since the end of the Arab-Israeli War of 1973, the region has served as an arena for U.S.-Soviet conflict, intraregional conflict, and internal instability, which have threatened the security interests of the United States and its allies. If the United States had faced a serious crisis in the region during the late 1970s and early 1980s that required the large-scale deployment of American military forces, it would have been hard pressed to respond.

The Arab oil embargo during the 1973 Arab-Israeli War proved that the West was vulnerable to a cutoff of the oil supply. The fall of the shah of Iran, followed by the Soviet invasion of Afghanistan in 1979, made it clear that the United States did not have the military capability to respond and restore stability to the region.

When President Carter proclaimed the "Carter Doctrine" in January 1980 and created the Rapid Deployment Joint Task Force (RDJTF) two months later, he sent a signal to the Soviet Union as well as to countries in Southwest Asia: the United States was prepared to intervene, with military force if necessary, to prevent outside influences from dominating the politics of the region. Although not specifically mentioned by name, the Soviet Union clearly was the target of Carter's statement.

The RDJTF was replaced by a more permanent command on January 1, 1983, with geographic responsibility for the nineteen-country region including parts of the Middle East, the Horn of Africa, and the Persian Gulf and extending to Pakistan and Afghanistan. The United States Central Command (or CENTCOM) was headquartered in Tampa, Florida, nearly 7,000 miles away from its area of responsibility. The challenge facing CENTCOM was how to deter, and if necessary fight, in the region given limited forces, serious logistical support shortfalls, and minimal access to countries in the region.

During the early to mid-1980s the United States embarked on an ambitious diplomatic effort to negotiate arrangements with countries in the Middle East, Persian Gulf, and the Horn of Africa to obtain critical support for an American deployment to the region in the event of war. The United States did negotiate limited arrangements with Egypt, Oman, Bahrain, Kenya, Somalia, and Israel. But Saudi Arabia —the most crucial from a strategic point of view—turned a deaf ear to American overtures. As a result, by the end of the 1980s, the U.S. ability to deploy forces to the region and support and sustain them in combat was not much improved from the situation in 1980, when the Carter Doctrine was first enunciated.

The Iraqi invasion of Kuwait on August 2, 1990, provided a critical test of these arrangements. Despite the lack of a formal access agreement, Saudi Arabia invited the United States to deploy several thousand troops on their soil, provided financial support for the American presence in the region, and agreed to expand their oil output to help deal with anticipated shortages.[3] Other Gulf states, including Oman, Bahrain, the United Arab Emirates, and Qatar, offered immediate support for the American troop deployments.[4] Even with the cooperation of its friends in the region, the deployment of thousands of troops and thousands of tons of military equipment to Saudi Arabia—code-named Operation Desert Shield—placed serious strains on U.S. capabilities.

The Negotiations on Logistical Support for the Persian Gulf

The use of American forces in the Persian Gulf depends upon successful diplomacy. Unlike the situation in Western Europe, in the Gulf region the United States maintains no formal alliance relationships that commit the parties to support each other in the event of crisis or war. Furthermore, there are few military bases and other military-useful infrastructure in the region capable of supporting American forces. This means that U.S. troops are required to bring logistical support with them, or depend upon countries in the region for support, in the event of a deployment to the Gulf.

In order to offset shortages in strategic airlift and sealift and to formalize access agreements and other logistical support arrangements between the United States and countries in the Persian Gulf, during the early 1980s the United States initiated negotiations with a number of the Arab states and Israel. The purpose of these negotiations was to discuss access to bases, joint exercise arrangements, and the acquisition of support from friendly governments in the region.

Although the United States, for planning purposes, aimed for formal written arrangements, many of the countries in the region were reluctant to sign formal agreements. Instead, they preferred an informal arrangement in which they pledged support to the United States in the event of a deployment of U.S. forces to the Gulf, without specifying the nature of the threat or the extent or location of support to be provided.

By the late 1980s the United States had little to show for its efforts. The Department of Defense still had no permanent base of its own in the Persian Gulf. America's greatest success has been with the sultanate of Oman. In 1980 the United States signed an agreement with Oman which provides the U.S. military with access to three Omani facilities: Masirah Island in the Indian Ocean, Seeb Air Base in the northern part of the country, and Thumrait Air Base in the south. These facilities are used for limited purposes in peacetime and presumably would be available to the United States, upon invitation by Oman, in wartime. The agreement was renewed in 1985. As part of this arrangement, the United States invested nearly $300 million in military construction in Oman. This investment was designed to upgrade runways and refueling areas and to build additional storage facilities. In addition, the United States military has prepositioned rations, trucks, jeeps, artillery shells, and air-to-air missiles in Oman and uses Omani bases for reconnaissance flights and for resupply of U.S. Navy vessels. Oman has also participated in joint military exercises with the United States. Still, there is no permanent U.S. military presence in Oman.[5]

The United States has been less successful in negotiating formal access agreements with other Gulf states. In Bahrain, for example, the government has been reluctant to permit a major U.S. presence. The United States Navy's Middle East Force is based in Bahrain, with its headquarters on a Middle East Force ship.[6] The United States leases housing and other facilities and airfield and port use in Bahrain.[7]

The United States also initiated negotiations with Kenya and Somalia in an effort to support U.S. strategy in the Persian Gulf. Although located on the Horn of Africa, some 1,400 miles from the Persian Gulf, Kenya and Somalia provide critical port and air base facilities in the event of a U.S. deployment to the region. In 1980 the United States signed an agreement with Kenya that provides for American use of the port of Mombasa and the Nanyuki Air Base in the event of war. Kenya also provides storage facilities and fuel, repair, and resupply services to U.S. ships and aircraft.[8] In support of this arrangement, the United States spent $30 million for dredging the harbor at Mombasa to accommodate aircraft carriers.[9]

In Somalia, the United States has access to two air and port facilities, at Berbera and Mogadishu, which could be used by the United States as staging bases. Similar to the arrangements with other countries, the United States has invested more than $50 million on runway improvements and warehouse construction in Somalia.[10]

The United States has also endeavored to negotiate similar arrangements with Egypt and Israel. Egypt has been unwilling to sign a formal written agreement, although Egyptian officials have pledged support to the United States in the event of crisis or war and fulfilled that pledge following the Iraqi invasion of Kuwait in August 1990. In addition, Egyptian military forces have participated in joint military exercises with U.S. forces.[11] The United States has signed an agreement with Israel, which provides for U.S. access to Israeli hospitals and the storage of medical supplies in Israel for use by American forces in the event of war in the region.[12]

The United States had the least success in dealing with the country deemed most critical for support of U.S. strategy in the Persian Gulf—Saudi Arabia. During the 1980s the government of Saudi Arabia was unwilling to permit the United States to have a base in their country and was reluctant to enter into written agreements with the United States, although, similar to the Egyptian case, Saudi officials offered verbal guarantees of support. The Saudi guarantees assumed the form of "overbuilding" their military facilities and military-related infrastructure to allow use by U.S. forces in the event of crisis or war.[13]

Negotiations between the United States and the Arab states and Israel concerning logistical support for a U.S. deployment to the Persian Gulf during the 1980s illustrate the problems involved in negotiating with friends—countries with which the United States does not have a formal alliance relationship. In the case of negotiations with the Arab states, the two sides were unable to reach consensus on the nature of the primary threat in the region and the specification of common interests and objectives. This complicated the negotiations and in some cases—Saudi Arabia the prime example—made negotiation of a formal agreement impossible.

Moreover, these cases illustrate the critical importance of the ongoing Middle East conflict for U.S. policy in the Persian Gulf. The U.S. commitment to the security of Israel and the feeling on the part of many Arabs that the United States was not pressing for resolution of the Palestinian problem were issues that directly affected the course of negotiations with the Arab states on logistical support for the Persian Gulf.

The case of Israel was different. The government of Israel encouraged American overtures and conducted the negotiations at a deliberate pace. Israel pressed for an arrangement that would permit the storage of U.S. support equipment and supplies in their country, which would be available to the United States in the event of a crisis or war in the Persian Gulf. For the United States, however, this kind of an arrangement would have presented political problems because of Arab concerns that this equipment might be used against them in the next Arab-Israeli war.[14]

In summary, the negotiations on logistical support for a U.S. deployment to the Persian Gulf demonstrate the problems of negotiation outside the context of a formal alliance or an adversarial relationship. Background factors, such as the history of relationships between the parties and cultural factors, and politics (both domestic and international) are crucial in explaining the relative lack of success experienced by American negotiators. Inability to define a common threat and identify common interests and objectives further complicated the consensus-building process during the 1970s and the 1980s.

The Decision to Negotiate

Question 1: What prompted the United States and its negotiating partners to enter into negotiations? In other words, what problem or situation brought the parties to the bargaining table?

The decision made by the United States to pursue negotiations about logistical support for the deployment of American forces to the Persian Gulf during crisis or war was a product of several factors. First, the Arab oil embargo that was imposed during the 1973 Arab-Israeli War demonstrated the importance of access to Gulf oil for the United States and, even more critically, for America's allies in Western Europe and Japan. During the early 1980s the United States depended on Persian Gulf suppliers for between 17 percent and 43 percent of its oil imports. American allies in Western Europe, in contrast, depended upon Gulf oil for between 47 percent and 81 percent of their oil imports. The situation in Japan was also critical. Imports from the Gulf made up 73 percent of Japanese oil imports in 1980.[15] Concern about the continued flow of oil from the Gulf prompted the United States to engage in discussions with the Arab states in that region.

Second, the fall of the shah of Iran in 1979 signaled the loss of a major American ally in the region. The United States had invested much time and other resources in developing a relationship with the shah and viewed him as a representative of U.S. interests in the region. Iran's strategic position offered bases to American troops in the event of crisis or war, and its location between the Gulf and the Soviet Union provided both a deterrent and a front line of defense against possible Soviet moves toward the Gulf.[16] The fall of the shah left a void in the region, and emergence of an Islamic revolution in the country did not bode well for American interests.[17]

Third, the strategic situation in the Gulf deteriorated even further when the Soviet Union invaded Afghanistan in December 1979. The invasion confirmed the fears of many in the United States that the Soviet Union had designs on the Gulf oil fields.[18] The expansion of the Soviet military threat to the region prompted an American response, beginning early in 1980.

On March 1, 1980, President Carter stated what later became known as the Carter Doctrine: "An attempt by any outside force to gain control of the Persian Gulf region will be regarded as an assault on the vital interests of the United States of America and such an assault will be repelled by any means necessary, including military force." [19] Although the Carter Doctrine was not directed toward a specific country, the clear understanding was that the Soviet Union was the target. In conjunction with promulgation of the Carter Doctrine, President Carter created the Rapid Deployment Joint Task Force, headquartered at the Readiness Command in Tampa, Florida, as the military instrument for implementation of the American commitment to the defense of U.S. interests in the Persian Gulf.

U.S. strategy in the Persian Gulf was designed, first, to deter a Soviet incursion and, second, if deterrence failed, to deploy air and ground forces to the region to stop the Soviet advance and end the conflict on

U.S. terms. This strategy was premised on mobility. Much like American strategy for the defense of Western Europe, the United States depended upon warning time and the ability to move troops quickly to the Gulf in the event of crisis or war. Geography posed a major obstacle for the United States. The Soviet Union, with its new presence in Afghanistan, had moved 300 miles closer to their objective of a port on the Arabian Sea, while the United States had no troops in the region.[20]

In 1980, when the RDJTF was created, there was consensus that the United States did not have the capability to enforce the Carter Doctrine. The United States lacked the airlift and fast sealift necessary to move forces quickly from the continental United States to the Persian Gulf in the event of crisis or war.[21] Creation of the RDJTF did not result in an expansion of U.S. force structure; in some cases, forces already committed to the defense of Western Europe became "dual-committed" to the defense of U.S. interests in the Persian Gulf. And this dual commitment applied to support forces as well as combat forces.

In 1980 the United States faced serious pressures on the defense budget. The Carter administration, after a decline in U.S. defense spending, had just begun to press for increases in the defense budget. But these increases would not be evident in American airlift and fast sealift capabilities for many years. In addition, the high cost of airlift in particular suggested that shortfalls would persist for some time. Just as the United States had decided during the same period to approach the Federal Republic of Germany about logistical support in NATO, so U.S. officials determined to approach the Arab states with requests for the negotiation of access rights to ports and airfields and logistical support arrangements.

What incentives brought the Arab states and Israel to the bargaining table in the early 1980s? For the Arab states, the incentives were few. The recent experience of the 1973 Arab-Israeli War had soured the Arabs on U.S. policy in the Middle East. Furthermore, the fall of the shah of Iran in 1979 and the assassination of Egyptian president Anwar Sadat in 1981 had convinced many Arab leaders that it was dangerous to associate too closely with the United States. The Arabs came to the bargaining table most reluctantly, hopeful that negotiations could be conducted in secret and that arrangements would remain verbal and informal. Some of the Arab states may have viewed negotiations with the United States as a means of achieving other objectives, such as foreign assistance, military sales, or military construction and the improvement of existing facilities in their countries. Others may have believed that cooperation with the United States would influence the American position in the Middle East conflict.[22]

Israel entered the negotiations later, prompted in part by the absence of U.S. success in its dealings with the Arab states. Israel clearly was not the United States's first choice. Geographically, Israel was far from CENTCOM's area of responsibility; politically, dealing with Israel could only make negotiations with the Arab states more difficult. But the United States had little choice. Saudi Arabia had closed the door on the negotiation of a formal agreement with the United States, Egypt was unwilling to consider a formal written accord, and the United States was making only limited progress with countries in the Gulf—Oman and Bahrain being the exceptions.

Interests and Objectives

Question 2: How did U.S. policymakers define their interests and objectives with respect to the negotiations? How did America's negotiating partners define their interests and objectives with respect to the negotiations? Were the parties able to define common interests and objectives?

Major differences in perceived interests and objectives among the United States, the Arab states, and Israel placed obstacles in the way of negotiations on logistical support for a U.S. deployment to the Persian Gulf. U.S. interests and objectives included (1) protecting the flow of oil from the Persian Gulf; (2) containing Soviet influence in the region, which became especially important following the Soviet invasion of Afghanistan; (3) ensuring regional stability; and (4) supporting the security of Israel.

Although the United States was far less dependent on oil from the Persian Gulf than the European allies and Japan, primary responsibility for the defense of the flow of oil from the Gulf fell to the United States. The American objective, as it pertained to the negotiations on logistical support for a U.S. deployment to the Gulf, was to devise formal access agreements and logistical support arrangements that would convince the Soviet Union that the U.S. commitment to the protection of the flow of oil from the Gulf was a serious commitment, one backed up by military capabilities.

Containing Soviet influence in the region was a primary objective of U.S. policy during the 1980s. The threat to stability in the region, as perceived by U.S. policymakers, was the Soviet Union. Soviet support of North Yemen and Ethiopia, and the presence of large numbers of Soviet troops in Afghanistan, raised the specter of a Soviet move in the Gulf.[23]

A third objective of U.S. policy in the Persian Gulf was ensuring regional stability, including the stability of major regional actors such as Saudi Arabia. The United States was concerned with the potential for Soviet or Soviet-sponsored efforts to destabilize governments in the region. In addition, the Islamic revolution in Iran and the Iranian commitment to spreading the revolution to other states raised concerns in Washington about the stability of governments such as Saudi Arabia. The prospect of internal strife in the oil-supplying states could threaten the flow of oil from the Persian Gulf just as much as Soviet intervention in the region.[24]

A fourth objective of the United States in the region, broadly defined, concerned the security of Israel. The U.S.-Israeli relationship was long-standing, and the American commitment to the security of Israel was a critical element of American policy. Israel, as its government's officials frequently reminded U.S. policymakers, was America's only democratic ally in the region. Strong domestic support for Israel in the United States limited the extent of cooperation between the United States and the Arab states. The U.S. commitment to the security of Israel has been viewed by some as an obstacle to the improvement of relations with the Arab states, including the negotiation of access rights and logistical support arrangements.

The interests and objectives of the Arab states were quite different. The major difference concerned perceptions of the greatest threat in the region. Unlike the United States, the Arab states did not view the

Soviet Union as the primary threat to the security of the Persian Gulf. For the Arabs, the state of Israel represented the major threat to their interests.[25] This focus on Israel, rather than the Soviet Union, was to complicate negotiations with the United States on access rights and logistical support for a U.S. deployment to the Persian Gulf.

A second concern on the part of the Arab states was the desire for development without Westernization. Particularly for the more conservative states in the region, such as Kuwait and Bahrain, opening their societies to Western influences was an undesirable side effect of Western-supported development efforts. These states wanted to reap the benefits of U.S. development assistance without the costs—that is, without diluting their cultural norms and standards of behavior.[26]

The Arab states had a more practical reason for wanting to minimize contact with the United States. Arab leaders noted the experience of the shah of Iran and Egyptian president Sadat. The fall of the shah and Sadat's assassination convinced many Arab leaders that there were serious, and unacceptable, costs associated with doing business with the United States. In the absence of compelling incentives, few Arab leaders wanted to deal openly with the United States.[27]

Israel had its own policy agenda. The United States and Israel shared overlapping, but not identical, views of the nature of threats to stability in the region. Both the United States and Israel viewed the Soviet Union as a major destabilizing influence. For Israel, however, the threat was more immediate and direct. Israel also viewed the Soviet Union as an indirect threat through their support of Syria, the Palestinians, and other Arab interests in the Middle East and the Persian Gulf.[28] This shared perception of the primary threat in the region facilitated discussions between the United States and Israel. But from the standpoint of satisfying U.S. military requirements in the region, the Arabs were much more critical than Israel. In the end, however, the domestic political requirements of U.S. policy in the region demanded a tilt toward Israel.

Negotiating Positions

Question 3: What factors influenced the formulation of negotiating positions? How did these positions change during the course of the negotiations? How did initial positions compare with the negotiated outcomes?

Negotiations between the United States and the Arab states and Israel about logistical support for the Persian Gulf focused on three major issues: (1) access to bases and facilities, (2) provisions for joint military exercises, and (3) acquisition of services and supplies from foreign governments, or contingency contracting. The U.S. approach to the negotiations was twofold. First, the United States pursued a political-level, government-to-government agreement that specified an in-principle commitment to cooperate. Second, representatives of the U.S. Department of Defense and their counterparts in one of the Arab states or Israel pursued the negotiation of technical implementing arrangements that specified the extent of access or types of support to be provided.

Access. The most difficult issue facing the parties to these negotiations was the question of access.[29] The only guaranteed access to the United States was at Diego Garcia, an island located 2,500 miles from the Strait of Hormuz, where the U.S. Navy had deployed eleven prepositioning ships to support U.S. forces in the event of deployment to the Persian Gulf.[30] The United States could count on no secure basing or prepositioning facilities in the Gulf itself.

The United States opened negotiations with Saudi Arabia, Egypt, and Oman in the early 1980s in an effort to acquire access to bases and facilities in the region. In each case the United States pressed for peacetime access for training, joint exercises, and prepositioning and for a formal agreement guaranteeing access and host nation support in wartime.

The desire for a formal written agreement stemmed from two concerns. First, military planners argued they could not plan effectively for a Persian Gulf contingency without an explicit statement of the extent of access and the type and amount of host nation support available to U.S. forces in the region. Whatever support was not guaranteed would have to be provided by American forces; this, in turn, would place additional burdens on already strapped airlift and sealift capabilities. And, second, a formal written agreement was required to secure congressional support for implementation of these arrangements. American negotiators believed that Congress would not fund the U.S. share of these programs without formal, written, government-to-government agreements.

The Saudi position was clear from the outset. Both superpowers should minimize their military involvement in the region and no foreign military bases should be permitted in the area. Although the Saudis had not allowed the United States to use airfields in their country since 1962, they did not object to the minimal U.S. presence in Oman or Bahrain.[31] The rationale for the Saudi position was complex and included fears that an American presence would have undesirable cultural and political effects. In addition, Saudi Arabia was concerned about the credibility of the American security commitment and the strength of American political leadership.

The United States was only slightly more successful in its negotiations with Egypt. President Anwar Sadat offered to permit U.S. access to facilities at Ras Banas on the Red Sea, but this offer was never formalized in a government-to-government agreement, for many of the same reasons expressed by the Saudis. The best that the United States was able to obtain from Egypt was an uncertain commitment in the form of a letter from President Sadat which said that "the Arab Republic of Egypt reaffirms its willingness to grant the Government of the United States of America temporary military facilities in Ras Banas for the purpose of assisting any Arab or Moslem country requesting such assistance."[32] That commitment was reiterated by the deputy prime minister of Egypt on November 26, 1982, following the assassination of President Sadat.[33]

The negotiations with the sultanate of Oman were more successful than negotiations with any other Arab state, resulting in a formal access agreement in 1980 that was renewed in 1985. Under the terms of this arrangement, the United States agreed to upgrade facilities at Masirah Island, Seeb, and Thumrait for the use of its military personnel, at American expense. Oman agreed to make these facilities available to U.S. forces on a temporary basis and to allow the prepositioning of equipment and other supplies in Oman. However, the sultanate of Oman retains the right to deny the U.S. access to these facilities at any time.[34]

On November 30, 1981, the press reported that the United States and Israel had signed a Memorandum of Understanding on Strategic Cooperation. The agreement reportedly committed the parties to cooperation in response to any threat to peace or security in the region by the Soviet Union or by Soviet-sponsored forces. In addition, the parties agreed to provide military assistance to each other in support of operations designed to cope with these threats. Third, the parties agreed to conduct joint military exercises in the eastern Mediterranean, involving the navy and air forces of both sides. Finally, the United States and Israel established a joint planning group to discuss access and the negotiation of specific military assistance arrangements.[35]

The 1981 agreement between the United States and Israel was permitted to lapse following the Israeli annexation of the Golan Heights in December 1981. In a move toward revitalizing the U.S.-Israeli relationship, provisions of the agreement were reaffirmed by President Reagan and Prime Minister Yitzhak Shamir in Washington, D.C., on November 29, 1983. In particular, the two sides agreed to create a Joint Politico-Military Group to engage in combined planning, joint exercises, and discussions about the prepositioning of equipment in Israel. In an effort to minimize the negative effects of U.S.-Israeli cooperation on U.S.-Arab relations, the two sides agreed that prepositioning of equipment in Israel would include only medical equipment and that joint exercises would be limited to air and sea exercises in the eastern Mediterranean.[36]

Joint Military Exercises. Negotiations between the United States and the Arab states and Israel focused on joint military exercises as well as on access to bases and facilities. The United States pursued arrangements with Saudi Arabia, Egypt, Oman, Israel, and other states in the region designed to facilitate joint military exercises.

American objectives in these negotiations were threefold. First, the United States wanted to expose units associated with the Rapid Deployment Joint Task Force to the desert conditions in which they would be fighting in the event of a crisis or war in the Persian Gulf. Second, military exercises that required the deployment of U.S. forces from their bases in the continental United States to the Persian Gulf would demonstrate both the American commitment to the security of countries in the region and the American capability to move these forces to the region in time of crisis or war. And, third, the negotiation of arrangements for joint military exercises would help both U.S. military forces and the forces of other participating states to assess the compatibility of their units, equipment, strategy, and tactics. The experience gained in these exercises would benefit all participants in the event of a crisis or war in the region.

Egypt, Oman, and the Sudan have participated in joint exercises with the United States in Southwest Asia. The most widely publicized of these exercises was the Bright Star series, which began in 1980. The first Operation Bright Star took place during ten days in November 1980 and involved the exercise of approximately 1,400 U.S. Army and Air Force troops in Egypt.[37] The second Operation Bright Star occurred in November and December 1981 and involved approximately 4,000 American troops as well as about 2,000 troops from Egypt, Oman, and the Sudan.[38] Bright Star now is conducted every two years; the 1987 exercise cost more than $75 million.[39]

The sensitivity of these exercises to the countries involved is reflected in two incidents. First, during Bright Star 1981 the sultanate of Oman asked for (and received) a dramatically reduced United States presence in their country. Although no official reasons were given, some observers suggested that Oman wanted to keep the exercise limited to avoid criticism from other Arab states that they were becoming too closely identified with the United States.[40] The second incident occurred in Egypt during the final phase of Bright Star 1981, when six U.S. B-52 bombers flew nonstop from their base in North Dakota and dropped live 500-pound bombs on an Egyptian training area as part of the exercise. The bombers were not permitted to land on Egyptian soil, and Egyptian president Hosni Mubarak did not attend—perhaps because he had been advised to avoid appearing too dependent on U.S. military forces.[41] In short, although the United States achieved its objective of negotiating agreements on joint military exercises with the

Arab states and Israel, none of the countries involved seemed anxious to participate in more than a minimal, low-key way.

Contingency Contracting. A third issue confronting the United States and the Arab states and Israel in negotiating logistical support for the Persian Gulf concerned acquisition from foreign governments, or contingency contracting. The experience of Operation Bright Star in 1981 and 1982 highlighted problems in acquiring goods and services from foreign governments during joint military exercises. The United States relies on host nation governments to secure needed supplies and services to support exercises and other programs, including the maintenance of prepositioned equipment. In part, CENTCOM is dependent upon host governments because the Persian Gulf is located 7,000 miles from the continental United States. Moreover, in time of crisis or war the United States would rely on host nation support early in the conflict because of shortfalls in airlift and fast sealift. And, in wartime, host governments probably would be the only reliable sources of needed supplies and services—few commercial alternatives exist in this part of the world.

For all of these reasons, CENTCOM pursued contract arrangements with the Arab states and Israel in support of joint military exercises and other programs. For example, CENTCOM negotiators pursued negotiations on an acquisition memorandum of understanding with Egypt to procure goods and services needed for exercises and wartime support of U.S. forces. CENTCOM also pursued negotiations with the sultanate of Oman on a "caretaker contract" governing maintenance of U.S. prepositioned equipment.

U.S. negotiators were bound, however, to operate under procedures established by the Federal Acquisition Regulation (FAR), which was approved on April 1, 1984, to replace the individual regulations of federal agencies. The FAR is a several-hundred-page document that specifies conditions that must be included in contracts between the United States government and other parties. The FAR was designed for use in the United States to govern U.S. government contracts with commercial contractors, but in practice it was applied worldwide to contracts with foreign governments as well as commercial firms.

Both Egypt and Oman raised major concerns about several provisions mandated by the FAR that were contained in draft contracts. These provisions were deemed unacceptable in a government-to-government agreement, and the Arab states refused to sign any contracts in which they were included. The three areas of dispute concerned (1) benefit to officials, (2) gratuities, and (3) contingent fees. The "officials not to benefit" clause essentially says that U.S. officials will accept no bribes in exchange for business. The "gratuities" clause says that if the contracting party offers gratuities, the U.S. government can terminate the contract, impose termination fees, and try the case in U.S. courts. The "contingent fees" clause requires the contracting party to promise that it did not bribe, lobby, or pay someone on a contingent basis to get the contract.[42]

While these provisions may represent good business practice when the United States government is dealing with a commercial firm, they were interpreted as an insult by Arab governments. The FAR presented a serious obstacle to the negotiation of contingency contracts in the Persian Gulf. The European members of NATO had received exemption or relief from these provisions. CENTCOM sought similar relief for nations within its area of responsibility during 1984 and 1985. In June 1985 the deputy under secretary of defense (acquisition management) authorized an exemption for CENTCOM, valid for a three-year period. This enabled the United States to negotiate contracts with the Arab states that excluded the offensive provisions.

Bargaining and Concession-making

Question 4: What strategies and tactics did the parties use during the negotiations? How did differences in bargaining style influence the process and outcome of the negotiations? What was the role of politics in the selection of strategies and tactics? If the negotiations resulted in the signing of a formal agreement, how did the process of concession-making occur?

The negotiations on logistical support for the Persian Gulf illustrate the critical role of politics in explaining the bargaining and concession-making process. In each case, a concession-convergence model of negotiation is less helpful than a political model in explaining the outcome.

The United States and the Arab states differed on the format of agreements concerning access and logistical support. The United States pressed for formal, written, government-to-government agreements, for both military and political reasons. In contrast, most of the Arab states were reluctant to sign a formal written agreement with the United States. The extent of their opposition and the reasons for it varied. In the case of Saudi Arabia, concerns about the reliability of an American commitment and the implications of a highly visible American presence in their country were primary factors. In Egypt, an access agreement that permitted a permanent U.S. presence on their soil was viewed as "an encroachment on their sovereignty," even by President Sadat, who had developed a close relationship with President Carter during the Camp David negotiations.[43] While the sultanate of Oman was willing to sign an access agreement with the United States, Oman reserved the right to deny access at any time. For Oman, the concerns were twofold. First, Oman—like Egypt—was concerned about an infringement on their sovereignty. And, second, Omani officials were concerned that a highly visible relationship with the United States could threaten internal stability and lead to the overthrow of the regime.[44]

In all three cases—Saudi Arabia, Egypt, and Oman—the U.S. relationship with Israel and failure to resolve the Palestinian issue played major roles in the bargaining and concession-making process. The Palestinian issue was critical for all of the Arab states. Concerns about the U.S. tilt toward Israel fueled doubts in the Arab states about the reliability of the United States. These doubts, in turn, discouraged Arab leaders from risking their political futures in a formal government-to-government agreement with the United States. As a result, the United States made major concessions during the course of these negotiations. The price for U.S. access in Southwest Asia was the willingness to live with informal arrangements and without the strategic consensus that the Reagan administration had deemed critical for the pursuit of U.S. objectives.[45]

The bargaining and concession-making process with Israel followed a different path, although political considerations dominated these discussions as well. Unlike the negotiations with the Arab states, discussions between the United States and Israel were premised on a shared perception of the threat. Both the United States and Israel were concerned about Soviet influence in the Middle East and Persian Gulf and viewed strategic cooperation as a means toward the end of containing the Soviet threat. Israeli officials recognized that the United States did not have the political access that they needed to fulfill military requirements for a deployment to the Gulf. This fact put Israel in a strong bargaining position with the United States on issues of strategic cooperation.

Implementation

Question 5: What additional action, if any, was required for implementation of the agreements? How did the implementation process reflect the role of background factors, context, substance, and politics?

Implementation of access agreements and logistical support arrangements for a U.S. deployment to the Persian Gulf required action by both the Department of Defense and the United States Congress. The Office of the Secretary of Defense, the Joint Chiefs of Staff, the military services, and CENTCOM played critical roles in ensuring that funds were included in service budget requests to support three aspects of the program: (1) U.S. share of operations and maintenance costs associated with these agreements; (2) military construction funds for upgrading bases and facilities in the region; and (3) procurement funds to support the purchase of equipment to be prepositioned in the region. Congress became involved during the defense appropriations process.

Ensuring support for the implementation of these programs was almost as difficult as the negotiations themselves. Within the Department of Defense, the Office of the Secretary of Defense (OSD) and CENTCOM served as champions of the programs during the defense budget process. OSD endeavored to mobilize the Washington community in support of CENTCOM's efforts to win funding for contingency support for a potential U.S. deployment to Southwest Asia. CENT-COM needed help because they were unable to directly influence the service budget requests and felt that those budgets were not responsive to their near-term needs.[46]

The separate military services—army, navy, and air force—are responsible for preparation of their budgets, under the guidance of the secretary of defense. The Organization of the Joint Chiefs of Staff (OJCS) and the commands (including CENTCOM) provide input to the budget process but have no direct influence over the service budget requests. Traditionally, the services have emphasized procurement of combat equipment, rather than support equipment.

Although the Joint Chiefs of Staff and the commander-in-chief of the United States Central Command (known as CINCCENT) argued strongly in the early 1980s for critically needed airlift and fast sealift to support a U.S. deployment to the Persian Gulf, they recognized that it would be years before increased funding for airlift and sealift was translated into actual military capabilities. In the meantime, they had to be prepared to fight the next day with existing military capabilities. For these reasons, CINCCENT placed a premium on funding for implementation of access agreements and other logistical support arrangements that would provide essential support to U.S. forces in Southwest Asia.

To increase the visibility of CENTCOM efforts, the Office of the Secretary of Defense established an interagency group called the Contingency Support Advisory Group (CSAG) in 1984. The purpose of the CSAG was to provide CENTCOM with a forum for raising their concerns about shortfalls in service funding and to mobilize support for CENTCOM's military objectives. The CSAG was chaired by the assistant secretary of defense (manpower, installations, and logistics) and included representatives of the Office of the Secretary of Defense, CENTCOM, the Joint Chiefs of Staff, the military services, the intelligence community, and the Department of State. Formally, the CSAG was intended to be a mechanism for focusing high-level interagency attention in Washington on implementation of U.S. strategy in Southwest Asia. Informally, the objective was to put increased pressure on the military services to respond to CENTCOM's needs.

Congressional involvement in the implementation of access agreements and logistical support arrangements for the Persian Gulf focused on the appropriation of funds for procurement, operations and maintenance, and military construction. The debate within the Congress on funding for military construction in Southwest Asia, in particular, highlights the role of political considerations in the implementation process.

Congress was reluctant to appropriate funds in support of these programs in the absence of a formal, written, government-to-government agreement that guaranteed U.S. access in time of crisis or war. It took many months of testimony by officials of the U.S. Departments of Defense and State before the Congress was willing to approve funding for new military construction and the improvement of existing facilities in Oman, Egypt, Kenya, and Somalia.[47] The primary congressional concern was that in the absence of a written agreement U.S. access could be denied at any time. As Congressman Ralph Regula (R-Ohio) noted during discussion of U.S. access to a classified base that had been formalized in a letter from the country involved: "I have seen that letter and that is a masterpiece of ambiguity. If that is all we have, I don't put much faith in that. Number one, the person who wrote it is no longer in charge."[48] Under these circumstances, Congress was reluctant to appropriate funds for the improvement of bases and existing facilities. The host country involved received the benefits of improved infrastructure that would remain long after U.S. forces departed, while the United States received only an informal pledge of access and support in the event of crisis or war.

The Department of Defense attempted to deal with congressional opposition to American funding of permanent military construction in the region by including funds for facilities upgrade in the services' operations and maintenance accounts, rather than the military construction accounts. For example, the U.S. Air Force defined some of these activities as repair projects, which are funded from operations and maintenance accounts and therefore do not require specific authority from the Congress.[49] Congress questioned whether a project could be considered repair when it substantially upgraded and reinforced a runway not originally designed for use by heavy aircraft.[50]

Another example involves the concept of "expeditionary construction." In order to deal with both the congressional objection to American funding of permanent facilities and the host country objection to a permanent U.S. presence on their soil, the U.S. Air Force proposed the use of modular, relocatable structures for aircraft maintenance hangars, maintenance shops, dining halls, and living quarters.[51] These structures could be dismantled and removed when U.S. forces departed the area. Expeditionary construction could be funded out of operation and maintenance accounts, rather than military construction, and technically satisfied the host country objection to a permanent American presence.

These debates within the U.S. government about implementation of access agreements and logistical support arrangements for Southwest Asia, although understandable, fueled Arab concerns about the reliability of the United States. They focused unwanted public attention on cooperation between the United States and the Arab states, at a time when the Arabs preferred to deal with the United States in private. As an unidentified Arab observed, "You Americans should learn how to treat your security partners more like private mistresses rather than public whores. In either case, you get your way, but in the former, at least the partner retains its dignity."[52]

Explaining Failure

Question 6: If the negotiations did not result in the signing of a formal agreement, to what extent can the framework account for failure?

From a military perspective, Saudi Arabia was the linchpin of American strategy in the Persian Gulf. Saudi Arabia was strategically located to support U.S. tactical aircraft operations throughout Iran. Moreover, U.S. military strategy depended upon access to the Saudi labor pool to provide support for U.S. forces in wartime.[53] Yet the United States made little progress in negotiations with the Saudis on access and other logistical support arrangements for a U.S. deployment to Southwest Asia. The best the United States could do was to elicit an agreement from Saudi Arabia to "overbuild"—that is, to make it feasible for the United States to use its facilities in a crisis—without any formal peacetime commitment to U.S. access in wartime.[54] What factors help explain the inability of the United States to negotiate a formal access agreement with Saudi Arabia?

First, the United States and Saudi Arabia had different perceptions of the threat to stability in Southwest Asia. For the Saudis, the primary threat was not direct Soviet intervention or even indirect Soviet influence: "The most immediate threats to Saudi security come not from Soviet-supported forces operating on the Horn of Africa, in the People's Democratic Republic of Yemen, or in Afghanistan, but rather from within the Persian Gulf region, if not from within Saudi Arabia itself."[55] A formal, visible security tie to the United States, particularly if it involved the presence of U.S. military forces in their country, could only exacerbate problems of internal and intraregional stability.

Moreover, Saudi Arabia viewed the Arab-Israeli conflict as a direct threat to their security. The Saudis did not expect an Israeli invasion, nor were they concerned about being drawn into the next Arab-Israeli war. But they were concerned about the potential for Soviet mischief realized by that conflict and the unresolved Palestinian issue, which had created opportunities for the Soviet Union to split the United States from the moderate Arab states.[56]

A third factor that undermined negotiations between the United States and Saudi Arabia on logistical support for the Persian Gulf was Saudi resentment of Israeli influence over U.S. arms sales policy in the region.[57] The United States government believed that better relations with Saudi Arabia would improve U.S. influence throughout the region and saw arms sales—particularly in the case of the airborne warning and control system (AWACS) and the F-15 fighter plane— as a means to that end. The sale of advanced military equipment to the Saudis would support certain U.S. military objectives because the equipment could support U.S. military operations in the event of war. Ultimately, establishing a military supplier-recipient relationship with Saudi Arabia might lead to formal access.

Every effort to sell advanced military equipment to Saudi Arabia during the 1970s and the 1980s met with vocal opposition in the United States Congress and among the public at large because of the possible negative effects on the security of Israel. In May–June 1980 Saudi Arabia requested that the United States upgrade the capabilities of F-15 fighter aircraft they had purchased from the United States in 1978. President Carter sensed opposition to the Saudi request in the Congress and postponed a decision on the issue until after the 1980 election. Following the election, the Saudis requested five AWACS planes in addition to the enhancement of the F-15. The Reagan administration approved this request but tied it to the concept of agreement on a strategic consensus for the region.[58]

Following approval of the AWACS sale, Congress undoubtedly expected Saudi Arabia to sign on to the strategic consensus pushed by the Reagan administration, which included support of the peace process initiated at Camp David and an explicit focus on the Soviet threat to the Persian Gulf. Congressional frustration with Saudi behavior was reflected in the following comments by Congressman Lee Hamilton (D-Ind.) of the House Foreign Affairs Committee: "We sold the AWACS to the Saudis last year. Since that time, Prince Fahd has canceled a visit to the United States. Saudi Arabia has reestablished relations with Libya. Their oil production has not increased, it has decreased. They have continued their support, very strong financial support, of the PLO. They continue to promote a peace plan that is in opposition to the Camp David peace process. They are financing more Syrian purchases of Soviet weapons. . . . Why was that sale so important to U.S. interests if we make the sale and they do all these things against our interests?"[59] These views have been mirrored in editorials in American newspapers, which ask "When will we get something in return for arms to Saudis?"[60]

The Saudi view, however, is that they owe the United States nothing in exchange for our agreement to sell them advanced military equipment. After all, they pay for the weapons they purchase; unlike Egypt and Israel, who receive substantial amounts of American foreign and military assistance from the United States as a result of the Camp David Accords, the Saudis pay their way. Efforts to dictate Saudi deployment and operation of weapons they have purchased and the view that they owe the United States something more than the price of the weapons strike the Saudis as an infringement on their sovereignty and unequal treatment.

In their dealings with Saudi Arabia during the 1980s, the United States failed to recognize that the Saudis were not strong leaders in the

Arab world. Traditionally, Saudi Arabia tried to stake out the middle ground in a political environment that posed serious threats to their security.[61] The United States failed in their efforts to negotiate access agreements and logistical support arrangements for the Persian Gulf because we expected Saudi Arabia to accept a strategic consensus that ran counter to their security interests. In other words, we ignored the politics of the negotiating environment. A direct military threat from the Soviet Union was not the major problem confronting the Saudi leadership. U.S. military requirements—which were premised on the worst case, Soviet threat—demanded a substantial commitment of host nation support. The idea of that commitment, and the rapid deployment forces themselves, posed more of a threat to the internal stability of Saudi Arabia than did the Soviet Union.

The situation changed dramatically following the Iraqi invasion of Kuwait in August 1990. The first crisis of the post–Cold War world posed a threat to the interests of both the United States and Saudi Arabia. For the United States, the Iraqi aggression threatened the principle of national self-determination, the lives of American hostages, and the world oil market. For Saudi Arabia, the Iraqi aggression posed a threat to their territorial security. A common definition of the threat facilitated the Saudi invitation to the United States to deploy thousands of troops on their soil, despite the absence of a formal access agreement.

Conclusion: The Politics of Logistical Support for the Persian Gulf

Negotiations between the United States and the Arab states and Israel about access agreements and logistical support arrangements for a U.S. deployment to the Persian Gulf demonstrate the problems of negotiating with friends. Unlike allies, friends often do not share a common perception of the threat. Because the negotiations take place in a vacuum, the parties may find it difficult to identify common interests and objectives. And the absence of a long-standing relationship between the parties increases the risk of misperception and raises doubts about intentions and the strength of commitments. These characteristics increase the complexity of negotiations between friends and may make those negotiations even more difficult than negotiations between adversaries.

Political considerations strongly influenced the process and outcome of negotiations between the United States and the Arab states on logistical support for the Persian Gulf. Domestic politics, both in the United States and in the Arab states, made it difficult for the parties to identify common interests and objectives and led to misinterpretations on both sides. Differences within the United States government fueled Arab concerns about the reliability of U.S. commitments. While there was general consensus within the U.S. defense establishment that access to the Arab states, and especially Saudi Arabia, was critical to the implementation of U.S. strategy, there were serious conflicts between the military services and CENTCOM about funding for these efforts. Congress expressed one bias in favor of formal written agreements and another in its perceived tilt toward Israel. Both President Carter and President Reagan let election-year politics influence their decisions about arms sales to Saudi Arabia.

All of these factors created the impression of disarray within the U.S. government that raised serious concerns in the Arab states about U.S. reliability. If the United States enters into a formal security commitment with an Arab state, will domestic political conditions allow a U.S. response in the event of crisis? And if a response is forthcoming, will the U.S. military have the capability to implement that decision?

The United States also failed to understand the complexities of cultural differences and regional politics in the Middle East and the Persian Gulf. Saudi Arabia was threatened as much by the Islamic revolution in Iran as they were by the Soviet Union. The Iranian revolution demonstrated the power of what has been called "Populist Islam," which challenges the "Establishment Islam" practiced by the Saudi ruling elite and many of the smaller Gulf states.[62] While Establishment Islam aims to preserve the status quo and is somewhat more willing to cooperate with the superpowers in maintaining it, Populist Islam aims to redress inequality and injustice, weed out corruption, and avoid any external influence in the affairs of the state. The growth of Populist Islamic movements within Saudi Arabia placed serious limits on the extent of U.S.-Saudi security cooperation; permanent American bases were unthinkable, and even formal access or prepositioning agreements would have threatened the stability of the regime. And the Saudi desire for private discussions with the United States conflicted with the Congress's need to know. The more the Congress pressed for formal commitments, the less willing were the Saudis to continue discussions.

The situation was somewhat different with respect to Israel. Negotiations between the United States and Israel on access and logistical support arrangements for a U.S. deployment to Southwest Asia benefited from the long-standing U.S.-Israeli relationship and a common perception of the threat—at least as regards the Soviet Union and Soviet influence in the region. The question in these negotiations was not whether Israel would permit U.S. access or provide logistical support for U.S. forces in wartime, but the implications of such an outcome for a balanced U.S. policy in the Middle East and the Persian Gulf.

The United States had to avoid the impression that they were putting all of their eggs in the Israeli basket. The price for access and logistical support arrangements with the Arab states was at a minimum a balanced U.S. policy in the region, which meant greater pressure on Israel to deal with the Palestinian problem. For domestic political reasons, the United States was unable to successfully press Israel on this issue; the result was little movement in negotiations with the Arab states on guaranteeing access and logistical support for a U.S. deployment to the Persian Gulf. The United States made every effort to separate the Arab-Israeli conflict from its policy and strategy for the Persian Gulf. The net effect, however, was to delink the Palestinian issue from U.S. strategy and military requirements in the Persian Gulf when one could not be resolved without the other.

In summary, the United States simply lacked the negotiating leverage necessary to bring these talks to a successful conclusion. In dealing with the Arab states, the United States had little flexibility on the Palestinian issue and failed to understand regional dynamics. In dealing with Israel, the United States found it difficult to say "No" because of lack of access in the Arab world. The result was misperception and misinterpretation by all the parties, and little success in negotiating formal access agreements and logistical support arrangements for the Persian Gulf.

By the late 1980s, however, the situation had begun to change. The success of Operation Earnest Will, which began with the reflagging and escort of Kuwaiti oil tankers by U.S. warships in the Persian Gulf in July 1987 and ended in late 1988 with the declared cease-fire between Iran and Iraq, greatly enhanced America's reputation with the Arab states. General H. Norman Schwarzkopf, commander-in-chief of the U.S. Central Command, has concluded that "our actions in the Gulf, including our measured responses to Iranian provocations, showed our friends in the region that the United States sticks to its commitments and is ready and able to wield military might to underscore those commitments."[63] Enhanced reputation was not translated into greater willingness on the part of the Arab states to sign formal access agreements and enter into logistical support arrangements with the United States. But it did shape the response of America's friends in the Gulf, and especially Saudi Arabia, to the Iraqi invasion of Kuwait in August 1990. The support provided by the Saudis, and others, for the U.S. deployment to the Gulf was a critical element of the multinational response to the Iraqi threat. The ability of the United States and its Arab friends to define a common threat and identify common interests and objectives was a necessary condition for strategic cooperation in Southwest Asia.

8. The Problem of "Mixed" Relationships

NATO and the "Out-of-Area" Question

Apart from clear-cut cases of direct Soviet intervention, as in Afghanistan, there is no convincing reason why the members of an Alliance which exists for the overriding purpose of providing security in Europe, should necessarily agree on issues in other regions of the world. To expect the contrary would be to subject allied solidarity to unnatural tests which risk jeopardizing agreement on NATO's more central security concerns.
— Marc Bentinck [1]

I am not inviting the Soviets in [to the Persian Gulf], and saying we won't start world war III, but why should we put our neck in the noose and say we will, particularly when our allies, the people who get the oil, Japan and Europe, are not willing to do much about it?
— Congressman Henry Reuss (D-Wis.) [2]

The out-of-area debate that occurred within NATO during the 1980s forced members of the alliance to balance their collective security interests against their individual political, economic, and defense needs. Although questions about the relevance of member out-of-area commitments and policies have been the subject of debate within the alliance since 1949, a series of events during the late 1970s and early 1980s engaged NATO in a highly visible, public discussion about the scope of allied responsibilities. The results of that discussion were reflected in the allied response to the Iraqi invasion of Kuwait in August 1990.

The Carter Doctrine, announced in January 1980, committed the United States to intervene in Southwest Asia, with military force if required, to protect the West's access to Persian Gulf oil. While the

United States was engaged in negotiations with the Arab states and Israel during the early 1980s to obtain access and critically needed logistical support for American forces in the event of a deployment to Southwest Asia, the issue of NATO burdensharing—both in the Gulf and in Europe—was being raised at home. Influential members of the Congress, notably Senator Sam Nunn (D-Ga.), argued that America's NATO allies were not carrying their fair share of the defense burden. Moreover, the Reagan administration, in several reports to the Congress by Secretary of Defense Caspar Weinberger, called for greater allied support for the common defense.[3] It was also during this period that the United States initiated negotiations with the allies concerning prepositioning and host nation support for U.S. forces in Europe.

The United States turned to its allies in Western Europe for support of America's strategy in the Persian Gulf. After much debate within the alliance during the early 1980s, the allies agreed to pursue conventional force improvements in Europe designed to compensate for any diversion of NATO-earmarked U.S. forces in the event of an American deployment to Southwest Asia. For its part, the United States dropped its early insistence on direct allied participation in support of the Persian Gulf strategy, choosing instead to pursue bilateral arrangements with individual members of the alliance.[4] By the mid- to late 1980s, the out-of-area debate within the alliance had subsided. While these discussions were less successful than U.S. policymakers had hoped, neither did they create permanent fissures in the alliance—as many observers on both sides of the Atlantic had feared in the early 1980s.

Allied support for the U.S. deployment of troops to Saudi Arabia in conjunction with a multinational response to the Iraqi invasion of Kuwait in August 1990 was a visible sign of Europe's commitment to the defense of Western interests in the Persian Gulf. This support was made possible by the end of the Cold War, transformation of the Soviet threat to the region, and widespread consensus that Saddam Hussein's aggression could not be allowed to succeed.

The Negotiations on NATO Support for Out-of-Area Contingencies

One might have expected negotiations with the European allies to be easier than negotiations with the Arab states and Israel. The United States and its allies shared a long-standing alliance relationship based on the common perception of threats to their security interests. Other things being equal, the history of cooperation among members of the alliance should have facilitated discussions about how to respond to the threat posed by the Soviet invasion of Afghanistan to the security interests of the member states.

The problem for the NATO alliance, however, concerned constraints imposed on its members by Article 6 of the North Atlantic Treaty, which defines the geographical scope of member responsibilities. Article 6 defines the NATO area as the territory of any member state in Europe and North America, Turkey, the Mediterranean Sea, and the North Atlantic north of the Tropic of Cancer.[5] Thus, Southwest Asia and the Persian Gulf fall outside of the scope of member responsibilities. The alliance has no responsibility to act collectively in the face of threats to the interests of any member outside of these geographical boundaries.

The inability of the United States and its European allies to solve the out-of-area issue to American satisfaction is reflected in the outcome of the discussions. During the early 1980s the United States failed in its efforts to convince members of the alliance that a threat to Western interests in the Persian Gulf or Southwest Asia demanded a collective response.[6] The allies continued to argue that any response must be based on the national decisions of individual members of the alliance. This sentiment is reflected in nearly every final communiqué issued by meetings of the North Atlantic Council and the Defence Planning Committee between 1980 and 1982.[7]

By 1983 and 1984 the focus of alliance discussion had shifted to compensatory measures—that is, measures that would be adopted by individual members of the alliance to take into account the possible diversion of U.S. forces earmarked for NATO during a contingency in Southwest Asia. The emphasis, however, was on "measures necessary to maintain deterrence and defence within the NATO area."[8]

The United States retained primary responsibility for out-of-area contingencies in the Persian Gulf and Southwest Asia. For their part, the European allies merely agreed to take up the slack created by an American deployment to Southwest Asia.

The United States pushed for NATO agreement to include a number of compensatory measures in NATO force goals for 1985–90.[9] However, little progress was made toward these goals during the late 1980s. The sense of crisis surrounding the alliance debate about out-of-area concerns had subsided by that time, and the allies were pursuing new opportunities for improvement in East-West relations created by Gorbachev's appearance on the political scene. The disappearance of the out-of-area issue from the NATO arena is illustrated by the fact that it was not raised in the final communiqués of North Atlantic Council or Defence Planning Committee meetings after 1986.

The negotiations between the United States and its European allies about NATO support for out-of-area contingencies illustrate the problems involved in dealing with "mixed" relationships. The concept of mixed relationship as applied to NATO describes debates about issues that fall outside the scope of traditional alliance responsibilities, as defined in the North Atlantic Treaty. While the United States and its European allies share a common perception of the threat to the NATO area, during the 1980s they did not share the same perception of threats to U.S. and European interests and objectives in Southwest Asia. The larger political environment—defined in terms of East-West relations and the ongoing Arab-Israeli conflict—strongly influenced positions taken by the United States and the Europeans in negotiations on the out-of-area issue. The domestic politics of the NATO burden-sharing issue in the United States further complicated the discussions. Finally, major shifts in the international political environment had occurred by the late 1980s. The Soviet Union was no longer perceived as the primary threat to the stability of Southwest Asia, even by the United States. And the Iraqi invasion of Kuwait in August 1990 served to rally the United States and Europe around the need for a multinational response to the first serious threat to Western interests in the post–Cold War world.

The Decision to Negotiate

Question 1: What prompted the United States and its negotiating partners to enter into negotiations? In other words, what problem or situation brought the parties to the negotiating table?

The United States initiated negotiations with the European allies about NATO support for out-of-area contingencies for a variety of military and political reasons. In the first place, allied support was required for implementation of American strategy in Southwest Asia. The Soviet invasion of Afghanistan had raised concerns about a possible Soviet move toward the Gulf. The Carter Doctrine, designed to deter Soviet aggression in the region, demanded the commitment of substantial resources, both military and economic, to succeed. U.S. policymakers believed that allied cooperation would enhance deterrence by increasing Soviet uncertainty about the likely Western response to Soviet aggression in Southwest Asia.

Second, the United States military needed allied support to move forces quickly to Southwest Asia in the event of crisis or war. At a minimum, American forces required en route access to allied facilities as they moved from the continental United States to the Persian Gulf. Allied support was critical given the reluctance of countries in the region to grant formal access to U.S. forces.[10] In the absence of guaranteed access to countries in Southwest Asia, the United States needed staging facilities in Western Europe.[11] Moreover, if the allies could be convinced to provide direct support—such as by making available military and civilian aircraft to move forces across the Atlantic, the United States could deploy its forces to the region more quickly. This capability would further strengthen deterrence.

Third, American policymakers were well aware that certain countries in the Persian Gulf and Southwest Asia might be more receptive to a European deployment to the region than to an American deployment. Several of the European members of NATO had long-standing relationships with countries in the region. The British relationship with Oman and the French relationship with Djibouti are two examples. Britain developed its ties with Oman in the eighteenth century, as a way of excluding other European states from activities in the Indian Ocean; the objectives changed in the nineteenth and twentieth centuries to protection of the lines of communication to India and support for British commercial interests.[12] The result was a close relationship between the military establishments of the two countries. France maintains nearly 4,000 troops in Djibouti, along with support facilities for France's Indian Ocean squadron. Djibouti also permits annual visits by both the French and American navies.[13] The United States wanted to capitalize on these relationships; if countries in the region were reluctant to provide access to the United States in a crisis, perhaps they would provide access to America's allies.

The fourth reason why the United States initiated discussions with the European allies on the out-of-area issue was strictly political. The United States Congress had expressed serious concerns about the wisdom of a unilateral American response to contingencies in Southwest Asia. In their view, the primary objective of U.S. strategy in the Persian Gulf was to protect the flow of oil to the West. And it was clear that America's European allies and Japan were much more dependent than the United States on the continued flow of oil from the Persian Gulf. "Why should the U.S. assume all of the risks to protect 'their' oil?" was an often-heard refrain in the halls of Congress.[14]

Explaining the decision of America's European allies to enter into discussions about out-of-area contingencies is more difficult. There were many reasons for allied reluctance to be drawn into discussions about the U.S. strategy for the Persian Gulf. First, the allies did not necessarily share the U.S. premise that the Soviet Union posed the most likely threat to the stability of the Persian Gulf and the flow of oil to the West. Like many countries in the region, the Europeans were more concerned about the impact of domestic instability and regional conflicts, such as the Iran-Iraq War, on the flow of oil from the Gulf. Moreover, many of the allies faced serious domestic economic and political pressures to cut defense spending; taking on new military commitments in support of the U.S. strategy for Southwest Asia could weaken European governments. And, finally, there were serious differences among members of the alliance about whether a military response to the situation was required. While the United States pressed for a military response, the allies argued for diplomatic and economic initiatives.[15]

If these factors mitigated against negotiations, what explains the European decision to consider the out-of-area issue? First, the Europeans were sensitive to growing pressures within the United States Congress on the issue of NATO burdensharing. During the early 1970s the Nixon and Ford administrations had successfully derailed congressional initiatives aimed at withdrawing U.S. troops from Europe. However, sentiments for greater allied contributions to the common defense continued to run strong in the Congress. By the early 1980s traditional supporters of the alliance on Capitol Hill were beginning to raise the issue again, especially as it concerned Southwest Asia. European members of the alliance clearly wanted to avoid the unilateral reduction of American troops from Europe, and being forthcoming on the out-of-area issue was one way to demonstrate their commitment to the United States.

Another major reason why the allies were willing to discuss the out-of-area issue was their concern that the United States might divert troops based in Western Europe or earmarked for the defense of Western Europe to the Persian Gulf in the event of crisis or war.[16] By participating in a discussion of U.S. strategy for the Persian Gulf, the Europeans hoped to influence American decision making on this sensitive issue. Engaging the United States in a debate about strategy for out-of-area contingencies might increase the probability that the European allies would be consulted in the event of a crisis.[17] The allies feared any unilateral American action that could weaken deterrence in Western Europe. Establishing the precedent of consultation would guard against this scenario.

In short, the United States was the demandeur in the negotiations with the allies on NATO support for out-of-area contingencies. The Europeans came to the negotiating table reluctantly, determined to minimize their association with the U.S. strategy for Southwest Asia. For the United States, in contrast, the negotiations offered the prospect of critically needed en route access and logistical support for an American deployment to the Persian Gulf.

Interests and Objectives

Question 2: How did U.S. policymakers define their interests and objectives with respect to the negotiations? How did America's negotiating partners define their interests and objectives with respect to the negotiations? Were the parties able to define common interests and objectives?

The debate about out-of-area issues within NATO has been characterized as a situation in which "European-American differences are rooted in real interests that diverge."[18] American policymakers pursued two major objectives in negotiations with the European allies on the out-of-area issue: (1) to win political-level support for the U.S. strategy in Southwest Asia and (2) to win military support for a U.S. deployment to the region.

The United States pressed for political-level support for its strategy in Southwest Asia in order to strengthen the administration's position with the Congress. Members of Congress had expressed reluctance to foot the entire bill for the defense of the Gulf, particularly when America's European allies and Japan were more dependent than the United States on the continued flow of oil from the Persian Gulf. Defense officials were concerned that their budget requests in support of Southwest Asia programs would be cut if they could not demonstrate that the European allies supported U.S. strategy in the region.

Second, the United States sorely needed the military support of its European allies in the event of the deployment of American troops to Southwest Asia. An immediate objective was to convince the Europeans to provide direct support for U.S. forces, including en route access to bases and facilities in Western Europe. The lack of American access in the region made en route access in Western Europe absolutely critical. But access, even in Western Europe, could not be guaranteed. Many U.S. officials remembered that, with the exception of Portugal, the allies had refused to grant refueling rights to U.S. forces engaged in an airlift to Israel during the 1973 Arab-Israeli War—a situation they did not want to see repeated during a Persian Gulf contingency.[19] The United States pressed for formal access agreements within the alliance as a way of avoiding similar events in the future.

Moreover—and this became the primary military issue for the alliance—the United States was also concerned about the implications for NATO defense of a diversion of U.S. forces to the Persian Gulf in the event of a crisis. The major military objective of the United States in these negotiations was to convince the allies to take up the slack, or make up for the possible diversion of U.S. conventional forces to Southwest Asia.[20] Defense officials had estimated that a Persian Gulf contingency could force the diversion of between 20 and 30 percent of U.S. forces earmarked for the defense of Europe. These shortfalls could lead the Soviet Union to believe that deterrence had been weakened.[21] The solution was for the European allies to "compensate" for these drawdowns by strengthening their conventional capabilities.

The compensation issue also allowed the United States to reiterate its support for needed improvements in NATO's conventional defense posture that had been agreed to by heads of state and government in 1978. Since 1978 the United States had pressed the Europeans on meeting the objectives of the Long Term Defense Program (LTDP) and the NATO agreement on 3 percent real annual increases in defense spending. Most of the allies had failed to meet the 3 percent goal during the early 1980s. West Germany met the goal in 1981, but not in 1982 or 1983, when defense spending declined in real terms. Belgium, Denmark, and the United Kingdom failed to meet the goal in all three years. The comparable figures for the United States were 4.7 percent real growth in 1981, 7.6 percent in 1982, and 7.4 percent in 1983.[22] The contrast between U.S. and allied performance on this measure of defense burdensharing fueled congressional concerns that the allies were not doing their fair share. Although the Europeans would support the U.S. strategy for Southwest Asia by strengthening their conventional capabilities, they could argue that they were simply fulfilling commitments concerning the defense of Europe made by the alliance in 1978.

While the allies expressed certain shared interests with the United States concerning out-of-area contingencies, their objectives in the negotiations reflected the unique political and economic environment in Western Europe. The Europeans had four objectives: (1) to maintain the flow of oil from the Gulf; (2) to avoid being drawn into a U.S.-Soviet conflict in Southwest Asia; (3) to maintain and expand

East-West détente; and (4) to avoid additional defense commitments that would require major investments of money and other resources.

Maintaining the flow of oil from the Gulf was the primary European objective. The Europeans were more dependent on Persian Gulf oil than the United States. Moreover, the allies and Japan were vulnerable in the short term to the cutoff of the oil supply. Unlike the United States, the allies and Japan did not produce enough of their own supplies or import enough from other regions to withstand the cutoff of the Persian Gulf supply.[23]

The United States and the Europeans differed, however, on the sources of possible disruption of the oil supply. The United States, especially during the early 1980s, viewed the Soviet Union as the major potential source of disruption of the oil flow; the Europeans, in contrast, believed that internal instability and regional conflicts in Southwest Asia were more likely to disrupt the flow of oil.[24] These differences in the perception of the threat were to have a major impact on the positions offered by the two sides during the negotiations.

Second, the Europeans wanted to avoid being drawn into a potential U.S.-Soviet conflict in Southwest Asia. U.S. military strategy for Southwest Asia was premised on the concept of preemption: a decision to deploy U.S. forces to the region would be based on warning of a Soviet move to the Gulf, not the fact of a Soviet invasion. Preemption was required for successful defense, given the geographical asymmetries that characterized the Soviet and American strategic situations. The Europeans were understandably concerned that a preemptive strategy would leave little time for consultation within the alliance.[25]

This concern pulled the Europeans in two directions. On the one hand, it discouraged the European members of NATO from agreeing to the concept of a collective response to out-of-area contingencies. On the other hand, it argued for an alliance response that might at least guarantee prior consultation by the United States in the event of a crisis in Southwest Asia.

A third European objective was to maintain and expand East-West détente. The European members of NATO, and West Germany in particular, wanted to expand the network of East-West ties. The concept of a collective alliance response to out-of-area contingencies could draw the Europeans into a direct confrontation with the Soviet Union in regions of the world that were not central to the defense of Europe, the primary objective of the alliance. In essence, the Europeans preferred a situation in which the United States unilaterally assumed responsibility for the defense of Western interests in Southwest Asia, while they were allowed to pursue the benefits of détente in Europe.[26]

Finally, European governments were experiencing strong domestic pressures to spend less money on defense, not more. Assuming additional defense responsibilities for the Persian Gulf could only increase the defense burden. During the early 1980s European governments confronted strong peace and antinuclear movements. The alliance's December 1979 decision to deploy new theater nuclear forces in Europe had already forced European governments to spend scarce political capital. There was little left to argue for increased defense spending in support of an American strategy for Southwest Asia that could draw the Europeans into a direct conflict with the Soviet Union.

In summary, the United States and their European allies entered into negotiations on support for out-of-area contingencies with certain shared interests but also with very different perceptions of the threat. The United States focused primarily on the threat posed by the Soviet Union to Western interests in Southwest Asia and argued strongly for a collective alliance response with emphasis on military force. The Europeans, for their part, focused on internal and regional threats to the flow of oil from the Gulf and argued for national initiatives and the use of diplomatic and economic, rather than military, tools of foreign policy. These differences were papered over, but never resolved, as the alliance pursued negotiations on the out-of-area issue.

Negotiating Positions

Question 3: What factors influenced the formulation of negotiating positions? How did these positions change during the course of the negotiations? How did initial positions compare with the negotiated outcome?

The negotiations between the United States and their European allies on out-of-area contingencies focused on four major issues: (1) whether military or political instruments of foreign policy were most appropriate; (2) whether the alliance should pursue collective responses or individual national responses to out-of-area contingencies; (3) requests by the United States for en route access and support for U.S. forces deploying to Southwest Asia in a crisis; and (4) discussion of the concept of allied compensation for dual-committed U.S. forces.

Military or Political Instruments? The first major debate within the alliance concerned whether the most appropriate response to out-of-area problems should emphasize military force or the use of diplomatic or economic instruments of foreign policy. The United States viewed the problem in military terms and saw the solution primarily in military terms as well. The out-of-area issue was tied in the minds of American policymakers to the fall of the shah of Iran, the Soviet invasion of Afghanistan, and promulgation of the Carter Doctrine, which threatened an American military response to "outside" threats to Southwest Asia. The organization and announcement of the Rapid Deployment Joint Task Force (RDJTF) early in 1980 was a tangible statement of the American perspective on Southwest Asia.

For their part, the Europeans were willing to agree in May 1980 that the situation in Southwest Asia had "serious implications for the security of member countries."[27] However, European foreign ministers argued for a low-key response that emphasized the use of diplomatic and economic instruments of foreign policy. The European focus on nonmilitary instruments reflected the reality of European military capabilities: with the exception of the United Kingdom and France, the allies simply did not have the military capabilities necessary to pursue an active involvement in the Persian Gulf and Southwest Asia. The nonmilitary focus also was consistent with the allied view that diplomatic initiatives would be more effective than military force in ensuring the continued flow of oil from the Gulf. It should not be surprising, then, that in December 1980 NATO foreign ministers indicated that "members of the Alliance are prepared to work for the reduction of tension in the area and, individually, to contribute to peace and stability for the region, while protecting their vital economic and strategic interests."[28]

The Europeans eventually came around to the American position that some military response was required. However, the allies insisted that a military response would be premised on decisions by individual members of the alliance to support U.S. strategy in Southwest Asia.[29] The United States was unable to convince the allies that the problem was, fundamentally, a military one that demanded a collective military solution. And the allies were unable to convince the United States that the primary threats to Western interests were internal and regional, rather than from external forces.

The Iraqi invasion of Kuwait in August 1990 influenced the positions of both sides on whether the most appropriate response to out-of-area problems should emphasize military force or diplomatic or economic instruments of foreign policy. For its part, the United States launched an intensive diplomatic effort within the United Nations to convince the Europeans, Japan, the Soviet Union, and other regions to participate in a multinational response to Iraqi aggression. At the same time, the United States responded to the Saudi request for American troops to deter an Iraqi move against their country. In addition to supporting a sustained diplomatic and economic embargo of Iraq through the United Nations, several European allies and Japan contributed troops or other resources to increase the military pressure on Iraq. Thus, by late 1990, both sides had concluded that an effective response to Western interests in the Gulf demanded diplomatic, economic, and military action. All of these initiatives were taken by individual governments, however, and not collectively by NATO.[30]

Collective or Individual Response? Perhaps the major issue for debate within the alliance on out-of-area contingencies concerned whether members of the alliance would commit themselves to collective action in response to a crisis in Southwest Asia. The United States argued strongly for a NATO agreement on a collective alliance response. U.S. policymakers believed that a collective response, instead of individual national activities, would send an important signal to the Soviet Union about NATO's commitment to the defense of its security interests in Southwest Asia. In addition, a collective response would send an equally important political signal to the United States Congress on the issue of NATO burdensharing.

The Europeans were opposed to any alliance commitment to a collective response in the event of a crisis in Southwest Asia. Some allies, such as Norway, Denmark, Iceland, Greece, and Turkey, were reluctant to discuss any out-of-area role for NATO. Others, including the United Kingdom and France, were willing to discuss bilateral arrangements with the United States.[31] As an alliance, however, NATO was unable to move beyond the commitment of individual members, based on national decisions, to provide support for the U.S. strategy in Southwest Asia. The language that appeared in NATO communiqués between 1980 and 1984 reflected this outcome: references to action out-of-area were linked to those members of the alliance "in a position to do so."[32]

The collective response issue was never fully resolved. The allies maintained their position that the North Atlantic Treaty prohibited collective action out-of-area. In June 1982, at the Bonn summit, NATO heads of state and government agreed "to examine collectively in the appropriate NATO bodies the requirements which may arise for the defence of the NATO area as a result of deployments by individual member states outside that area."[33] Thus, the best that the United States could do was to convince the allies to address collectively the impact of an American deployment to Southwest Asia on the defense of Western Europe. By late 1990, however, that question had become a "non-issue" in the face of the end of the Cold War, the unification of Germany, and the signing of a conventional arms control agreement designed to dismantle the military confrontation in Europe.

En Route Access and Support. The third major issue concerned the American request for en route access and support from the allies in the event of a deployment of U.S. forces to Southwest Asia. The United States argued that they could not effectively deploy troops to the Persian Gulf in the event of crisis without the support of the allies. When it became clear that agreement on a collective response would not be forthcoming, the United States pressed individual members of the alliance for en route access and support. The United Kingdom and Portugal were obvious candidates for American overtures.

The United Kingdom agreed to permit the United States use of its facilities at Diego Garcia, an island in the Indian Ocean nearly 2,500 miles from the Persian Gulf. In the absence of access to countries in the region, Diego Garcia serves as a prepositioning site for CENT-COM troops and a staging base for ships and aircraft deploying to the Gulf.[34] The United States also approached Portugal with a request to use the air base at Lajes for en route refueling and support.[35] In both cases, the allies agreed to the American request, although the price of that commitment was U.S. agreement to modernize the existing facilities. The United States was less successful in obtaining en route access and support from other allies.

Compensation. The final issue in the out-of-area debate between the United States and the allies concerned compensation for the diversion of NATO-earmarked American forces to the Persian Gulf in the event of crisis or war. Initially, the United States pressed for direct allied support for U.S. strategy in Southwest Asia. When it became clear that the allies were unwilling to agree to direct support for out-of-area contingencies, the debate shifted to compensation. In fact, the concept of compensation had been raised by Chancellor Helmut Schmidt in February 1980 as an alternative to direct allied participation in out-of-area activities.[36]

Compensation solved a military problem for the United States and a political problem for European members of the alliance. It gave American defense planners greater flexibility in the allocation of scarce forces in the event of a contingency in Southwest Asia. And it allowed the Europeans to argue that they were supporting the U.S. strategy in Southwest Asia without the risks associated with direct participation in military planning for a Persian Gulf contingency.

The need for compensatory measures was recognized by the alliance as early as December 1980, when the Defence Planning Committee indicated that members of the alliance should "prepare against the eventuality of a diversion of NATO-allocated forces the United States and other countries might be compelled to make in order to safeguard the vital interests of member nations outside the North Atlantic Treaty area."[37] At the time, NATO highlighted "host nation support to facilitate the reception and employment of reinforcement forces."[38] This support would be provided to U.S. forces in Europe to enable critically needed U.S. support forces to deploy to Southwest Asia, where little or no host nation support was available.

By 1983 and 1984 the United States and the European allies were formally considering measures to enhance the conventional defense of Europe in the event of a U.S. deployment to Southwest Asia. The Defence Planning Committee formally adopted force goals for 1985–90 relating to compensation.[39] However, like many of the commitments made by members of the alliance in the late 1970s, these force goals were not fully implemented because of growing political and economic pressures to scale back defense spending in the West. And, by 1990, the end of the Cold War and the transformation of the Soviet threat made it clear that the force goals process had been overtaken by events.

Bargaining and Concession-making

Question 4: What strategies and tactics did the parties use during the negotiations? How did differences in bargaining style influence the process and outcome of the negotiations? What was the role of politics in the selection of strategies and tactics?

U.S. policymakers were determined to address the out-of-area issue in formal NATO decision-making bodies, such as the North Atlantic Council (NAC) and the Defence Planning Committee (DPC). The United States believed they could put more pressure on the allies in the NATO context than through bilateral diplomatic channels. The NAC and the DPC meet in ministerial session twice each year and issue communiqués following those meetings. These communiqués—which receive widespread press, particularly in Western Europe—allowed the United States to raise the visibility of the out-of-area issue with the public while keeping it on the NATO policy agenda in private. Pursuing the out-of-area issue through these NATO bodies also supported the American objective of a collective alliance response.

The going-in position of American diplomats was to push for direct support for U.S. strategy in Southwest Asia. During 1980 the Carter administration raised the issue of joint military action outside of the NATO area with the allies. By the fall of 1980, however, the European allies had convinced the United States of their opposition to any joint military force operating outside of the area defined by Article 6 of the North Atlantic Treaty. At that point, American policymakers lowered their expectations of the allies, and talk shifted to the concept of compensation for U.S. out-of-area activities that might impact unfavorably on the defense of Europe.[40] Other efforts to win allied support for direct action were pursued through bilateral diplomatic channels.

From the beginning, the allies were reluctant to pursue the out-of-area issue in NATO's formal decision-making bodies. Initially there was no response from Europe to the announcement of the Carter Doctrine in January 1980 and the Rapid Deployment Joint Task Force in March 1980. In April 1980 Robert Komer, the under secretary of defense for policy, briefed the Europeans on U.S. strategy for Southwest Asia and elicited their support for the military and financial burdens involved in planning for the deployment of U.S. forces to Southwest Asia.[41]

The European response was predictable. They viewed the Carter administration's unilateral announcements in January and March 1980 with concern. The European fear was that if they agreed, even if only in principle, to support the U.S. strategy in Southwest Asia, they could be drawn into a Soviet-American confrontation in the region without their explicit consent.[42] For this reason, the European strategy was to push for consultation within the alliance framework. Although consultation would permit discussion of the out-of-area issue within the alliance, it might also decrease the likelihood that the United States would involve the Europeans in a conflict in Southwest Asia without their consent. The NATO strategy of consultation was reflected in the language of every NAC and DPC communiqué that addressed Southwest Asia between 1980 and 1984.

The Europeans also managed to redirect discussion away from the American proposal for direct military support and toward compensation for U.S. out-of-area activities. The allies agreed to compensate for the possible diversion of U.S. NATO-earmarked forces in the context of the Long Term Defense Program and the alliance commitment to 3 percent real growth in defense spending, to which they had already agreed in 1978. In other words, the European strategy was to avoid any new defense commitments in support of their interests in the Persian Gulf and Southwest Asia. This could be done by characterizing earlier commitments to improve the alliance's conventional force capabilities in Europe as support—albeit indirect—for European and American security interests in the Persian Gulf and Southwest Asia.

Although the European arguments against direct involvement in out-of-area issues focused on Article 6 of the North Atlantic Treaty, their bargaining strategies and tactics were based primarily on political considerations. These considerations included the need to maintain access to Gulf oil and concern about the military thrust of U.S. strategy for the Gulf region. Politics influenced U.S. strategies and tactics as well. The United States began by pushing for direct support but backed off when it became clear that the alliance, qua alliance, would not be persuaded. When direct support was not forthcoming, American policymakers shifted their focus to compensation; they used allied commitments that had already been made to improve conventional capabilities as leverage to coax increased support from the allies for the common defense effort.

Explaining Failure

Question 6: If the negotiations did not result in the signing of a formal agreement, to what extent can the framework account for failure?

The United States seemed to make most of the concessions in these negotiations. They moved from an initial demand for direct support from the allies to an agreement on consultation within the alliance framework and compensation for U.S. out-of-area activities. The United States failed in their objective of eliciting a collective alliance military response to the demands of U.S. strategy in the Persian Gulf and Southwest Asia. In terms of direct military support, American negotiators were forced to pursue bilateral arrangements with individual NATO allies. For their part, the Europeans achieved their objective of consultation while avoiding either a political commitment or a new military commitment in support of U.S. strategy in Southwest Asia. The allies convinced the United States to accept the notion of compensation, in Europe, for U.S. activities out-of-area.

What explains the American failure to achieve their primary objectives on the out-of-area issue? The interests of the allies clearly were at stake in Southwest Asia; continued flow of oil from the Middle East and the Persian Gulf was essential for the economic security of Europe and Japan. The United States needed access and logistical support from the Europeans in order to defend Western interests in the region; the absence of access in the region left the United States no choice. Officials in the executive branch had to demonstrate allied support for U.S. strategy in Southwest Asia to win congressional support for defense budget requests. Despite these converging, if not common, interests, the United States and the European allies were unable to reach formal agreement on the out-of-area issue.

Political considerations help explain the failure of the United States to achieve its objectives in these negotiations. In the first place, although the United States and the European allies identified converging interests in the Persian Gulf and Southwest Asia, they disagreed on the nature and source of threats to those interests and the appropriate strategies for dealing with them. The United States defined the problem in terms of the Soviet threat to stability and the flow of oil from the Gulf, while the Europeans defined the problem in terms of internal stability and regional conflicts. Moreover, the United States argued for the primacy of a military response to the threat, while the Europeans pressed for diplomatic and economic initiatives. These differences increased the reluctance of the Europeans to discuss the out-of-area issue in the context of the alliance and mitigated against a collective alliance response to the problem.

Second, the allies expressed grave concerns about the impact of a high-profile role in the Persian Gulf and Southwest Asia for East-West relations generally and the pursuit of détente in Europe in particular. The Europeans believed that acceptance of the American strategy in Southwest Asia would lead them into direct confrontation with the Soviet Union and that this confrontation—even if it was strictly political, not military—would have adverse effects on East-West relations.

Third, several European governments were faced with strong peace and antinuclear movements during the early 1980s. The December 1979 NATO decision to deploy new theater nuclear weapons in Europe had not been taken without political cost to European governments. The Soviet Union had initiated a serious propaganda campaign during the early 1980s directed at European publics, with the objective of derailing the deployment decision. The political situation in Europe was exhibiting strains created by the debate about intermediate-range nuclear forces, and European governments calculated that they could not withstand the additional pressure that would be created by active diplomatic or military support of U.S. strategy in the Persian Gulf and Southwest Asia.

A final reason for the U.S. failure to achieve their objectives on the out-of-area issue concerns the economic burden of defense in Europe and the political consequences of that burden. During the early 1980s vocal elements of European publics pressured their governments for cuts in defense spending. These pressures were reflected in the inability of some NATO governments to meet the agreed 3 percent real increase in defense spending and other objectives associated with the Long Term Defense Program. There were also concerns that the declining pool of draft-eligible Europeans would put pressure on their defense establishments. Collectively, these trends made it unlikely that European governments would be willing to take on additional defense burdens out of area.

In 1990 the end of the Cold War and the unification of Germany eliminated whatever incentives still existed for increased defense spending in Europe. Despite the absence of formal, negotiated agreements on out-of-area contingencies, however, the new threat posed by the Iraqi invasion of Kuwait did generate a multinational response—although outside of the NATO framework—and included military or financial commitments by the Europeans and Japan in support of the deployment of troops to Saudi Arabia.

Conclusion: The Politics of the "Out-of-Area" Question

The negotiations between the United States and the European allies about access and logistical support for U.S. strategy in the Persian Gulf and Southwest Asia dramatically illustrate the problems of mixed relationships. Although the issues were framed in legal terms—that is, what activities were or were not permitted by Article 6 of the North

Atlantic Treaty—in fact the major issues were highly political. The absence of an alliance consensus on how to deal with out-of-area issues made it especially difficult for the United States to pursue its objective of a collective alliance response. The United States was successful in channeling the debate through formal NATO decision-making bodies, such as the North Atlantic Council and the Defence Planning Committee. But these deliberations failed to produce the desired result; discussion remained focused on consultation (a European priority) and compensation, with direct support for U.S. strategy in Southwest Asia left to national decisions.

Out-of-area issues were not new to the alliance in the early 1980s. During the 1950s the European governments were in the position of demandeur. The United States wanted to disassociate itself from the vestiges of European colonialism and criticized European intervention in the Third World to protect their colonial empires. For their part, the Europeans—and particularly the French—were equally vocal in their efforts to win alliance support for the defense of their colonial territories. By the 1960s the situation had changed, with the United States pressing for allied support of American policy in Vietnam and the European governments arguing for a strict reading of the constraints imposed by Article 6 of the North Atlantic Treaty.[43]

What made the situation different in the 1980s was the political context in which the negotiations on out-of-area issues occurred. Unlike the debates of the 1950s and the 1960s, the 1980s debate about U.S. strategy in Southwest Asia had the potential of leading to an East-West confrontation in which the allies would be dragged into a conflict between the United States and the Soviet Union. Moreover, the 1980s debate raised concerns about the implications of support for the U.S. strategy in Southwest Asia for deterrence and defense in Europe. Concerns about the adequacy of both American and European military forces for the defense of Europe were heightened by talk of diversion and the assumption of new military commitments out-of-area.

Despite the U.S. lack of success during the early 1980s in extracting a collective commitment from NATO for direct support of out-of-area activities in the Persian Gulf and Southwest Asia, by 1987 the political situation had changed sufficiently to allow several European governments to participate directly (although they claimed not in support of the United States) in military operations in the Persian Gulf. In response to attacks by Iran on ships in the Persian Gulf in early 1987, Kuwait requested that its oil tankers be reflagged and escorted by the United States Navy.[44] The United Kingdom, France, Belgium, the Netherlands, and Italy ultimately stepped up their naval presence in the Gulf, providing escorts and minesweepers to protect their own ships.[45] But these actions were taken by those nations as independent actors and not in the context of a NATO response.

The international political situation had changed by 1987. Gorbachev had emerged on the political scene in the Soviet Union. The United States and the Soviet Union were approaching an agreement on intermediate-range nuclear weapons in Europe. By this time, also, some American policymakers had reassessed their earlier view that the Soviet Union posed the primary threat to the flow of oil from the Gulf. The progress of the Iran-Iraq War demonstrated that regional threats were at least as likely as Soviet intervention to interrupt the flow of oil. In short, by 1987 American and European perceptions of the nature of the threat to the region had begun to converge. At the same time, the United States was even then unable to press for a coordinated alliance response to the situation in the Gulf. The American, British, and French actions were taken based on national, not alliance, decisions.

If the political situation had changed by 1987, the world had been transformed by the end of 1990. The emergence of democratic regimes in Eastern Europe, the fall of the Berlin Wall, and the unification of Germany signaled the end of the postwar order and the beginning of a new era in international relations. The Iraqi invasion of Kuwait on August 2, 1990, posed a threat to all nations, East and West, developed and less developed. Iraqi aggression was met by a multinational response, including a United Nations embargo and the deployment of American, European, and Arab state forces to the region. While a coordinated alliance response to the crisis was not forthcoming, individual members of the alliance contributed military forces or other support in the defense of Western interests.

In summary, the United States and the European allies confronted difficult obstacles in dealing with the out-of-area issue. Bilateral agreements and unilateral initiatives have substituted for a coordinated response to out-of-area threats to the security interests of the members of the alliance. This should not be surprising, given the history of NATO and the alliance's traditional focus on the security of Europe. Political considerations, both in the United States and in Western Europe, will continue to influence the alliance debate on the out-of-area problem. Reassessment of the role of NATO itself in the post–Cold War world will further complicate the debate about out-of-area issues. As American and European policymakers focus their attention on the problem of restructuring European security, domestic economic challenges, demographic trends, and increasing pressures to cut defense spending, it may become even more difficult to convince members of the alliance to assume additional defense commitments out of area. The fault lies not with the negotiators but in the political context of negotiations on out-of-area issues in the 1990s.

Part V   **Conclusions**

During the past forty-five years, the world has moved from "hot war" to Cold War to "warm peace." Although the new security order is not yet in place, the old order no longer provides a framework for international negotiation. Negotiating security after the Cold War will require an understanding of the present and of the past, as America deals with allies, adversaries, and friends.

The concluding chapter reviews generalizations about the process and outcome of negotiations with allies, adversaries, and friends during the Cold War and suggests how an understanding of the political dynamics of negotiating during the Cold War may help American policymakers deal with the security challenges of the twenty-first century.

The United States will rely more heavily on international negotiation to achieve its national security objectives in the future. While this increased reliance on diplomacy is due to the transformation of the Cold War framework within which negotiation has occurred during the last forty years, it is also due to the emergence of new actors and issues. The United States will deal with friends and mixed situations more than traditional allies and adversaries in the future. Politics at all levels—bureaucratic, domestic, and international—will dominate international negotiation.

9. The Politics of Negotiation

Implications

for Policy

Negotiation is one of the most important processes of international conflict management. . . . What distinguishes negotiation from other kinds of international action is the recognition by the parties that they are mutually dependent on one another, that they cannot achieve their purposes unilaterally, through independent action. It is this interdependence of interests among states that creates the opportunity for international negotiation.

—Janice Gross Stein [1]

On July 6, 1990, members of NATO issued a declaration following their summit meeting in London in which they proposed "to the member states of the Warsaw Treaty Organization a joint declaration in which we solemnly state that we are no longer adversaries."[2] This declaration symbolized the end of the Cold War and the beginning of a new era in which negotiation will assume a central role in building a new security order.

As of early 1991 the structure of that security order remained uncertain. Some have argued that NATO and the Warsaw Pact should be merged to create a new security arrangement for Europe. Others have suggested that the answer lies in the Conference on Security and Co-operation in Europe, while still others have proposed a new "Concert of Europe" within the CSCE structures.[3]

The process of developing new security arrangements in the post–Cold War era will be difficult because of the fluidity of the situation in Europe and the Soviet Union. For more than forty years, the Cold War environment was characterized by clearly defined relationships between international actors. We knew who our enemies were and who our friends were. Issues were defined in East-West or U.S.-Soviet terms. The structure of alliances—in particular, NATO and the Warsaw Pact—was built around the assumptions of the Cold War. America's dealings with its allies and adversaries, in general, were predictable, if not always peaceful.

In contrast, the emerging international security environment will be characterized by the redefinition of relationships between countries that saw themselves as allies or adversaries during the Cold War. In the interim, some countries (particularly those in Europe, as well as the United States and the Soviet Union) are more likely to see one another as friends—sharing certain interests and objectives in the international arena but lacking the predictable relationships of allies or adversaries. During this period of uncertainty and political transformation, the United States will rely less on traditional formal alliance structures such as NATO, with their roots in the Cold War, and more on informal bilateral and multilateral negotiations.

The purposes of this book have been to examine selected negotiations between the United States and its allies, adversaries, and friends during the 1970s and the 1980s and to draw conclusions about the impact of background factors, context, interests and objectives, and politics on the process and outcome of international negotiation. Although the Cold War context of these negotiations is disintegrating and the new context is not yet clear, I believe that the experience of the past offers important lessons for the future. Effective negotiation demands both a clear understanding of the situation at hand and an awareness of the dynamics of America's previous experience in dealing with allies, adversaries, and friends. This chapter highlights the lessons of these cases and discusses the policy implications of our conclusions for negotiating security after the Cold War.

Bargaining with Allies

The negotiations between the United States and the Federal Republic of Germany on wartime host nation support and between the United States and its European allies about deploying theater nuclear forces in Europe illustrate how the existence of an alliance relationship can facilitate negotiations on security issues. In the case of wartime host nation support, both sides shared the objective of strengthening deterrence and supporting the rapid deployment of U.S. forces to Europe in the event of crisis or war. The WHNS program allowed both sides to achieve their objectives at a relatively cheap cost. The United States acquired sorely needed logistic support for its forces in Europe, and the Europeans won the U.S. commitment to deploy ten divisions to the theater in ten days, in the event of crisis or war. Debates between American and West German policymakers focused on how best to implement the program; these discussions translated into debates about the nature of the WHNS model, equipment sourcing, and reinforcement exercises.

Although more visible to publics on both sides of the Atlantic, the debate within NATO about the deployment of theater nuclear forces in Europe was also facilitated by the existence of an alliance relationship. Similar to the WHNS case, the United States and the European allies shared a commitment to extended deterrence and the role of nuclear weapons in Europe. Although there were differences of emphasis in the U.S. and European perspectives, those differences existed in the context of a shared belief in the strategy of flexible response that was adopted by the alliance in 1967. The debate within the alliance focused on the configuration of weapons and the role of arms control in the decision.

However, the cases presented in Part II also demonstrate that negotiations between allies are not problem free. Despite the existence of common interests and objectives, negotiation between allies requires consensus-building, both domestically and internationally. In the case of the U.S.-German wartime host nation support program, the failure of the U.S. executive branch to win the support of the Congress for the program before the WHNS Agreement was signed led to serious problems in implementation. Congress was reluctant to appropriate funds for the program because they believed that the allies were not carrying their fair share of the defense burden. This is not to say that prior consultation would have eliminated opposition to the program on Capitol Hill. But it seems clear that prior consultation would have minimized the opposition and avoided misunderstandings with West German officials about the strength of the American commitment to the program and to their security interests.

The United States and the European allies were able to forge the interallied consensus necessary to implement the December 1979 decision despite elaborate efforts by the Soviet Union to convince the allies to renege on their agreement to accept new theater nuclear forces on European soil. In part, the consensus evolved because NATO made the INF deployment decision a public test of alliance strength and commitment. The political consequences of failure to deal with the theater nuclear forces problem were unacceptable, both to the United States and to the European allies. Thus, although the consensus may have been forced, it evolved and was sustained because to do otherwise could have threatened the existence of the alliance. (This situation contrasts markedly with the debate within NATO about out-of-area issues, where the subject under discussion was not deemed critical to the central mission of the alliance.)

In short, negotiations between allies were facilitated by the existence of a long-standing relationship between the parties and shared perceptions of the threat, but they were not problem free. Multiple interests and objectives came into play on both sides. Consensus-building, both at home and among the parties, remains critical for the successful negotiation of international agreements between allies and for their implementation.

In the future, negotiations between the United States and its European allies will be complicated by the disintegration of the Soviet and Warsaw Pact threat that facilitated consensus-building during the Cold War. It will be more difficult for the United States and the Europeans to reach agreement on interests and objectives in a security environment in which the primary Cold War security structure—NATO—is undergoing fundamental change. The emergence of new security structures, perhaps within the framework of CSCE, the Western European Union (WEU), or the European Community (EC), will promote European independence. Within these structures, in which relationships are not defined by the Cold War stereotypes that have characterized NATO and the Warsaw Pact, the United States will exercise less influence over the Europeans. This means that the United States will be less likely to get its way in future negotiations with the Europeans.

Negotiating with Adversaries

The negotiations between members of NATO and the Warsaw Pact on conventional arms control in Europe during the 1970s and the 1980s illustrate the dynamics of negotiations between adversaries. For both sides, the objectives when the Mutual and Balanced Force Reductions negotiations began in 1973 were not directly related to achieving a formal agreement. For the West, the objective was to avoid the unilateral reduction of American troops; for the East, the objective was to win U.S. acceptance of and participation in the Conference on Security and Cooperation in Europe. By the time that both sides began to focus seriously on conventional arms control in the late 1980s, it was clear that structural problems within MBFR—notably the exclusion of France and the western military districts of the Soviet Union—made it an inappropriate arena.

The Treaty on Intermediate-Range Nuclear Forces demonstrates what can be achieved when adversaries pursue arms control in a serious way. Neither the United States nor the Soviet Union really wanted an agreement on INF when those negotiations began in 1980. For both parties, the target audience for the negotiations was Europe. The Soviet Union pursued arms control talks with the United States because they believed they could convince the European allies to renege on the December 1979 deployment decision. The United States entered into arms control discussions grudgingly, as the price to be paid for implementation of the December 1979 decision. Decisions by both parties to pursue arms control seriously between 1985 and 1987 were prompted primarily by political considerations. But the case illustrates that negotiations between adversaries can succeed when the parties see a mutuality of interests and the political conditions are favorable.

In summary, negotiations between the United States and its adversaries during the 1970s and the 1980s were difficult, but not impossible. Unlike the situation for allies, the heaviest burden in negotiations between adversaries is the identification of common interests and objectives. For this reason, and because of the absence of trust between the parties, adversaries are more likely to negotiate about positions, rather than interests. Negotiating about positions tends to lock the parties into a conflictual relationship and concession-making becomes more difficult. Thus, for adversaries, decisions to compromise are likely to be held hostage to favorable political conditions. And concession-convergence models are less useful than politics in explaining the process and outcome of negotiations.

Progress on conventional arms control in 1990 was tied to the dramatic political and economic changes in the Soviet Union and Eastern Europe. The unification of Germany, in particular, allowed both sides—East and West—to deal with the conventional military confrontation in Europe. Movement toward resolution of "the German problem," which had complicated arms control negotiations during the 1970s and the 1980s, provided the necessary political momentum. The situation regarding Germany clearly was different by 1990, when Chancellor Kohl said he would be prepared to negotiate limits on the size of the military establishment in a unified Germany, in the context of the conventional arms control talks taking place in Vienna.[4] This changed environment, more than any other consideration, propelled East and West to the signing of a conventional arms control agreement in November 1990.

Dealing with Friends and the Problem of "Mixed" Relationships

The negotiations between the United States and the Arab states and Israel about access and logistical support for a U.S. deployment to Southwest Asia illustrate the problems involved in negotiating with friends. The United States and Israel shared the view that the Soviet Union represented the major threat to stability in the region—either through direct intervention or through the support of radical Arab states. This facilitated negotiations with Israel but complicated negotiations with the Arab states. The Arabs believed that Israel was the primary threat to stability in the region, with regional conflicts and domestic unrest serving as contributing factors. Inability to agree on the nature of the threat made it difficult for the United States to sell Arab leaders on the existence of common interests and objectives in the region. And Arab concern about the future reliability of the United

States—particularly after the experience of the shah of Iran—made them reluctant to enter into any formal written agreements with the United States that might expose them to Soviet or Arab reprisals.

Negotiations between allies on nontraditional issues, or the problem of "mixed" relationships, exhibit their own political dynamics. The out-of-area issue demonstrates the problems that emerge when nontraditional issues are debated within an alliance framework. The United States and its European allies were unable to reach agreement on the nature of the threat to the flow of oil from the Gulf. During the 1980s the United States believed that the Soviet Union was the primary threat, while the allies believed that regional conflict and domestic instability posed more likely threats. Moreover, the allies were concerned about the impact of their support of U.S. strategy in the Gulf region for East-West relations and the pursuit of détente in Europe. Allied concerns were viewed by some in the United States, particularly on Capitol Hill, as evidence that the allied commitment to Western security was weakening. These strains made negotiations difficult and ultimately prompted the United States to pursue compensation and the negotiation of bilateral arrangements, rather than a coordinated alliance response.

In the future, negotiations with friends and with allies about issues that fall outside of formal alliance commitments will comprise more of America's foreign policy agenda. The end of the Cold War has removed many of these issues from the East-West, U.S.-Soviet, and Communist-democratic frameworks within which they have been addressed for the past forty years. While this will complicate policymakers' understanding of interests and objectives, it will also enable them to deal with issues independent of the rhetoric and confrontation associated with the Cold War.

Politics: International, Domestic, and Bureaucratic

It should be clear from the case studies presented in this book that political considerations dominate the process and outcome of international negotiations. Beginning with the decision to negotiate, to the formulation of interests, objectives, and negotiating positions, to the bargaining and concession-making process, and, finally, to the implementation of agreements, politics is the critical factor. The explanation of success and failure in international negotiation—both in the past and for the future—depends upon an understanding of the impact of international politics, domestic politics, and bureaucratic politics.

International Politics. Perceptions of the balance of power, the status of regional conflicts, and other factors have traditionally been cited as important influences on international negotiation. The "realist" perspective on international affairs would argue that considerations of international politics are the most important influences on international negotiation.[5] The cases presented in this book demonstrate the influence of international politics on negotiation. The perceptions that negotiators and political leaders have about the nature of the balance of power and the sources of global and regional instability clearly influence their decisions to negotiate, definitions of interests and objectives, and bargaining and concession-making strategies.

The international context in which events occur is critical. The debate within NATO during the late 1970s about the impact of the Soviet deployment of the SS-20 ballistic missile and the Backfire bomber illustrates the point. These deployments did not represent a new threat because the Soviet Union had long deployed theater nuclear forces in Eastern Europe capable of targeting the same cities and military facilities as the SS-20 and the Backfire. But what had changed by the late 1970s was the perception of the strategic balance. The emergence of strategic nuclear parity between the United States and the Soviet Union placed these new deployments in an entirely different context— one that demanded an alliance response.

Similarly, on the regional level, discussions between the United States and the Arab states about access and logistical support for a U.S. deployment to Southwest Asia could not be separated from the situation in the Middle East and the perception on the part of the Arab states that the United States was not engaged in a serious effort to resolve the Palestinian problem. One of the reasons the United States experienced limited success in these negotiations is that they attempted to divorce the Southwest Asia issue from the U.S. commitment to the security of Israel, while for the Arab states the role of Israel in the Middle East *was* the problem.

Domestic Politics. These cases also illustrate several ways in which domestic politics influences the process and outcome of international negotiation. First, negotiations are more complex when they occur between nations with different political systems.[6] The negotiations between East and West on conventional arms control and between the United States and the Soviet Union on intermediate-range nuclear forces demonstrate the point. The role of public opinion in the West and the function of the United States Senate in the ratification and interpretation of treaties created obstacles to the negotiation of agreements in both MBFR and INF. However, the parties were able to overcome this obstacle in INF because of other domestic political considerations that pushed the United States and the Soviet Union toward agreement.

The negotiations between the United States and the Arab states on access and logistical support for a U.S. deployment to Southwest Asia also illustrate the difficulties in dealing with different political systems. Clearly, cultural factors operated as well, but disagreements arose because of a lack of understanding by the United States of the constraints under which the Arab governments operated and lack of understanding by the Arabs of the role of the Congress and public opinion in the United States. Even when dealing with allies, the nature of the political system can have an impact on the process and outcome of negotiations. During the implementation of the WHNS program, West German officials were startled to learn that agreement by the U.S. executive branch did not carry with it a commitment by the United States Congress to fund the program.

Second, and independent of the first influence, public opinion affects the process and outcome of international negotiation.[7] In all of these cases, public opinion in the United States played a critical role. In some of the cases, opinion in Western Europe was at least as critical in explaining the success or failure of the negotiations. The reserve and National Guard lobby in the United States influenced the position of the U.S. Congress on funding the WHNS program. The nuclear-freeze movement in the United States and the antinuclear movements in Western Europe clearly influenced the arms control track of NATO's December 1979 decision.

Although less visible than on the nuclear issue, public opinion on defense spending and the presence of large numbers of U.S. troops in Western Europe influenced both U.S. and European positions in the MBFR negotiations. Both the United States and the Soviet Union reassessed their negotiating positions in the INF talks in response to, or in an effort to influence, European public opinion. And the U.S. stance in its dealings with the Arab states, Israel, and the European allies on access and logistical support for a U.S. deployment to Southwest Asia was strongly influenced by the views of the Israeli lobby in the United States.

Finally, domestic politics influences the process and outcome of international negotiation through the electoral process.[8] Every four years American presidents run for reelection. As administrations enter their third year, they begin to focus on the contributions that foreign policy successes can make to the political campaign. Not surprisingly, American presidents (and their advisers) look to international negotiation for some of those successes. Negotiations with adversaries, in particular, offer valuable opportunities to add to an American president's political capital. The history of arms control negotiations between the United States and the Soviet Union is littered with examples of the use of arms control as a political tool. During the MBFR negotiations, more than one American president used MBFR for political purposes. And the Reagan administration clearly used the INF talks to achieve both personal and political objectives.

Bureaucratic Politics. Bureaucratic politics explanations of foreign policy became popular in the 1960s, when Graham Allison introduced alternative models of decision making during the Cuban missile crisis.[9] The bureaucratic model of foreign policy-making has earned a respected place in the literature on American politics and foreign policy. However, bureaucratic politics explanations have yet to earn a comparable position in the literature on international negotiation. The cases presented in this book demonstrate that international negotiation involves multiple, rather than unitary, actors who pursue multiple interests and objectives. In all of the cases, the existence of multiple actors complicated the identification of common interests and objectives and the process of bargaining and concession-making.

In negotiations with adversaries, military actors are likely to join forces in arguing with their respective governments for a "military" definition of the problem; arms control interests are likely to engage in similar behavior, defining the problem in terms that lead toward a negotiated solution. In negotiations between adversaries, military players on both sides are likely to argue for caution in whatever arrangements are ultimately negotiated.

However, military players may also differ among themselves in terms of how they define national security problems and their solutions. During the negotiation and implementation of the U.S.-German Wartime Host Nation Support Agreement, military officers representing the Department of the Army argued against funding the near-term operations and maintenance and procurement costs of the WHNS program at the expense of long-term service investment programs. Representatives of the U.S. European Command, in contrast, lobbied hard for support of the WHNS program, which would provide near-term support for U.S. troops in Europe in the event of crisis or war. A similar debate emerged between the Department of the Army and the U.S. Central Command concerning funding for near-term logistical support for a U.S. deployment to Southwest Asia.[10]

In negotiations between friends, where there is less political-level consensus on how to deal with the issue, bureaucratic politics is likely to dominate the debate. The absence of an overarching framework within which to assess interests, objectives, and negotiating positions increases the leverage of bureaucrats in policy-making and negotiation.

In short, politics seems to dominate international negotiation. Whether dealing with allies, adversaries, or friends, political considerations influence whether the United States succeeds or fails. What are the implications of these conclusions for American security policy and the use of negotiation as an instrument of that policy in the future?

Implications for Negotiating Security after the Cold War

Transformations in the postwar political environment have made the process of international negotiation even more difficult. Traditional definitions of allies and adversaries are breaking down, along with the security structures associated with the Cold War, and the United States is increasingly confronted with negotiations between friends and mixed relationships. Allies are becoming friends, as the American-European and American-Japanese relationships feel the strains of economic conflict. Adversaries are also becoming friends—as illustrated by the changing relationships between the United States and the Soviet Union as well as among the Europeans. This means that the traditional assumptions about negotiation that applied when dealing with allies and adversaries will be less relevant in the future. At the same time, the difficult and time-consuming negotiations that characterize relationships between friends will comprise more of the foreign policy agenda of the United States.

The end of the Cold War has brought with it a new international security agenda—one that highlights the necessity of negotiation as a means of resolving differences between nations. This new agenda, which defines such problems as pollution of the environment, overpopulation, trade imbalances and fiscal deficits, drug use, and acquired immune deficiency syndrome (AIDS) as international security concerns, joins the older agenda of regional conflicts, political instability, proliferation of nuclear, chemical, and advanced conventional technologies, and terrorism.[11] The older agenda has changed as well, as regional conflicts and other issues are divorced from the Cold War context in which they were considered for the past forty years.

These trends will have important effects on the process and outcome of international negotiation. In the first place, the absence of common perspectives that characterize traditional relationships between allies and adversaries mean that perceptions of external threats will be difficult to sustain. Consider the problem confronting American policymakers as they attempt to generate the same level of public concern about the security threat posed by environmental pollution as was mobilized against the Soviet Union during the Cold War.

Second, it will become more difficult for allies to identify common interests and objectives; at the same time, it will become less difficult for adversaries to do so. However, the evolution of relationships between negotiating partners will also lead to misperceptions and misunderstandings, further complicating already difficult negotiations. In this uncertain period of transition, as the Cold War evolves into a warm peace, American policymakers will be challenged to walk a fine line in dealing with former adversaries who are not yet allies.

Third, politics—which already play a critical role in the process and outcome of negotiations—will become even more important in the future. Domestic politics, in particular, will become more influential in explaining decisions to negotiate, the expression of interests, objectives, and negotiating positions, and the selection of bargaining and concession-making strategies. Consensus-building at home will capture the attention of policymakers and negotiators alike; this will increase the difficulty of developing and sustaining an international consensus.

What are the implications of these trends for policy-making? What can the United States expect to achieve through international negotiation? Negotiation is not a substitute for adequate defense preparations. However, it can and should influence the nature of relationships between adversaries. There is something to be said for the contribution that negotiation, for the sake of negotiation, can make to U.S. security. If the process of negotiation helps to shape the relationship between the United States and its adversaries—both old and new—in favorable ways, so much the better.

At the same time, we should avoid creating unrealistic expectations for negotiation. Negotiation may resolve conflicts between nations, but it will not eliminate conflict between them. In short, there is no magic formula for the resolution of conflict through negotiation. Negotiation can enhance, but not substitute for, other instruments of foreign and defense policy. However, with the challenges confronting the United States in the future, we cannot afford to neglect negotiation in the pursuit of security.

Notes

Chapter 1

1. Winham, "Multilateral Economic Negotiation," p. 188.

2. See Maynes, "America without the Cold War"; Nunn, "Challenges to NATO in the 1990s"; Howard, "The Remaking of Europe"; Mandelbaum, "Reconstructing the European Security Order"; and Foreign Policy Institute Policy Study Group, *Changing Roles and Shifting Burdens in the Atlantic Alliance*.

3. "Text of the Declaration after the NATO Talks," *New York Times*, July 7, 1990, p. 5.

4. For examples of the historical approach, see Lall, *How Communist China Negotiates*, and E. Sheehan, *The Arabs, Israelis, and Kissinger*. One of the best treatments of bargaining and negotiation by an economist is Schelling, *The Strategy of Conflict*. See, also, Cross, *The Economics of Bargaining*. For the sociological perspective, see Bartos, "Simple Model of Negotiation." Psychology is represented by Spector, "Negotiation as a Psychological Process." For the political science approach, see Miller, "Politics over Promise," and Quandt, "The Electoral Cycle and the Conduct of Foreign Policy."

5. Lall has drawn heavily from his background in international law and knowledge of international institutions such as the United Nations to produce *Modern International Negotiation*. Lall assumes that negotiations will not occur unless the parties believe a problem exists that needs to be addressed, suggesting that negotiation is part of the broad context of relations between states.

6. An example of this approach is Ikle's *How Nations Negotiate*. According to Ikle, negotiations may result in formal agreements or treaties, but often they affect the mutual relations of the parties in other ways. For example, the parties may reassess their national interests or assume additional political burdens imposed by domestic or international public opinion, as a result of international negotiation.

7. Young examines the post–Korean War American experience in negotiating with the Chinese Communists in *Negotiating with the Chinese Communists*. M. Blaker blends political and historical analysis in *Japanese International Negotiating Style*, in which he surveys Japanese attitudes toward diplomacy and international negotiation, the role of domestic politics in shaping Japanese bargaining style, and the impact of Japanese cultural norms on negotiating strategies and tactics.

8. Nicolson suggests that there are two currents in diplomatic theory: the warrior or heroic theory, in which diplomacy is viewed as war by other means, and the mercantile or shopkeeper's theory, in which diplomacy is viewed as an aid to commerce. There are important differences in the theory and practice of negotiation by the "Great Powers." Some, such as Great Britain, have been more successful in their foreign relations because they have adopted the shopkeeper model; others, such as Germany, have been less successful because they have adopted the warrior model. See Nicolson, *Diplomacy*, p. 128.

9. The American track record in negotiating arms control arrangements with the Soviet Union illustrates the point. In his personal recollections of the Strategic Arms Limitation Talks (SALT) between the United States and the Soviet Union, Ambassador Gerard Smith reflects that these discussions were not negotiations between two unitary actors but discussions at multiple levels involving the diplomatic and military establishments of the two sides. See G. Smith, *Doubletalk*.

10. For example, President Carter has described the holding of American hostages in Iran as "the most gripping and politically important issue" facing him during the election year. See Carter, *Keeping Faith*, p. 557.

11. See Raiffa, *The Art and Science of Negotiation*. Raiffa examines three types of negotiating situations, or games: (1) negotiations involving two parties and one issue, (2) negotiations involving two parties and many issues, and (3) negotiations involving many parties and many issues.

12. A recent effort to combine insights from the historical record with the results of scientific analyses of negotiation is *The Practical Negotiator* by Zartman and Berman. Their analysis is based on the assumption that every negotiation can be divided into three stages or phases—diagnosis, formula, and details— each of which has appropriate strategies, tactics, and behaviors that can be learned by practitioners.

13. Perhaps the best-known popular analysis of negotiation is *Getting to Yes* by Fisher and Ury. An underlying premise of their approach is that, in very fundamental ways, negotiating an international agreement is similar to labor-management negotiations, landlord-tenant negotiations, real estate dealings, or the process of buying a used car.

14. Zartman, "The Analysis of Negotiation," p. 18.

15. A classic example of this approach is Thomas Schelling's work on bargaining and negotiation. Schelling assumes that parties to a negotiation behave rationally and that each party's best choice of action in a bargaining situation depends upon how the other party is expected to behave. Schelling terms this principle the "theory of interdependent decisions." See Schelling, *The Strategy of Conflict*, p. 15.

16. Propositions set forth by Bartos in *Process and Outcome of Negotiations* illustrate the tendency to think in terms of unitary actors. Although Bartos

offers several propositions relevant to multiparty negotiations, these conclusions refer to the behavior of multiple unitary actors (that is, to multilateral negotiations), rather than to the behavior of members of a single negotiating team.

17. In Anatol Rapoport's game between two nuclear powers, the parties engage in an arms race because the costs of unilateral disarmament in a situation of mistrust are too high. Such factors as the relative military capabilities of the two powers, the nature of their political systems, and the personal beliefs of their heads of state do not enter into the analysis. See Rapoport, *Strategy and Conscience*, pp. 48–52.

18. The idea of concession-convergence has been proposed by Martin, "The 'Practical' and the 'Theoretical' Split," p. 51.

19. Zartman and Berman believe that the experiences of negotiators fit into a pattern from which we can derive a set of propositions, knowledge, and teachable skills. See Zartman and Berman, *The Practical Negotiator*, pp. 8–9.

20. DeCallieres, *On the Manner of Negotiating with Princes*, p. 57.

21. For example, Druckman has examined the behavior of children from India, Argentina, and the United States and finds that bargaining behavior and the effects of age and sex vary dramatically among cultures. See Druckman, Benton, Ali, and Bagur, "Cultural Differences in Bargaining Behavior," p. 413.

22. Zartman and Berman, *The Practical Negotiator*, is one of the best examples.

Chapter 2

1. G. Smith, *Doubletalk*, p. 454.

2. Alexander George has characterized this approach as "structured, focused comparison." See George, "Case Studies and Theory Development," p. 50.

3. George and Smoke, *Deterrence in American Foreign Policy*, p. 95.

4. Ibid., p. 97.

5. Ibid., p. 96.

6. Craig, *The Germans*, p. 15.

7. Kissinger, *White House Years*, p. 54.

8. Neustadt and May, *Thinking in Time*.

9. Nicolson, for example, argues that European states exhibit different styles of diplomatic behavior, which can be traced to their historical experiences and cultural roots. See Nicolson, *Diplomacy*, p. 151.

10. Young, *Negotiating with the Chinese Communists*, p. 350.

11. Ibid., p. 345.

12. Quandt, *Saudi Arabia in the 1980s*, p. 150.

13. S. Salmore, M. Hermann, C. Hermann, and B. Salmore, "Conclusion: Toward Integrating the Perspectives," pp. 199–200.

14. Janosik, "Rethinking the Culture-Negotiation Link," p. 391. Elgstrom, "Norms, Culture, and Cognitive Patterns," p. 154, also makes the case that the impact of culture on negotiation is situation specific.

15. M. Hermann, "Effects of Personal Characteristics," p. 52.

16. Reed, *Germany and NATO*, p. 184.

17. Stoertz, "Observations on Soviet Negotiating Practice," p. 46.

18. Greenhalgh, "Relationships in Negotiations," p. 236.

19. Lewicki and Litterer, *Negotiation*, p. 15.

20. Pruitt, *Negotiation Behavior*, p. 6.

21. Greenhalgh, "Relationships in Negotiations," p. 237.

22. These factors, interpreted as ways of describing foreign policy behavior, are evaluated in Callahan, Brady, and M. Hermann, *Describing Foreign Policy Behavior*.

23. For a discussion of affect as it relates to the foreign policy behavior of nations, see M. Hermann, C. Hermann, and Hutchins, "Affect."

24. Commitment is described in Callahan, "Commitment," p. 182.

25. East and M. Hermann, in "Scope of Action," present an alternative conceptualization of scope, defined in terms of the target or recipient of foreign policy behavior.

26. Osgood, *Alliances and American Foreign Policy*, p. 17.

27. Ibid., p. 18.

28. Slocombe, "Negotiating with the Soviets," p. 65.

29. Ibid. On the problem of leverage in U.S.-Soviet arms control negotiations, see Einhorn, *Negotiating from Strength*, p. 56.

30. Ikle, *How Nations Negotiate*, p. 6.

31. Fisher, *International Conflict for Beginners*, p. 88.

32. Ikle, *How Nations Negotiate*, p. 2.

33. Nicolson, *Diplomacy*, p. 151.

34. See Hoffmann, *Gulliver's Troubles*, pp. 345–48, on American interests.

35. The process of prenegotiation is analyzed in Stein, *Getting to the Table*. On the relationship between situation, problem, and occasion for decision, see Brady, "The Situation and Foreign Policy."

36. On the bureaucratic politics approach to the analysis of foreign policy, see Allison, *Essence of Decision*, and Halperin, *Bureaucratic Politics and Foreign Policy*.

37. Allison, *Essence of Decision*, p. 176.

38. Garthoff, "Negotiating with the Russians," p. 19.

39. Ikle, *How Nations Negotiate*, p. 122.

40. Fisher and Ury, *Getting to Yes*, pp. 42–51.

41. M. Sheehan, *Arms Control*, p. 116.

42. Martin, "The 'Practical' and the 'Theoretical' Split," p. 51.

43. Ibid., pp. 51–52.

44. See Raiffa, *The Art and Science of Negotiation*; Zartman and Berman, *The Practical Negotiator*; and Schelling, *The Strategy of Conflict*, for examples of this approach.

45. Sloss and Davis, in *A Game for High Stakes*, discuss Soviet negotiating style and practice as well as lessons learned in negotiating with the Soviets in bilateral and multilateral settings. See, also, R. Smith, *Negotiating with the Soviets*, based on his State Department experience in dealing with Soviet counterparts.

46. Schelling would offer this advice, based on principles discussed in *The Strategy of Conflict*.

47. Druckman and Mahoney, "Processes and Consequences of International Negotiations," p. 72.

48. Ibid., p. 83.

49. M. Sheehan, *Arms Control*, p. 111.

50. Talbott, *Master of the Game*, pp. 126–27.

51. Quandt, *Camp David*, p. 336.

52. Zartman, "The Analysis of Negotiation," p. 33.

53. Miller, "Politics over Promise," pp. 88–89.

54. Winham, "Multilateral Economic Negotiation," p. 177.

55. Druckman, "Boundary Role Conflict," p. 87.

56. Ibid., p. 100.

57. Saunders, "International Relationships," p. 246.

58. M. Hermann, "Commentary," p. 281.

59. H. Smith, *The Power Game*, p. 545.

60. Lamb, *How to Think about Arms Control, Disarmament, and Defense*, p. 166.

Chapter 3

1. Rogers, "Statement for Insertion in the Record of the Hearings before the Subcommittee on Defense, House Appropriations Committee," *Department of Defense Appropriations for Fiscal Year 1983*, 97th Cong., 2d sess., May 3, 1982.

2. Stevens, *Fiscal Year 1983 Supplemental Request for Department of Defense*, Hearing before the Senate Appropriations Committee, 98th Cong., 1st sess., p. 34.

3. Corterier, "Quo Vadis NATO?," p. 141.

4. For a discussion of these trends, see Brady and Kaufman, *NATO in the 1980s*.

5. The formal title of this agreement is "Agreement between the Government of the United States of America and the Government of the Federal Republic of Germany Concerning Host Nation Support during Crisis or War."

6. Thus, the POMCUS program (Prepositioned Overseas Materiel Config-

ured to Unit Sets) was born. By 1983 the United States had begun to preposition equipment for four U.S. divisions in the Federal Republic of Germany (Division Sets 1–4) and had won agreement from Belgium and the Netherlands to provide the facilities to house equipment for an additional two divisions (Division Sets 5 and 6).

7. Brady and Fleck, "Transatlantische militarische Zusammenarbeit in Krisenzeiten," pp. 585–86. See, also, Charles W. Groover, Deputy Assistant Secretary of Defense (Program Integration), *Fiscal Year 1983 Supplemental Request for Department of Defense*, Hearings before the Defense Subcommittee of the Senate Appropriations Committee, 98th Cong., 1st sess., May 4, 1983, pp. 36–37.

8. These issues are discussed in *Department of Defense Appropriations for Fiscal Year 1983*, Hearings before the Defense Subcommittee of the House Appropriations Committee, 97th Cong., 2d sess., May 3, 1982, pp. 860–63.

9. In testimony before the House Appropriations Committee, Groover stated that the Department of Defense estimated "that these 93,000 German Reservists will cost about one-tenth of what it would cost to provide the same capability with U.S. Reserve Component units and less than one-fortieth of what it would cost to provide that capability with U.S. active forces." See "Statement before the Subcommittee on Military Installations and Facilities, House Appropriations Committee," *Department of Defense Appropriations for Fiscal Year 1983*, Hearings, 97th Cong., 2d sess., March 23, 1982, p. 3. If the costs of procuring additional airlift to move U.S. support units (either active or reserve) from the United States to Europe in a crisis or war were included, the Department of Defense estimated the cost advantage of the wartime host nation support program over the use of U.S. forces to be greater than 200 to 1. See Lawrence J. Korb, Assistant Secretary of Defense (Manpower, Reserve Affairs, and Logistics), in *Department of Defense Appropriations for Fiscal Year 1983*, Hearings before the Defense Subcommittee of the House Appropriations Committee, 97th Cong., 2d sess., p. 848.

10. Addabbo, *Department of Defense Appropriations for Fiscal Year 1983*, Hearings before the Defense Subcommittee of the House Appropriations Committee, 97th Cong., 2d sess., pt. 3, p. 854.

11. Ibid., p. 855.

12. Ibid., pp. 852–53. See, also, Senator Ted Stevens, *Fiscal Year 1983 Supplemental Request for Department of Defense*, Hearings before the Senate Appropriations Committee, 98th Cong., 1st sess., p. 41.

13. Wartime Host Nation Support Agreement, Annex 1.

14. Information Paper on U.S.-Germany Wartime Host Nation Support, February 7, 1989.

15. Wartime Host Nation Support Agreement, Article 3, Paragraph 5.

16. Information Paper on U.S.-Germany Wartime Host Nation Support, February 7, 1989.

17. Wartime Host Nation Support Agreement, Article 3, Paragraph 6.

18. Groover, "Statement before the Subcommittee on Military Installations and Facilities, House Appropriations Committee," *Department of Defense Appropriations for Fiscal Year 1983*, Hearings, 97th Cong., 2d sess., March 23, 1982, p. 4; Korb, "Statement before the Subcommittee on Department of Defense Appropriations, House Appropriations Committee," *Department of Defense Appropriations for Fiscal Year 1983*, Hearings, 97th Cong., 2d sess., May 3, 1982, p. 848.

19. Information Paper on U.S.-Germany Wartime Host Nation Support, February 7, 1989.

20. In Fiscal Year 1983, the first year of the program, the Department of Defense request for $44 million to pay the U.S. share of the costs was denied by the House and Senate Appropriations committees. Both committees argued that the Federal Republic of Germany should pay a greater share of the costs associated with the WHNS program. Start-up funds for the WHNS program were denied by the Department of Defense Appropriations Act of Fiscal Year 1983, which considered it inappropriate to buy equipment for foreign reserve units when U.S. reserve units continued to report equipment shortages. The Congress finally agreed to appropriate start-up funds for the program in the Supplemental Appropriations Bill for 1983, although at levels far below those requested by the Department of Defense.

21. Information Paper on U.S.-Germany Wartime Host Nation Support, February 7, 1989.

22. Wartime Host Nation Support Agreement, Article 3, Paragraph 6.

23. *Strategic Survey 1982–83*, p. 57.

24. Ibid., p. 45.

25. *Supplemental Appropriations for 1983*, Hearings before the Defense Subcommittee of the House Appropriations Committee, 98th Cong., 1st sess., pp. 335–36.

26. Ibid.

27. Information Paper on U.S.-Germany Wartime Host Nation Support, February 7, 1989.

28. The agreement was signed in Bonn, West Germany, by Lawrence J. Korb, representing the U.S. secretary of defense, and Hans-Joachim Hildebrandt, representing the West German minister of defense.

29. Reinforcement Exercises Agreement, Article 1, Paragraph 2.

30. Ibid., Article 7, Paragraph 1. Although the focus of this provision was on the resolution of civilian complaints, matters of "military interest" could be considered as well.

31. Wartime Host Nation Support Agreement, Article 2, Paragraph 1.

32. *Supplemental Appropriations for 1983*, Hearings before the Defense Subcommittee of the House Appropriations Committee, 98th Cong., 1st sess., p. 338.

33. Information Paper, U.S.-Germany Wartime Host Nation Support, February 7, 1989.

34. Joffe, "Once More: The German Question," p. 136.

35. Ibid., p. 138.

Chapter 4

1. M. Clarke, "West European Politics and Extended Deterrence," pp. 201 and 203.

2. "We are not America's Guinea Pigs" appeared on signs during a protest at Hyde Park in London on October 24, 1981. See "Thousands in London Protest Nuclear Arms," *Washington Post*, October 25, 1981, p. A1. The second slogan, the official slogan of a Dutch antinuclear group, Interchurch Council on Matters of Peace and War (IKV), is cited in Weers, "The Nuclear Debate in the Netherlands," p. 69.

3. Strategic nuclear weapons are those systems with ranges greater than 5,500 kilometers. Theater nuclear weapons (intermediate-range nuclear forces, or INF, in the Reagan administration) are those systems with ranges between 1,000 and 5,500 kilometers. Shorter-range theater nuclear forces (or tactical nuclear forces) are those systems with ranges less than 1,000 kilometers. Battlefield nuclear weapons are those with ranges less than 200 kilometers.

4. Daalder and Kelleher, "Ban Land-Based Nukes in Europe," p. 18.

5. Final Communiqué, Special Meeting of Foreign and Defense Ministers, December 12, 1979. Reprinted in *NATO Review* 28, no. 1 (February 1980): 25–26.

6. See Cotter, "NATO Theater Nuclear Forces," p. 44.

7. Final Communiqué, Special Meeting of Foreign and Defense Ministers, Paragraph 7.

8. Garthoff, *Détente and Confrontation*, pp. 865–66.

9. Schmidt, "The 1977 Alastair Buchan Memorial Lecture."

10. On the origins and evolution of flexible response, see Schwartz, *NATO's Nuclear Dilemmas*.

11. On this tension, see ibid., and Sigal, *Nuclear Forces in Europe*.

12. Dean, *Watershed in Europe*, p. 149.

13. Treverton, "Nuclear Weapons in Europe," pp. 58–59.

14. Garthoff, *Détente and Confrontation*, p. 853.

15. Ibid., p. 854.

16. Haig, "NATO—An Agenda for the Future," p. 4.

17. Ibid., p. 5.

18. Apel, in "Apel Interviewed on Euromissiles, Other Issues," in U.S. Infor-

mation Agency, Foreign Broadcast Information Service (FBIS), *Daily Report: Western Europe*, October 30, 1979, p. C1.

19. Garthoff, *Détente and Confrontation*, p. 855.

20. Ibid., p. 854.

21. Schwartz, *NATO's Nuclear Dilemmas*, p. 221.

22. Bertram, "The Implications of Theater Nuclear Weapons in Europe," p. 310.

23. LeGloannec, "West German Security," p. 172.

24. See Schwartz, *NATO's Nuclear Dilemmas*, p. 6.

25. Talbott, *Deadly Gambits*, p. 33.

26. Ibid., p. 35.

27. Schwartz, *NATO's Nuclear Dilemmas*, p. 226.

28. Garthoff, *Détente and Confrontation*, p. 862.

29. Ibid., p. 862.

30. Weers, "The Nuclear Debate in the Netherlands," p. 68; Sigal, *Nuclear Forces in Europe*, pp. 98–103.

31. Garthoff, *Détente and Confrontation*, pp. 859–60.

32. Schwartz, *NATO's Nuclear Dilemmas*, pp. 231–32.

33. See Garthoff, *Détente and Confrontation*, pp. 858–65, for a detailed discussion of the HLG work program. See, also, Buteux, *The Politics of Nuclear Consultation in NATO*, chaps. 5 and 6.

34. For a discussion of the general problems associated with asking the Europeans to take the lead on nuclear issues, see Treverton, "Nuclear Weapons in Europe," and Bertram, "The Implications of Theater Nuclear Weapons in Europe." On the neutron issue, a specific example of the problem, see Wasserman, *The Neutron Bomb Controversy*, and Strong and Zeringue, "The Carter Administration and the Neutron Bomb."

35. On the Integrated Decision Document, see Schwartz, *NATO's Nuclear Dilemmas*, pp. 232–33.

36. Initial reaction to Brezhnev's speech includes "Government Has Qualified Welcome for Brezhnev Offer," FBIS, *Daily Report: Western Europe*, October 15, 1979, p. F3; "Government, Political Leaders Comment on Brezhnev Proposal," FBIS, *Daily Report: Western Europe*, October 15, 1979, pp. J1–J2; "Genscher Interviewed on Brezhnev Speech, Arms Control," FBIS, *Daily Report: Western Europe*, October 17, 1979, pp. J5–J7; and "Military Chief Calls Brezhnev Proposal 'Poor Deal,'" FBIS, *Daily Report: Western Europe*, October 30, 1979, p. C1.

37. Reported in "Schmidt Receives Brezhnev Letter on Disarmament Proposals," in FBIS, *Daily Report: Western Europe*, October 17, 1979, p. J1.

38. See, for example, "Der Spiegel Interviews Zagladin, Falin on Brezhnev Initiative," in FBIS, *Daily Report: USSR*, November 7, 1979, pp. AA1–AA18.

39. See chapter 6 for a discussion of Soviet strategy in the INF talks.

40. Ruhle, "The Theater Nuclear Issue in German Politics," p. 55. For an especially good analysis of the period from decision to deployment, see McCausland, "Dual Track or Double Paralysis?"

41. Sigal, *Nuclear Forces in Europe*, p. 84. See, also, Pond, "Federal Republic of Germany," p. 227.

42. Sigal, *Nuclear Forces in Europe*, p. 93.

43. McCausland, "Dual Track or Double Paralysis?," p. 446.

44. Ibid., p. 444.

45. Sigal, *Nuclear Forces in Europe*, pp. 87–90. See, also, McCausland, "Dual Track or Double Paralysis?," pp. 443–44; Stuart, "NATO in the 1980s," p. 427; and Viotti, "European Peace Movements and Missile Deployments," p. 516.

46. For a discussion of the difficulty in maintaining a consensus within the Netherlands on security policy, particularly on nuclear issues in NATO, see Domke, "The Netherlands: Strategy Options and Change," and Kroes, "Cruise Missiles and the Western Party System."

Chapter 5

1. Warnke, "Lessons Learned in Bilateral Negotiations," p. 55.

2. Blacker, "The MBFR Experience," p. 136.

3. Blackwill, "Conceptual Problems of Conventional Arms Control," p. 29.

4. For background on the CFE talks, see "Breaking with Convention: The State of New European Force Talks," pp. 3–9.

5. "U.S. and Soviets Sign Pact Paring Arms in Europe," *New York Times*, November 20, 1990, p. Al.

6. Dean, *Watershed in Europe*, p. xiii.

7. Final Communiqué, Preparatory Consultations, June 28, 1973, Paragraph 3.

8. On the role of plenaries and informals in the MBFR negotiations, see Dean, "East-West Arms Control Negotiations," pp. 94–96.

9. Representatives of the United States, the United Kingdom, and the Federal Republic of Germany met periodically to discuss next steps in MBFR. These meetings were called "trilaterals."

10. Blacker points to the absence of mutuality of interests in MBFR as the major reason the parties were unable to reach agreement. See Blacker, "The MBFR Experience," pp. 135–38. Eastern representatives in Vienna often pointed to the absence of "political will" on the part of the West as an obstacle to progress in the negotiations.

11. Keliher, *The Negotiations on Mutual and Balanced Force Reductions*, pp. 40–41.

12. Blacker and Duffy, *International Arms Control*, p. 297.

13. Blacker, "The MBFR Experience," p. 126.

14. Ibid.

15. Dean, *Watershed in Europe*, discusses the West's objectives in MBFR. See, especially, pp. 153–58.

16. For a sampling of the literature on assessing the military balance, including the problems associated with static models, see the following: Posen, "Measuring the European Conventional Balance"; Biddle, "The European Conventional Balance"; Chalmers and Unterseher, "Is There a Tank Gap?"; Cohen, "Toward Better Net Assessment"; Mearsheimer, "Assessing the Conventional Balance"; and Epstein, "The 3:1 Rule."

17. Resor, "MBFR Aims at Security and Stability," p. 5.

18. See Bertram, *Mutual Force Reductions in Europe*, p. 4, for a discussion of the interests of flank states in MBFR. Arguments made by the flank states in support of their participation in the negotiations are also addressed in Dean, "East-West Arms Control Negotiations," p. 93.

19. Blackwill, "Conceptual Problems of Conventional Arms Control," p. 32.

20. Keliher, *The Negotiations on Mutual and Balanced Force Reductions*, p. 112.

21. Bertram, *Mutual Force Reductions in Europe*, p. 3.

22. Soviet objectives in MBFR are described in Van Oudenaren, "Conventional Arms Control in Europe," pp. 45–46.

23. Ibid., pp. 46–47.

24. The point on defense cooperation is made by Bertram, "Mutual Force Reductions in Europe," pp. 6–7. Soviet concern about controlling Germany, and the Bundeswehr in particular, is reflected in comments made by Soviet negotiators in Vienna. More than once, members of the Soviet delegation confided to their American counterparts that the purpose of these negotiations was to "control Germany." "You control your Germans and we will control ours" was the unspoken understanding.

25. Keliher, *The Negotiations on Mutual and Balanced Force Reductions*, p. 81.

26. Ibid., p. 87.

27. See chapter 3 for a discussion of the importance of prepositioning of equipment for the implementation of NATO's defense strategy.

28. See Blacker, "The MBFR Experience," p. 128; Keliher, *The Negotiations on Mutual and Balanced Force Reductions*, p. 99.

29. Keliher, *The Negotiations on Mutual and Balanced Force Reductions*, p. 81.

30. Ibid., p. 87.

31. Ibid.

32. Ibid., p. 81.

33. Dean, *Watershed in Europe*, p. 178.

34. Brady, "Negotiating European Security," pp. 196 and 198.

35. Ibid., p. 199.

36. Dean, *Watershed in Europe*, p. 178.

37. Blackwill, "The Security Implications of Conventional Arms Control," p. 125.

38. Ibid., pp. 125–26.

39. Final Communiqué, Preparatory Consultations, June 28, 1973, Paragraph 3.

40. Blacker and Duffy, *International Arms Control*, p. 304. For a discussion of points of agreement and disagreement between East and West on these measures, see Dean, *Watershed in Europe*, pp. 161–62.

41. Brady, "Negotiating European Security," p. 203.

42. Ibid., p. 202.

43. The associated measures tabled by the Warsaw Pact are listed in Canby, "Arms Control, Confidence-Building Measures, and Verification," p. 201.

44. *Strategic Survey 1986–87*, p. 70.

45. The "Mandate for Negotiation on Conventional Armed Forces in Europe" is reprinted in *Arms Control Today*, March 1989, pp. 18–19.

46. The NATO organization in support of MBFR is diagrammed in Resor, "MBFR Aims at Security and Stability," pp. 4–5.

47. Soviet representatives in Vienna on more than one occasion revealed to U.S. representatives their concerns about the West German Bundeswehr. The Soviet Union has long viewed the presence of at least some American troops in West Germany as important for stability, just as they see the presence of Soviet troops in East Germany as contributing to stability in Central Europe.

48. See chapter 4 for a discussion of Soviet efforts to convince the European members of NATO to withdraw their support for the December 1979 decision.

49. See Canby, "Mutual Force Reductions," pp. 129–31.

50. Keliher, *The Negotiations on Mutual and Balanced Force Reductions*, pp. 126–27.

51. Dean, *Watershed in Europe*, pp. 153–54.

52. On the importance of a focus on equipment, see Blackwill, "Conventional Stability Talks," pp. 437–39.

53. Dean, *Watershed in Europe*, p. 168.

54. CSCE has a long history. For background, see Blacker and Duffy, *International Arms Control*, pp. 294–96, and Goodby, "The Stockholm Conference."

55. Dean, *Watershed in Europe*, pp. 170–71.

56. Blacker and Duffy, *International Arms Control*, p. 301.

57. Canby, "Arms Control, Confidence-Building Measures, and Verification," p. 187.

Chapter 6

1. M. Sheehan, *Arms Control*, p. 163.
2. Davis, "Lessons of the INF Treaty," p. 725.
3. See "Treaty between the United States of America and the Union of Soviet Socialist Republics on the Elimination of Their Intermediate-Range and Shorter-Range Nuclear Missiles" for the detailed provisions.
4. Kirkey, "The NATO Alliance and the INF Treaty," pp. 288–89; G. Smith, "From Arms Control to Arms Reductions," p. 118.
5. Final Communiqué, Special Meeting of Foreign and Defense Ministers, Paragraph 4. The communiqué is reprinted in *NATO Review* 28, no. 1 (February 1980): 25–26.
6. Gliksman, "Control of Nuclear Weapons in Europe," p. 44.
7. Garthoff, "The TNF Tangle," p. 83.
8. Ibid.
9. Goldberg, "Moscow's INF Experience," p. 106.
10. National Academy of Sciences, *Nuclear Arms Control*, p. 112.
11. On the growing strength of the antinuclear movement in Europe in late 1981 and 1982, see "150,000 in London Rally against Bomb," *New York Times*, October 25, 1981, p. 3; "Antinuclear Protest Spreads in Europe," *Washington Post*, October 26, 1981, p. A1; "'Ban the Bomb' Movement Is Bouncing Back in Britain," *New York Times*, November 13, 1981, p. A2; and "Bonn Rally during Reagan Visit Is a Focal Point of Antinuclear Movement," *New York Times*, June 3, 1982, p. A10.
12. National Academy of Sciences, *Nuclear Arms Control*, p. 113; Talbott, *Deadly Gambits*, p. 71.
13. "Negotiators Shuttle in Silence Up and Down Geneva Street," *International Herald Tribune*, December 7, 1981, p. 2.
14. *New York Times*, November 31, 1981, p. A12. The United States did not include the Pershing I ballistic missile and British and French nuclear weapons in its count.
15. Eagleburger, "The U.S. Approach to the Negotiations on Intermediate-Range Nuclear Forces," p. 8.
16. Yuri Andropov had assumed power, following Brezhnev's death, on November 10, 1982. Andropov died on February 9, 1984, and was replaced by Konstantin Chernenko on February 13, 1984. Mikhail Gorbachev assumed power on March 11, 1985, following the death of Chernenko.
17. Korb and Daggett, "The Defense Budget and Strategic Planning," pp. 44–46.
18. Reagan had characterized the Soviet Union as an "evil empire" in a speech to a religious group in Orlando, Florida, on March 8, 1983.
19. The German view was reflected in the Final Communiqué of Foreign and Defense Ministers issued on December 12, 1979. See Paragraph 9B of

the communiqué. The German position is presented in detail in Genscher, "Intermediate Range Missiles—Moscow Holds the Key to Disarmament," pp. 1–7.

20. "Negotiators Shuttle in Silence Up and Down Geneva Street," *International Herald Tribune*, December 7, 1981, p. 2.

21. Sigal, *Nuclear Forces in Europe*, pp. 148–49.

22. One Dutch view is presented in Bar, "Views of Church Groups in the Netherlands on War and Peace," pp. 23–27.

23. *New York Times*, November 31, 1981, p. A12.

24. Talbott, *Deadly Gambits*, p. 124; Goldberg, "Moscow's INF Experience," p. 112.

25. Talbott, *The Master of the Game*, pp. 369–70.

26. National Academy of Sciences, *Nuclear Arms Control*, p. 111.

27. "Reagan Offers 4-Point Plan for U.S.-Soviet Missile Curbs and Force Limits in Europe," *New York Times*, November 19, 1981, p. A1.

28. These principles were agreed on in discussions within the NATO Special Consultative Group, the mechanism established by the alliance to ensure allied input into the formulation of U.S. negotiating positions. See Hanmer, "NATO's Long-Range Theatre Nuclear Forces," pp. 5–6.

29. *Strategic Survey 1982–83*, pp. 21–22.

30. The best widely available description of the "walk in the woods" is Talbott, *Deadly Gambits*, pp. 116–51.

31. *Strategic Survey 1983–84*, p. 29.

32. *Strategic Survey 1986–87*, p. 63.

33. *Strategic Survey 1985–86*, p. 56.

34. *Strategic Survey 1986–87*, pp. 60–63.

35. Ibid.

36. *Strategic Survey 1987–88*, p. 14.

37. Talbott, *Deadly Gambits*, p. 65, describes these measures as "collateral restraints."

38. Ibid., p. 183.

39. *New York Times*, November 30, 1981, p. A12.

40. "Gorbachev Offers to Render Europe Clear of Missiles," *New York Times*, April 15, 1987, p. 1.

41. Talbott, *Deadly Gambits*, p. 125.

42. "The Double Zero," *Christian Science Monitor*, May 4, 1987, p. 21.

43. "Europe Seeks Common Stand," *Christian Science Monitor*, April 3, 1987, p. 12.

44. "Kohl Urges Shorter-Range U.S. Missiles," *Atlanta Constitution*, April 8, 1987, p. 3A; "West Germany Waffles over Issue of Shorter-Range Missiles," *Christian Science Monitor*, April 28, 1987, p. 11; "Hard Bargaining Replaces Rhetoric in Arms Control," *Christian Science Monitor*, May 8, 1987, p. 9.

45. "Gorbachev OKs Reagan Stand on Missile Cuts," *Atlanta Journal*, July 23, 1987, p. 1A.

46. "Soviets Using Pershing 1A Missiles to Divide W. Germany, NATO Allies," *Atlanta Journal and Constitution*, August 22, 1987, p. 4A.

47. "West Germany Vows to Scrap Arms under Pact," *Atlanta Journal*, August 26, 1987, p. 1A.

48. M. Sheehan, *Arms Control*, p. 124. See, also, Kunzendorff, *Verification in Conventional Arms Control*, pp. 6–7.

49. Eagleburger, "The U.S. Approach to the Negotiations on Intermediate-Range Nuclear Forces," p. 10.

50. "U.S. Charges New Soviet Arms Violations," *Washington Times*, December 23, 1985, p. 4.

51. *Strategic Survey 1986–87*, p. 61.

52. "Missile Treaty Will Stand or Fall on Verification Provisions," *Atlanta Journal and Constitution*, November 29, 1987, p. 26A; "Verification Could Spell Trouble for Planned Treaty," *Christian Science Monitor*, September 11, 1987, p. 3.

53. *Strategic Survey 1987–88*, p. 239.

54. "U.S., Soviets Reported Stuck on Verification of Arms Treaty," *Atlanta Journal*, November 18, 1987, p. 3A.

55. "U.S., Soviets Focus on Missile Inspection Issue," *Atlanta Journal and Constitution*, November 22, 1987, p. 7C; "Arms Pact Verification System Is Most Far-Reaching Ever," *Christian Science Monitor*, November 27, 1987, p. 15.

56. Talbott, *Deadly Gambits*, p. 59.

57. *Strategic Survey 1982–83*, p. 157.

58. "Two Sides Far Apart as Arms Talks Near," *Washington Post*, March 10, 1985, p. 1.

59. "The Wrong Way to Treat Moscow," *New York Times*, March 3, 1985, p. E21, points to Soviet concerns about continuation of the offensive arms race and fears that the propaganda advantage was shifting to the West for the Soviet decision to return to the negotiations.

60. *Strategic Survey 1987–88*, p. 22.

61. Einhorn, *Negotiating from Strength*, pp. 1–2.

62. The Supreme Soviet's consideration of the INF Treaty was pro forma compared with the United States Senate's. See "As Expected, Supreme Soviet Gives INF Treaty Warm Welcome," p. 22.

63. "Shultz Lobbies for INF Accord as Hearings Start," *Atlanta Journal*, January 25, 1988, p. 1A; "U.S. Arms Negotiator Denies INF Accord Could Harm NATO," *Atlanta Journal*, January 26, 1988, p. 3A.

64. Crowe, "Why the Joint Chiefs Support the INF Treaty," p. 6.

65. "NATO Chief: INF Treaty 'Worth the Risks,'" *Christian Science Monitor*, February 12, 1988, p. 12.

66. "Kohl: Ratify INF without Amendments," *Atlanta Journal*, February 19, 1988, p. 3D.

67. "Officials, Experts Praise Treaty in Senate Hearings," pp. 19–20.

68. "Foreign Relations Committee Approves INF Treaty 17-2," p. 26.

69. "Dispute on Verification Clouds Arms Negotiation as Moscow Talks Near," *Atlanta Journal*, April 28, 1988, p. 18A; "Dispute with Soviets May Stall INF Ratification," *Atlanta Journal and Constitution*, May 1, 1988, p. 4A.

70. "Shultz, Soviet Meet to Mend INF Pact Rift," *Atlanta Journal*, May 11, 1988, p. 1A; "U.S., Soviets Debate What They Agreed to on INF," *Christian Science Monitor*, May 11, 1988, p. 1; "U.S., Soviet Negotiators Clearing Up Sticking Points on INF Missile Treaty," *Atlanta Journal*, May 12, 1988, p. 3A; "U.S. and Soviets Say Missile Pact Issue Has Been Resolved," *New York Times*, May 13, 1988, p. 1; "'Hard Bargainers,' Shultz Says as INF Flap Settled," *Atlanta Journal*, May 13, 1988, p. 1A; "Senate Opening INF Debate as Inspection Dispute Settled," *Atlanta Journal*, May 17, 1988, p. 4A.

71. "Officials, Experts Praise Treaty in Senate Hearings," p. 21.

72. "Senate Turns Back Three GOP Challenges to Missile Pact," *Atlanta Journal*, May 24, 1988, p. 4A.

73. On the debate between advocates of the "broad" and "narrow" interpretations of the ABM Treaty, see Talbott, *The Master of the Game*, pp. 231–49.

74. "INF Treaty Embroiled in Constitutional Controversy," p. 19.

75. "Shultz Affirms INF Testimony as 'Authoritative,'" *Atlanta Journal*, February 10, 1988, p. 1A; "Nunn, Byrd Drop Attempt to Delay Hearings on the INF Treaty," *Atlanta Journal*, February 11, 1988, p. 4A.

76. "Foreign Relations Committee Approves INF Treaty 17-2," p. 18. The full text of the Senate's condition is reprinted in "Senate Conditions on the INF Treaty," p. 23.

77. Talbott, *The Master of the Game*, p. 369.

78. Ibid., p. 296.

79. Ibid., p. 347.

Chapter 7

1. Kupchan, *The Persian Gulf and the West*, p. 99.

2. Response to a written question submitted for the record, *Department of Defense Appropriations for 1990*, Hearings before the Defense Subcommittee of the House Appropriations Committee, 101st Cong., 1st sess., pt. 2, February 7, 1989, p. 316.

3. "Bush Sends U.S. Force to Saudi Arabia as Kingdom Agrees to Confront Iraq," *New York Times*, August 8, 1990, p. A1.

4. "Cheney, on Quick Tour, Reaches Agreement on More Bases in Gulf," *New York Times*, August 21, 1990, p. A1.

5. The Omani agreement is described in "U.S. Government Builds Gulf Military Network—Just in Case," *Christian Science Monitor*, January 19, 1988, p. 36, and "Superpowers Jostle in Gulf," *Christian Science Monitor*, July 6, 1987, p. 1. See, also, *U.S. Policy toward the Persian Gulf*, Hearing before the Subcommittee on Europe and the Middle East of the House Committee on Foreign Affairs, and the Joint Economic Committee, 97th Cong., 2d sess., May 10, 1982, p. 32; and Response to a written question submitted for the record, *Department of Defense Appropriations for Fiscal Year 1983*, Hearings before the Senate Appropriations Committee, 97th Cong., 2d sess., pt. 3, May 12, 1982, p. 268.

6. "U.S. Government Builds Gulf Military Network—Just in Case," *Christian Science Monitor*, January 19, 1988, p. 36.

7. Response to a written question submitted for the record, *Department of Defense Appropriations for 1990*, Hearings before the Defense Subcommittee of the House Appropriations Committee, 101st Cong., 1st sess., pt. 2, February 7, 1989, p. 317.

8. Ibid., p. 345.

9. "U.S. Government Builds Gulf Military Network—Just in Case," *Christian Science Monitor*, January 19, 1988, p. 36.

10. Ibid.

11. "Facilities Access—Southwest Asia," *Military Construction Appropriations for Fiscal Year 1984*, Hearings before the Military Construction Subcommittee of the House Appropriations Committee, 98th Cong., 1st sess., February 16, 1983, p. 116. See, also, McNaugher, *Arms and Oil*, pp. 16–17.

12. "Closer U.S.-Israeli Cooperation Seen," *Washington Post*, November 8, 1983, p. A1; "U.S. and Israelis Expand Strategic and Political Ties," *Washington Post*, November 30, 1983, p. A1; and "U.S.-Israeli Military Pact to Start Soon," *New York Times*, January 15, 1984, p. 10.

13. Testimony by Frank C. Carlucci, Deputy Secretary of Defense, *Department of Defense Appropriations for Fiscal Year 1983*, Hearings before the Senate Appropriations Committee, 97th Cong., 2d sess., pt. 3, June 10, 1982, p. 287. See, also, Kupchan, *The Persian Gulf and the West*, p. 143.

14. On the sensitivity of this issue, see "U.S.: Kingston Sums Up Bright Star."

15. Cordesman, *The Gulf and the Search for Strategic Stability*, p. 11.

16. Kupchan, *The Persian Gulf and the West*, pp. 69–75.

17. Ibid., p. 74; see, also, Bill, "Resurgent Islam."

18. Kupchan, *The Persian Gulf and the West*, pp. 75–77.

19. Quoted in McNaugher, *Arms and Oil*, p. 3.

20. Record, *The Rapid Deployment Force and U.S. Military Intervention in the Persian Gulf*, p. 9.

21. Ibid., p. 3. Record rightly points out that strategic mobility is not enough.

22. Arab objectives in negotiating with the United States (or in choosing not to negotiate) vary widely. For background on the critical Gulf states, see Cordesman, *The Gulf and the Search for Strategic Stability*.

23. See Papp, *Soviet Policies toward the Developing World during the 1980s*, pp. 241–54, for an analysis of Soviet policies in the Middle East and the Persian Gulf during the 1980s.

24. Some observers have argued that direct Soviet intervention in the region may be the least likely scenario and that the United States should pay more attention to other threats to the flow of oil from the Persian Gulf. See, for example, Van Hollen, "Don't Engulf the Gulf," pp. 1068–71.

25. On the Saudi perspective, see Quandt, *Saudi Arabia in the 1980s*, pp. 30–33.

26. Concern about the undesirable effects of greater cooperation with the West are discussed in Van Hollen, "Don't Engulf the Gulf," p. 1069; Bill, "Resurgent Islam," p. 113.

27. On American reliability, see Lawrence, *U.S. Policy in Southwest Asia*, pp. 43–49.

28. Shamir, "Israel's Role in a Changing Middle East," p. 799.

29. The importance of access to the Arab states, and Saudi Arabia in particular, for executing a U.S. deployment to the Persian Gulf is discussed in "Superpowers Jostle in Gulf," *Christian Science Monitor*, July 6, 1987, p. 1, and "U.S. Builds Gulf Military Network—Just in Case," *Christian Science Monitor*, January 19, 1988, p. 36. See, also, "No Permanent Bases in Gulf Area Limits U.S.," *Christian Science Monitor*, May 28, 1987, p. 1.

30. Kupchan, *The Persian Gulf and the West*, p. 120.

31. Quandt, *Saudi Arabia in the 1980s*, p. 55.

32. "Facilities Access—Southwest Asia," *Military Construction Appropriations for FY 1984*, Hearings before the Military Construction Subcommittee of the House Appropriations Committee, 98th Cong., 1st sess., February 16, 1983, p. 116.

33. Ibid.

34. "U.S. Builds Gulf Military Network—Just in Case," *Christian Science Monitor*, January 19, 1988, p. 36; "No Permanent Bases in Gulf Area Limits U.S.," *Christian Science Monitor*, May 28, 1987, p. 1; "Superpowers Jostle in Gulf," *Christian Science Monitor*, July 6, 1987, p. 1.

35. "Closer U.S.-Israeli Cooperation Seen," *Washington Post*, November 8, 1983, p. A1; "U.S. and Israelis Expand Strategic and Political Ties," *Washington Post*, November 30, 1983, p. A1; "U.S.-Israeli Military Pact to Start Soon," *New York Times*, January 15, 1984, p. 10.

36. "U.S. and Israelis Expand Strategic and Political Ties," *Washington Post*, November 30, 1983, p. A10.

37. U.S. Department of Defense, *Annual Report to the Congress, Fiscal Year 1982*, p. 194.

38. Ibid. See, also, Cordesman, *The Gulf and the Search for Strategic Stability*, p. 812.

39. *Department of Defense Appropriations for 1990*, Hearings before the Defense Subcommittee of the House Appropriations Committee, 101st Cong., 1st sess., pt. 2, February 7, 1989, p. 364.

40. "Oman Reported to Tell U.S. to Scale Down Its Landing Exercises There," *Baltimore Sun*, November 6, 1981.

41. "Oman Landing Winds Up Well-Received 'Bright Star,' " *Baltimore Sun*, December 7, 1981, p. 1.

42. For reference, these statutes are Officials Not to Benefit (FAR 3.102, 41 USC 22), Gratuities (FAR 3.2, 10 USC 2207), and Covenant Against Contingent Fees (FAR 3.4, 10 USC 2306[b]).

43. Van Hollen, "Don't Engulf the Gulf," p. 1072.

44. Ibid., p. 1070.

45. For a discussion of the Reagan administration's concept of a strategic consensus for the Persian Gulf, see Safran, *Saudi Arabia*, pp. 327–28.

46. This remains a problem, as illustrated in congressional testimony by General H. Norman Schwarzkopf, commander-in-chief, U.S. Central Command. See *Department of Defense Appropriations for 1990*, Hearings before the Defense Subcommittee of the House Appropriations Committee, 101st Cong., 1st sess., pt. 2, February 7, 1989, pp. 304–5.

47. Lawrence, *U.S. Policy in Southwest Asia*, p. 23.

48. "Facilities Access—Southwest Asia," *Military Construction Appropriations for FY 1984*, Hearings before the Military Construction Subcommittee of the House Appropriations Committee, 98th Cong., 1st sess., February 16, 1983, p. 74.

49. Ibid., p. 84.

50. Ibid., p. 85.

51. Ibid., p. 66.

52. Lawrence, *U.S. Policy in Southwest Asia*, p. 36.

53. Kupchan, *The Persian Gulf and the West*, p. 131.

54. Ibid., p. 143. McNaugher, *Arms and Oil*, p. 55, reports that Saudi Arabia stocks excess air-delivered munitions, support equipment for the F-15 fighter aircraft, and fuel.

55. Kuniholm, "What the Saudis Really Want," p. 120.

56. Quandt, *Saudi Arabia in the 1980s*, p. 66.

57. Ibid., p. 143.

58. Safran, *Saudi Arabia*, pp. 327–28.

59. *U.S. Policy toward the Persian Gulf*, Hearing before the Subcommittee on Europe and the Middle East of the House Committee on Foreign Affairs, and

the Joint Economic Committee, 97th Cong., 2d sess., May 10, 1982, pp. 21–22.

60. "When Will We Get Something in Return for Arms to Saudis," *Atlanta Journal*, August 18, 1987, p. 22A.

61. Quandt, *Saudi Arabia in the 1980s*, pp. 12 and 34.

62. Bill, "Resurgent Islam."

63. Response to a written question submitted for the record, *Department of Defense Appropriations for 1990*, Hearings before the Defense Subcommittee of the House Appropriations Committee, 101st Cong., 1st sess., pt. 2, February 7, 1989, pp. 311–12.

Chapter 8

1. Bentinck, *NATO's Out-of-Area Problem*, p. 44.

2. *U.S. Policy Toward the Persian Gulf*, Hearing before the Subcommittee on Europe and the Middle East of the House Committee on Foreign Affairs, and the Joint Economic Committee, 97th Cong., 2d sess., May 10, 1982, p. 15.

3. This Department of Defense document, *Report on Allied Contributions to the Common Defense*, is known as the Burdensharing Report.

4. The problems faced by the United States in trying to persuade NATO to respond as an alliance to threats in the Persian Gulf are described in Sherwood, *Allies in Crisis*, pp. 149–83.

5. Article 6 of the North Atlantic Treaty reads in part: "An armed attack on one or more of the Parties is deemed to include an armed attack on the territory of any of the Parties in Europe or North America, on the Algerian Departments of France, on the occupation forces of any Party in Europe, on the islands under the jurisdiction of any Party in the North Atlantic area north of the Tropic of Cancer or on the vessels or aircraft in this area of the parties." See Sloan, *NATO's Future*, pp. 200–201.

6. Farrar-Hockley, "Problems of Over-extension," p. 57.

7. See the following communiqués: Defence Planning Committee, Final Communiqué, May 14, 1980. The complete text is reprinted in *NATO Review* 28, no. 3 (June 1980): 31–33. Also, Defence Planning Committee, Final Communiqué, December 10, 1980, reprinted in *NATO Review* 29, no. 1 (February 1981): 28–29; North Atlantic Council, Final Communiqué, May 18, 1982, reprinted in *NATO Review* 30, no. 3 (June 1982): 27–29; and "Document on Integrated NATO Defence," issued by Heads of State and Government participating in the meeting of the North Atlantic Council, June 10, 1982, reprinted in *NATO Review* 30, no. 3 (June 1982): 27.

8. Defence Planning Committee, Final Communiqué, December 5, 1984, reprinted in *NATO Review* 32, no. 6 (December 1984): 24–26.

9. Ibid.

10. On the military requirement for allied support for a U.S. deployment to Southwest Asia, see Brown, *Thinking about National Security*, p. 158.

11. James R. Blaker portrays alternative staging routes in "The Out-of-Area Question and NATO Burdensharing," p. 51.

12. Peterson, *Oman in the Twentieth Century*, pp. 137–38.

13. Cordesman, *The Gulf and the Search for Strategic Stability*, p. 796.

14. This sentiment is reflected in *U.S. Policy Toward the Persian Gulf*, Hearing before the Subcommittee on Europe and the Middle East of the House Committee on Foreign Affairs, and the Joint Economic Committee, 97th Cong., 2d sess., May 10, 1982.

15. Sherwood, *Allies in Crisis*, p. 160; Hunter, "NATO's Future," pp. 325–26.

16. Sherwood, *Allies in Crisis*, pp. 151 and 159.

17. See ibid., p. 175, on German concerns about timely consultation.

18. Treverton, "Defence beyond Europe," p. 217.

19. Kupchan, *The Persian Gulf and the West*, pp. 172–73. See, also, Record, *The Rapid Deployment Force and U.S. Military Intervention in the Persian Gulf*, p. 29.

20. Hunter, "NATO's Future," p. 331.

21. U.S. Congressional Budget Office, *Rapid Deployment Forces*, pp. 24–25. See, also, Record, *The Rapid Deployment Force and U.S. Military Intervention in the Persian Gulf*, pp. 33–36.

22. U.S. Department of Defense, *Report on Allied Contributions to the Common Defense*, March 1985, p. 53.

23. See Cordesman, *The Gulf and the Search for Strategic Stability*, pp. 3–32, on the strategic implications of Gulf oil.

24. Kupchan, *The Persian Gulf and the West*, pp. 194–95. The Iraqi invasion of Kuwait in August 1990 seems to support the European view about the most likely source of disruption of the oil supply.

25. J. Blaker, "The Out-of-Area Question and NATO Burdensharing," p. 43.

26. Kupchan, *The Persian Gulf and the West*, p. 194.

27. Defence Planning Committee, Final Communiqué, May 14, 1980, p. 32, reprinted in *NATO Review* 28, no. 3 (June 1980): 31–33.

28. North Atlantic Council, Final Communiqué, December 12, 1980, reprinted in *NATO Review* 29, no. 1 (February 1981): 25–27.

29. North Atlantic Council, Final Communiqué, May 18, 1982, reprinted in *NATO Review* 30, no. 3 (June 1982): 27–29.

30. For the U.S. rationale, see "Bush's Aims: Deter Attack, Send a Signal," *New York Times*, August 8, 1990, p. A1. For the European rationale, see "More Europeans to Join Gulf Force," *New York Times*, August 22, 1990, p. A7.

31. Komer, "Problems of Over-extension," p. 62.

32. See, for example, North Atlantic Council, Final Communiqué, May 18, 1982, reprinted in *NATO Review* 30, no. 3 (June 1982): 27–29.

33. "Document on Integrated NATO Defence," issued by Heads of State and Government participating in the meeting of the North Atlantic Council, June 10, 1982, reprinted in *NATO Review* 30, no. 3 (June 1982): 27.

34. McNaugher, *Arms and Oil*, pp. 66, 79–80.

35. J. Blaker, "The Out-of-Area Question and NATO Burdensharing," p. 50.

36. Komer, "Problems of Over-extension," p. 63.

37. Defence Planning Committee, Final Communiqué, December 10, 1980, reprinted in *NATO Review* 29, no. 1 (February 1981): 28–29.

38. Ibid.

39. Defence Planning Committee, Final Communiqué, December 5, 1984, reprinted in *NATO Review* 32, no. 6 (December 1984): 24–26.

40. Kupchan, *The Persian Gulf and the West*, p. 185.

41. Ibid., pp. 182–83.

42. J. Blaker, "The Out-of-Area Question and NATO Burdensharing," p. 43.

43. Kupchan, *The Persian Gulf and the West*, p. 163. See, also, Bentinck, *NATO's Out-of-Area Problem*, pp. 6–22.

44. For a detailed discussion of this episode, see Sherwood, *Allies in Crisis*, pp. 177–83.

45. "European Powers Step Up Gulf Role," *Christian Science Monitor*, July 27, 1987, p. 1; "France Sends Fleet to Gulf as Warning to Iran," *Atlanta Journal*, July 30, 1987, p. 3A; "Sixth Mine Discovered in Gulf of Oman as U.S., Other Nations Conduct Sweep," *Atlanta Journal*, August 13, 1987, p. 7A.

Chapter 9

1. Stein, "International Negotiation," p. 221.

2. "Text of the Declaration after the NATO Talks," *New York Times*, July 7, 1990, p. 5.

3. On alternative approaches to new security structures in Europe, see Snyder, "Averting Anarchy in the New Europe"; Mueller, "A New Concert of Europe"; Layne, "Superpower Disengagement"; Brenner, "Finding America's Place"; and Holt, "Europe's Security: In the EC, Not NATO."

4. See "Western Leaders Call for New NATO to Assure Soviets," *New York Times*, July 6, 1990, p. 5.

5. See Dougherty and Pfaltzgraff, *Contending Theories of International Relations*, pp. 92–119, for a discussion of realism in the twentieth century.

6. B. Salmore and S. Salmore, "Political Regimes and Foreign Policy," pp. 103–22.

7. The impact of public opinion on foreign policy, generally, is discussed in Bliss and Johnson, *Beyond the Water's Edge*, pp. 206–15.

8. Quandt makes a persuasive case for the role of election-year political considerations in foreign policy-making in "The Electoral Cycle and the Conduct of Foreign Policy."

9. Allison, *Essence of Decision.*

10. On tensions within the military establishment concerning the allocation of resources, see D. Clarke, *American Defense and Foreign Policy Institutions*, pp. 126–27.

11. See Marttila, "American Public Opinion," for an analysis of emerging perspectives on security issues.

Bibliography

Books and Reports

Allison, Graham T. *Essence of Decision*. Boston: Little, Brown and Company, 1971.

Bartos, Otomar J. *Process and Outcome of Negotiations*. New York: Columbia University Press, 1974.

Bentinck, Marc. *NATO's Out-of-Area Problem*. Adelphi Papers, no. 211. London: International Institute for Strategic Studies, Autumn 1986.

Bertram, Christoph. *Mutual Force Reductions in Europe: The Political Aspects*. Adelphi Papers, no. 84. London: International Institute for Strategic Studies, January 1972.

Blacker, Coit D., and Gloria Duffy, eds. *International Arms Control: Issues and Agreements*. 2d ed. Stanford: Stanford University Press, 1984.

Blaker, Michael. *Japanese International Negotiating Style*. New York: Columbia University Press, 1977.

Bliss, Howard, and M. Glen Johnson. *Beyond the Water's Edge: America's Foreign Policies*. Philadelphia: J. B. Lippincott Company, 1975.

Brady, Linda P., and Joyce P. Kaufman, eds. *NATO in the 1980s: Challenges and Responses*. New York: Praeger Publishers, 1985.

Brown, Harold. *Thinking about National Security*. Boulder, Colo.: Westview Press, 1983.

Buteux, Paul. *The Politics of Nuclear Consultation in NATO 1965–1980*. New York: Cambridge University Press, 1983.

Callahan, Patrick, Linda P. Brady, and Margaret G. Hermann, eds. *Describing Foreign Policy Behavior*. Beverly Hills, Calif.: Sage Publications, 1982.

Carter, Jimmy. *Keeping Faith*. New York: Bantam Books, 1982.

Clarke, Duncan L. *American Defense and Foreign Policy Institutions*. New York: Harper and Row, 1989.

Cordesman, Anthony H. *The Gulf and the Search for Strategic Stability*. Boulder, Colo.: Westview Press, 1984.

Craig, Gordon A. *The Germans*. New York: New American Library, 1982.

Cross, J. G. *The Economics of Bargaining*. New York: Basic Books, 1969.

Dean, Jonathan. *Watershed in Europe: Dismantling the East-West Military Confrontation*. Lexington, Mass.: Lexington Books, D. C. Heath and Company, 1987.

DeCallieres, Monsieur. *On the Manner of Negotiating with Princes.* Translated by A. F. Whyte. South Bend, Ind.: University of Notre Dame Press, 1963.

Dougherty, James E., and Robert L. Pfaltzgraff, Jr. *Contending Theories of International Relations.* 3d ed. New York: Harper and Row, 1990.

Einhorn, Robert J. *Negotiating from Strength.* New York: Praeger Publishers, 1985.

Fisher, Roger. *International Conflict for Beginners.* New York: Harper and Row, 1969.

Fisher, Roger, and William L. Ury. *Getting to Yes.* Boston: Houghton Mifflin, 1981.

Foreign Policy Institute Policy Study Group. *Changing Roles and Shifting Burdens in the Atlantic Alliance.* Washington, D.C.: Foreign Policy Institute, April 1990.

Garthoff, Raymond L. *Détente and Confrontation.* Washington, D.C.: Brookings Institution, 1985.

George, Alexander L., and Richard Smoke. *Deterrence in American Foreign Policy: Theory and Practice.* New York: Columbia University Press, 1974.

Halperin, Morton H. *Bureaucratic Politics and Foreign Policy.* Washington, D.C.: Brookings Institution, 1974.

Hoffmann, Stanley. *Gulliver's Troubles or the Setting of American Foreign Policy.* New York: McGraw-Hill, 1968.

Ikle, Fred Charles. *How Nations Negotiate.* New York: Harper and Row, 1964.

Keliher, John G. *The Negotiations on Mutual and Balanced Force Reductions.* New York: Pergamon Press, [1980].

Kissinger, Henry. *White House Years.* Boston: Little, Brown and Company, 1979.

Kunzendorff, Volker. *Verification in Conventional Arms Control.* Adelphi Papers #245. London: International Institute for Strategic Studies, Winter 1989.

Kupchan, Charles A. *The Persian Gulf and the West: The Dilemmas of Security.* Boston: Allen and Unwin, 1987.

Lall, Arthur. *How Communist China Negotiates.* New York: Columbia University Press, 1968.

———. *Modern International Negotiation: Principles and Practice.* New York: Columbia University Press, 1966.

Lamb, Christopher J. *How to Think about Arms Control, Disarmament, and Defense.* Englewood Cliffs, N.J.: Prentice-Hall, 1988.

Lawrence, Robert G. *U.S. Policy in Southwest Asia: A Failure in Perspective.* Washington, D.C.: National Defense University Press, 1984.

Lewicki, Roy J., and Joseph A. Litterer. *Negotiation.* Homewood, Ill.: Richard D. Irwin, 1985.

McNaugher, Thomas L. *Arms and Oil: U.S. Military Strategy and the Persian Gulf.* Washington, D.C.: Brookings Institution, 1985.

National Academy of Sciences. *Nuclear Arms Control: Background and Issues.* Washington, D.C.: National Academy Press, 1985.

Neustadt, Richard E., and Ernest R. May. *Thinking in Time: The Uses of History for Decision-makers.* New York: Free Press, 1986.

Nicolson, Harold. *Diplomacy.* New York: Harcourt, Brace and Company, 1939.

Osgood, Robert E. *Alliances and American Foreign Policy.* Baltimore: Johns Hopkins University Press, 1968.

Papp, Daniel S. *Soviet Policies toward the Developing World during the 1980s.* Maxwell Air Force Base, Ala.: Air University Press, 1986.

Peterson, J. E. *Oman in the Twentieth Century.* New York: Barnes and Noble Books, 1978.

Pruitt, Dean G. *Negotiation Behavior.* New York: Academic Press, 1981.

Quandt, William B. *Camp David: Peacemaking and Politics.* Washington, D.C.: Brookings Institution, 1986.

———. *Saudi Arabia in the 1980s.* Washington, D.C.: Brookings Institution, 1981.

Raiffa, Howard. *The Art and Science of Negotiation.* Cambridge: Harvard University Press, 1982.

Rapoport, Anatol. *Strategy and Conscience.* New York: Schocken Books, 1964.

Record, Jeffrey. *The Rapid Deployment Force and U.S. Military Intervention in the Persian Gulf.* 2d ed. Cambridge, Mass.: Institute for Foreign Policy Analysis, May 1983.

Reed, John A., Jr. *Germany and NATO.* Washington, D.C.: National Defense University Press, 1987.

Safran, Nadav. *Saudi Arabia: The Ceaseless Quest for Security.* Ithaca, N.Y.: Cornell University Press, 1985.

Schelling, Thomas C. *The Strategy of Conflict.* New York: Oxford University Press, 1963.

Schwartz, David N. *NATO's Nuclear Dilemmas.* Washington, D.C.: Brookings Institution, 1983.

Sheehan, Edward R. F. *The Arabs, Israelis, and Kissinger.* New York: Reader's Digest Press, 1976.

Sheehan, Michael J. *Arms Control: Theory and Practice.* New York: Basil Blackwell, 1988.

Sherwood, Elizabeth D. *Allies in Crisis: Meeting Global Challenges to Western Security.* New Haven: Yale University Press, 1990.

Sigal, Leon V. *Nuclear Forces in Europe.* Washington, D.C.: Brookings Institution, 1984.

Sloan, Stanley R. *NATO's Future: Toward a New Transatlantic Bargain.* Washington, D.C.: National Defense University Press, 1985.

Sloss, Leon, and M. Scott Davis, eds. *A Game for High Stakes: Lessons Learned*

in Negotiating with the Soviet Union. Cambridge, Mass.: Ballinger Publishing
Company, 1986.

Smith, Gerard. *Doubletalk: The Story of SALT I.* Lanham, Md.: University
Press of America, 1985.

Smith, Hedrick. *The Power Game.* New York: Random House, 1988.

Smith, Raymond F. *Negotiating with the Soviets.* Bloomington: Indiana
University Press, 1989.

Stein, Janice Gross, ed. *Getting to the Table: The Processes of International
Prenegotiation.* Baltimore: Johns Hopkins University Press, 1989.

Talbott, Strobe. *Deadly Gambits.* New York: Alfred A. Knopf, 1984.

————. *The Master of the Game.* New York: Alfred A. Knopf, 1988.

Wasserman, Sherri L. *The Neutron Bomb Controversy.* New York: Praeger
Publishers, 1983.

Young, Kenneth T. *Negotiating with the Chinese Communists: The United States
Experience, 1953–1967.* New York: McGraw-Hill, 1968.

Zartman, I. William, and Maureen R. Berman. *The Practical Negotiator.* New
Haven: Yale University Press, 1982.

Articles

"As Expected, Supreme Soviet Gives INF Treaty Warm Welcome." *Arms
Control Today* 18, no. 3 (April 1988): 22.

Bar, R. P. "Views of Church Groups in the Netherlands on War and Peace."
NATO Review 30, no. 1 (February 1982): 23–27.

Bartos, Otomar J. "Simple Model of Negotiation: A Sociological Point of
View." In *The Negotiation Process: Theories and Applications,* edited by
I. William Zartman, pp. 13–27. Beverly Hills, Calif.: Sage
Publications, 1978.

Bertram, Christoph. "The Implications of Theater Nuclear Weapons in
Europe." *Foreign Affairs* 60, no. 2 (Winter 1981/82): 305–26.

Biddle, Stephen D. "The European Conventional Balance: A
Reinterpretation of the Debate." *Survival* 30, no. 2 (March/April 1988):
99–121.

Bill, James A. "Resurgent Islam." *Foreign Affairs* 63, no. 1 (Fall 1984):
108–27.

Blacker, Coit D. "The MBFR Experience." In *U.S.-Soviet Security Cooperation,*
edited by Alexander L. George, Philip J. Farley, and Alexander Dallin,
pp. 123–43. New York: Oxford University Press, 1988.

Blackwill, Robert D. "Conceptual Problems of Conventional Arms Control."
International Security 12, no. 4 (Spring 1988): 28–47.

————. "Conventional Stability Talks: Specific Approaches to Conventional

Arms Control in Europe." *Survival* 30, no. 5 (September/October 1988): 429–47.

———. "The Security Implications of Conventional Arms Control." In *Conventional Arms Control and the Security of Europe*, edited by Uwe Nerlich and James A. Thomson, pp. 123–35. Boulder, Colo.: Westview Press, 1988.

Blaker, James R. "The Out-of-Area Question and NATO Burdensharing." In *NATO in the 1980s: Challenges and Responses*, edited by Linda P. Brady and Joyce P. Kaufman, pp. 39–55. New York: Praeger Publishers, 1985.

Brady, Linda P. "Negotiating European Security: Mutual and Balanced Force Reductions." *International Security Review* 6, no. 2 (Summer 1981): 189–208.

———. "The Situation and Foreign Policy." In *Why Nations Act: Theoretical Perspectives for Comparative Foreign Policy Studies*, edited by Maurice A. East, Stephen A. Salmore, and Charles F. Hermann, pp. 173–90. Beverly Hills, Calif.: Sage Publications, 1978.

Brady, Linda P., and Dieter Fleck. "Transatlantische militarische Zusammenarbeit in Krisenzeiten." *Europa Archiv* 10 (October 1983): 581–88.

"Breaking with Convention: The State of New European Force Talks." *Arms Control Today* 19, no. 3 (April 1989): 3–9.

Brenner, Michael J. "Finding America's Place." *Foreign Policy*, no. 79 (Summer 1990): 25–43.

Callahan, Patrick. "Commitment." In *Describing Foreign Policy Behavior*, edited by Patrick Callahan, Linda P. Brady, and Margaret G. Hermann, pp. 177–206. Beverly Hills, Calif.: Sage Publications, 1982.

Canby, Steven L. "Arms Control, Confidence-Building Measures, and Verification." In *Arms Control: The Multilateral Alternative*, edited by Edward C. Luck, pp. 198–212. New York: New York University Press, 1983.

———. "Mutual Force Reductions: A Military Perspective." *International Security* 2, no. 3 (Winter 1978): 122–35.

Chalmers, Malcolm, and Lutz Unterseher. "Is There a Tank Gap? Comparing NATO and Warsaw Pact Tank Fleets." *International Security* 13, no. 1 (Summer 1988): 5–49.

Clarke, Michael. "West European Politics and Extended Deterrence." In *Nuclear Deterrence: New Risks, New Opportunities*, edited by Catherine McArdle Kelleher, Frank J. Kerr, and George H. Quester, pp. 201–13. Washington, D.C.: Pergamon-Brassey's, 1986.

Cohen, Eliot A. "Toward Better Net Assessment: Rethinking the European Conventional Balance." *International Security* 13, no. 1 (Summer 1988): 50–89.

Corterier, Peter. "Quo Vadis NATO?" *Survival* 32, no. 2 (March/April 1990): 141–56.

Cotter, Donald R. "NATO Theater Nuclear Forces: An Enveloping Military Concept." *Strategic Review* 9, no. 2 (Spring 1981): 44–53.

Crowe, William J., Jr. "Why the Joint Chiefs Support the INF Treaty." *Arms Control Today* 18, no. 3 (April 1988): 3–6.

Daalder, Ivo H., and Catherine M. Kelleher. "Ban Land-Based Nukes in Europe." *Christian Science Monitor*, May 1, 1990, p. 18.

Davis, Lynn E. "Lessons of the INF Treaty." *Foreign Affairs* 66, no. 4 (Spring 1988): 720–34.

Dean, Jonathan. "East-West Arms Control Negotiations: The Multi-lateral Dimension." In *A Game for High Stakes*, edited by Leon Sloss and M. Scott Davis, pp. 79–106. Cambridge, Mass.: Ballinger Publishing Company, 1986.

Domke, William K. "The Netherlands: Strategy Options and Change." In *Evolving European Defense Policies*, edited by Catherine McArdle Kelleher and Gale A. Mattox, pp. 273–94. Lexington, Mass.: Lexington Books, D. C. Heath and Company, 1987.

Druckman, Daniel. "Boundary Role Conflict: Negotiation as Dual Responsiveness." In *The Negotiation Process: Theories and Applications*, edited by I. William Zartman, pp. 87–110. Beverly Hills, Calif.: Sage Publications, 1977.

Druckman, Daniel, Alan A. Benton, Faizunisa Ali, and J. Susana Bagur. "Cultural Differences in Bargaining Behavior: India, Argentina, and the United States." *The Journal of Conflict Resolution* 20, no. 3 (September 1976): 413–52.

Druckman, Daniel, and Robert Mahoney. "Processes and Consequences of International Negotiations." *Journal of Social Issues* 33, no. 1 (Winter 1977): 60–87.

Eagleburger, Lawrence S. "The U.S. Approach to the Negotiations on Intermediate-Range Nuclear Forces." *NATO Review* 30, no. 1 (February 1982): 7–11.

East, Maurice A., and Margaret G. Hermann. "Scope of Action: Targets in Foreign Policy Behavior." In *Describing Foreign Policy Behavior*, edited by Patrick Callahan, Linda P. Brady, and Margaret G. Hermann, pp. 115–33. Beverly Hills, Calif.: Sage Publications, 1982.

Elgstrom, Ole. "Norms, Culture, and Cognitive Patterns." *Negotiation Journal* 6, no. 2 (April 1990): 147–59.

Epstein, Joshua M. "The 3:1 Rule, the Adaptive Dynamic Model, and the Future of Security Studies." *International Security* 13, no. 4 (Spring 1989): 90–127.

Farrar-Hockley, General Sir Anthony. "Problems of Over-extension: Reconciling NATO Defence and Out-of-Area Contingencies: Part I." In

Power and Policy: Doctrine, the Alliance and Arms Control, Part III, pp. 54–59. Adelphi Papers, no. 207. London: International Institute for Strategic Studies, Spring 1986.

"Foreign Relations Committee Approves INF Treaty 17-2." *Arms Control Today* 18, no. 4 (May 1988): 18, 26.

Garthoff, Raymond L. "Negotiating with the Russians: Some Lessons from SALT." *International Security* 1, no. 4 (Spring 1977): 3–24.

———. "The TNF Tangle." *Foreign Policy*, no. 41 (Winter 1980–81): 82–94.

Genscher, Hans-Dietrich. "Intermediate Range Missiles—Moscow Holds the Key to Disarmament." *NATO Review* 31, no. 3/4 (October 1983): 1–7.

George, Alexander L. "Case Studies and Theory Development: The Method of Structured, Focused Comparison." In *Diplomacy: New Approaches in History, Theory, and Policy*, edited by Paul Gorden Lauren, pp. 43–68. New York: Free Press, 1979.

Gliksman, Alex. "Control of Nuclear Weapons in Europe." *National Defense* 66, no. 377 (April 1982): 43–49.

Goldberg, Andrew C. "Moscow's INF Experience." In *The Other Side of the Table: The Soviet Approach to Arms Control*, pp. 89–119. New York: Council on Foreign Relations Press, 1990.

Goodby, James E. "The Stockholm Conference: Negotiating a Cooperative Security System for Europe." In *U.S.-Soviet Security Cooperation*, edited by Alexander L. George, Philip J. Farley, and Alexander Dallin, pp. 144–72. New York: Oxford University Press, 1988.

Greenhalgh, Leonard. "Relationships in Negotiations." *Negotiation Journal* 3, no. 3 (July 1987): 235–43.

Haig, Alexander. "NATO—An Agenda for the Future." *NATO Review* 27, no. 3 (June 1979): 3–5.

Hanmer, Stephen R., Jr. "NATO's Long-Range Theatre Nuclear Forces: Modernization in Parallel with Arms Control." *NATO Review* 28, no. 1 (February 1980): 1–6.

Hermann, Margaret G. "Commentary: A Call for a New Type of Diplomat." *Negotiation Journal* 3, no. 3 (July 1987): 279–82.

———. "Effects of Personal Characteristics of Political Leaders on Foreign Policy." In *Why Nations Act: Theoretical Perspectives for Comparative Foreign Policy Studies*, edited by Maurice A. East, Stephen A. Salmore, and Charles F. Hermann, pp. 49–68. Beverly Hills, Calif.: Sage Publications, 1978.

Hermann, Margaret G., Charles F. Hermann, and Gerald L. Hutchins. "Affect." In *Describing Foreign Policy Behavior*, edited by Patrick Callahan, Linda P. Brady, and Margaret G. Hermann, pp. 207–22. Beverly Hills, Calif.: Sage Publications, 1982.

Holt, Pat M. "Europe's Security: In the EC, not NATO." *Christian Science Monitor*, July 11, 1990, p. 18.

Howard, Michael. "The Remaking of Europe." *Survival* 32, no. 2 (March/April 1990): 99–106.

Hunter, Robert E. "NATO's Future: The Out-of-Area Problem." In *NATO in the 1990s*, edited by Stanley R. Sloan, pp. 315–33. Washington, D.C.: Pergamon-Brassey's, 1989.

"INF Treaty Embroiled in Constitutional Controversy." *Arms Control Today* 18, no. 2 (March 1988): 19, 26.

Janosik, Robert J. "Rethinking the Culture-Negotiation Link." *Negotiation Journal* 3, no. 4 (October 1987): 385–95.

Joffe, Josef. "Once More: The German Question." *Survival* 32, no. 2 (March/April 1990): 129–40.

Kirkey, Christopher. "The NATO Alliance and the INF Treaty." *Armed Forces and Society* 16, no. 2 (Winter 1990): 287–305.

Komer, Robert W. "Problems of Over-extension: Reconciling NATO Defence and Out-of-Area Contingencies: Part II." In *Power and Policy: Doctrine, the Alliance and Arms Control, Part III*, pp. 60–67. Adelphi Papers, no. 207. London: International Institute for Strategic Studies, Spring 1986.

Korb, Lawrence J., and Stephen Daggett. "The Defense Budget and Strategic Planning." In *American Defense Annual 1988–89*, edited by Joseph Kruzel, pp. 43–66. Lexington, Mass.: Lexington Books, D. C. Heath and Company, 1988.

Kroes, Rob. "Cruise Missiles and the Western Party System: Some Dutch Lessons." *Armed Forces and Society* 12, no. 4 (Summer 1986): 581–90.

Kuniholm, Bruce R. "What the Saudis Really Want: A Primer for the Reagan Administration." *Orbis* 25, no. 1 (Spring 1981): 107–21.

Layne, Christopher. "Superpower Disengagement." *Foreign Policy*, no. 77 (Winter 1989–90): 17–40.

LeGloannec, Anne-Marie. "West German Security: Less of a Consensus?" In *Evolving European Defense Policies*, edited by Catherine McArdle Kelleher and Gale A. Mattox, pp. 169–84. Lexington, Mass.: Lexington Books, D. C. Heath and Company, 1987.

McCausland, Jeff. "Dual Track or Double Paralysis? The Politics of INF." *Armed Forces and Society* 12, no. 3 (Spring 1986): 431–52.

Mandelbaum, Michael. "Reconstructing the European Security Order." *Critical Issues 1990*, no. 1 (1990): 9–29.

Martin, Geoffrey R. "The 'Practical' and the 'Theoretical' Split in Modern Negotiation Literature." *Negotiation Journal* 4, no. 1 (January 1988): 45–54.

Marttila, John. "American Public Opinion: Evolving Definitions of National Security." In *America's Global Interests: A New Agenda*, edited by Edward K. Hamilton, pp. 261–315. New York: W. W. Norton, 1989.

Maynes, Charles William. "America without the Cold War." *Foreign Policy*, no. 78 (Spring 1990): 3–25.

Mearsheimer, John J. "Assessing the Conventional Balance: The 3:1 Rule and Its Critics." *International Security* 13, no. 4 (Spring 1989): 54–89.

Miller, Steven E. "Politics over Promise: Domestic Impediments to Arms Control." *International Security* 8, no. 4 (Spring 1984): 67–90.

Mueller, John. "A New Concert of Europe." *Foreign Policy*, no. 77 (Winter 1989/90): 3–16.

Nunn, Sam. "Challenges to NATO in the 1990s." *Survival* 32, no. 1 (January/February 1990): 3–13.

"Officials, Experts Praise Treaty in Senate Hearings." *Arms Control Today* 18, no. 2 (March 1988): 19–21.

Pond, Elizabeth. "Federal Republic of Germany: Westpolitik, Ostpolitik, and Security." In *Evolving European Defense Policies*, edited by Catherine McArdle Kelleher and Gale A. Mattox, pp. 223–44. Lexington, Mass.: Lexington Books, D. C. Heath and Company, 1987.

Posen, Barry R. "Measuring the European Conventional Balance: Coping with Complexity in Threat Assessment." *International Security* 9, no. 3 (Winter 1984–85): 47–88.

Quandt, William B. "The Electoral Cycle and the Conduct of Foreign Policy." *Political Science Quarterly* 101, no. 5 (1986): 825–37.

Resor, Stanley. "MBFR Aims at Security and Stability." *Commanders Digest* 16, no. 20 (November 14, 1974): 4–8.

Ruhle, Hans. "The Theater Nuclear Issue in German Politics." *Strategic Review* 9, no. 2 (Spring 1981): 54–60.

Salmore, Barbara G., and Stephen A. Salmore. "Political Regimes and Foreign Policy." In *Why Nations Act: Theoretical Perspectives for Comparative Foreign Policy Studies*, edited by Maurice A. East, Stephen A. Salmore, and Charles F. Hermann, pp. 103–42. Beverly Hills, Calif.: Sage Publications, 1978.

Salmore, Stephen A., Margaret G. Hermann, Charles F. Hermann, and Barbara G. Salmore. "Conclusion: Toward Integrating the Perspectives." In *Why Nations Act: Theoretical Perspectives for Comparative Foreign Policy Studies*, edited by Maurice A. East, Stephen A. Salmore, and Charles F. Hermann, pp. 191–209. Beverly Hills, Calif.: Sage Publications, 1978.

Saunders, Harold. "International Relationships—It's Time to Go Beyond 'We' and 'They.'" *Negotiation Journal* 3, no. 3 (July 1987): 245–74.

Schmidt, Helmut. "The 1977 Alastair Buchan Memorial Lecture." *Survival* 20 (January–February 1978): 2–10.

"Senate Conditions on the INF Treaty." *Arms Control Today* 18, no. 6 (July/August 1988): 23.

Shamir, Yitzhak. "Israel's Role in a Changing Middle East." *Foreign Affairs* 60, no. 4 (Spring 1982): 789–801.

Slocombe, Walter. "Negotiating with the Soviets: Getting Past No." In *A Game for High Stakes*, edited by Leon Sloss and M. Scott Davis, pp. 63–72. Cambridge, Mass.: Ballinger Publishing Company, 1986.

Smith, Gerard C. "From Arms Control to Arms Reductions: Achievements and Perspectives." In *The Changing Strategic Landscape, Part II*, pp. 116–24. Adelphi Papers, no. 236. London: International Institute for Strategic Studies, Spring 1989.

Snyder, Jack. "Averting Anarchy in the New Europe." *International Security* 14, no. 4 (Spring 1990): 5–41.

Spector, Bertram I. "Negotiation as a Psychological Process." In *The Negotiation Process: Theories and Applications*, edited by I. William Zartman, pp. 55–66. Beverly Hills, Calif.: Sage Publications, 1978.

Stein, Janice Gross. "International Negotiation: A Multidisciplinary Perspective." *Negotiation Journal* 4, no. 3 (July 1988): 221–31.

Stoertz, Howard, Jr. "Observations on Soviet Negotiating Practice." In *A Game for High Stakes*, edited by Leon Sloss and M. Scott Davis, pp. 43–46. Cambridge, Mass.: Ballinger Publishing Company, 1986.

Strong, Robert A., and Marshal Zeringue. "The Carter Administration and the Neutron Bomb." *Southeastern Political Review* 16, no. 1 (Spring 1988): 147–73.

Stuart, Douglas. "NATO in the 1980s: Between European Pillar and European Home." *Armed Forces and Society* 16, no. 3 (Spring 1990): 421–36.

Treverton, Gregory. "Defence beyond Europe." *Survival* 25, no. 5 (September/October 1983): 216–26.

———. "Nuclear Weapons in Europe." In *Nuclear Weapons and European Security*, edited by Robert Nurick, pp. 38–71. New York: St. Martin's Press, 1984.

"U.S.: Kingston Sums Up Bright Star." *Defense and Foreign Affairs Daily*, December 4, 1981.

Van Hollen, Christopher. "Don't Engulf the Gulf." *Foreign Affairs* 59, no. 5 (Summer 1981): 1064–78.

Van Oudenaren, John. "Conventional Arms Control in Europe: Soviet Policy and Objectives." In *Conventional Arms Control and the Security of Europe*, edited by Uwe Nerlich and James A. Thomson, pp. 40–64. Boulder, Colo.: Westview Press, 1988.

Viotti, Paul R. "European Peace Movements and Missile Deployments." *Armed Forces and Society* 11, no. 4 (Summer 1985): 505–21.

Warnke, Paul. "Lessons Learned in Bilateral Negotiations." In *A Game for High Stakes*, edited by Leon Sloss and M. Scott Davis, pp. 55–61. Cambridge, Mass.: Ballinger Publishing Company, 1986.

Weers, Col. Mozes W. A. "The Nuclear Debate in the Netherlands." *Strategic Review* 9, no. 2 (Spring 1981): 67–77.

Winham, Gilbert R. "Multilateral Economic Negotiation." *Negotiation Journal* 3, no. 2 (April 1987): 175–89.

Zartman, I. William. "The Analysis of Negotiation." In *The 50% Solution*, edited by I. William Zartman, pp. 1–41. New Haven: Yale University Press, 1976.

Public Documents

Agreement between the Government of the United States of America and the Government of the Federal Republic of Germany Concerning Host Nation Support during Crisis or War, April 15, 1982. Bonn, Federal Republic of Germany. Provided to the author by the Office of the Assistant Secretary of Defense, Manpower, Installations and Logistics.

Agreement between the Secretary of Defense of the United States of America and the Federal Minister of Defense of the Federal Republic of Germany Concerning the Preparation for and Execution and Support of Reinforcement Exercises and Other Related Exercises, January 21, 1983. Bonn, Federal Republic of Germany. Provided to the author by the Office of the Assistant Secretary of Defense, Manpower, Installations and Logistics.

Final Communiqué, Preparatory Consultations, June 28, 1973. Vienna, Austria. Reprinted in *NATO Review* 21, no. 4 (1973): 25.

Final Communiqué, Special Meeting of Foreign and Defense Ministers, December 12, 1979. Brussels, Belgium. Reprinted in *NATO Review* 28, no. 1 (February 1980): 25–26.

Information Paper on U.S.-German Wartime Host Nation Support (WHNS), February 7, 1989. Provided to the author by the Department of the Army, Office of the Deputy Chief of Staff, Logistics.

Treaty between the United States of America and the Union of Soviet Socialist Republics on the Elimination of Their Intermediate-Range and Shorter-Range Missiles, December 8, 1987. Washington, D.C. Provided to the author by the U.S. Arms Control and Disarmament Agency.

U.S. Congress. Congressional Budget Office. *Rapid Deployment Forces: Policy and Budgetary Implications*. Washington, D.C.: Government Printing Office, 1983.

U.S. Congress. House. Committee on Appropriations. Subcommittee on Defense. *Department of Defense Appropriations for Fiscal Year 1983*. Hearings. 97th Cong., 2d sess. Washington, D.C.: Government Printing Office, 1982.

———. *Department of Defense Appropriations for 1990*. Hearings. 101st Cong., 1st sess., pt. 2. Washington, D.C.: Government Printing Office, 1989.

———. *Supplemental Appropriations for 1983*. Hearings. 98th Cong., 2d sess. Washington, D.C.: Government Printing Office, 1983.

————. Subcommittee on Military Construction. "Facilities Access—Southwest Asia." *Military Construction Appropriations for Fiscal Year 1984.* Hearing. 98th Cong., 1st sess. Washington, D.C.: Government Printing Office, 1983.

————. Subcommittee on Military Installations and Facilities. *Department of Defense Appropriations for Fiscal Year 1983.* Hearings. 97th Cong., 2d sess. Washington, D.C.: Government Printing Office, 1982.

U.S. Congress. House. Committee on Foreign Affairs (Subcommittee on Europe and the Middle East) and the Joint Economic Committee. *U.S. Policy toward the Persian Gulf.* Hearing. 97th Cong., 2d sess. Washington, D.C.: Government Printing Office, 1982.

U.S. Congress. Senate. Committee on Appropriations. *Department of Defense Appropriations for Fiscal Year 1983.* Hearings. 97th Cong., 2d sess., pt. 3. Washington, D.C.: Government Printing Office, 1982.

————. *Fiscal Year 1983 Supplemental Request for Department of Defense.* Hearing. 98th Cong., 1st sess. Washington, D.C.: Government Printing Office, 1983.

————. Subcommittee on Defense. *Fiscal Year 1983 Supplemental Request for Department of Defense.* Hearings. 98th Cong., 1st sess. Washington, D.C.: Government Printing Office, 1983.

U.S. Department of Defense. *Annual Report to the Congress, Fiscal Year 1982.* Washington, D.C.: Government Printing Office, 1981.

————. *Report on Allied Contributions to the Common Defense.* Washington, D.C.: Government Printing Office, March 1985.

U.S. Information Agency. Foreign Broadcast Information Service. *Daily Report: USSR.*

————. *Daily Report: Western Europe.*

Newspapers and Frequently Consulted Periodicals

Arms Control Today. Published by the Arms Control Association, Washington, D.C.

Atlanta Journal and Constitution

Baltimore Sun

Christian Science Monitor

International Herald Tribune

NATO Review, 1979–89. Published by the Atlantic Council of the United States, Washington, D.C.

New York Times

Strategic Survey, 1982–83 to 1988–89. Published by the International Institute for Strategic Studies, London.

Washington Post

Washington Times

Index